Twelve Doors to the Soul

Twelve Doors

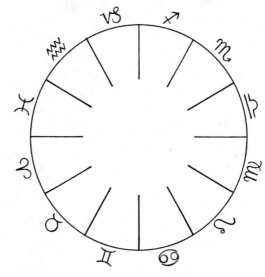

Cover art by the author

to the Soul

Astrology of the Inner Self

By
JANE A. EVANS

This publication made possible
with the assistance of the Kern Foundation

The Theosophical Publishing House
Wheaton, Ill. U. S. A.
Madras, India/London, England

Published by The Theosophical Publishing House, a department
of The Theosophical Society in America.

Library of Congress Cataloging in Publication Data

Evans, Jane 1917-
    Twelve doors to the soul.

    (A Quest book)
    Bibliography: p.
    1. Astrology. 2. Reincarnation. 3. Karma
I. Title.
BF1708.1.E94   133.5   78-64907
ISBN 0-8356-0521-3

Printed in the United States of America

To Virginia and Joy
who gave me the opportunity.

CONTENTS

INTRODUCTION

Only very recently has Astrology been deliberately used as a technique for furthering the psychological and spiritual development of individuals. Although in some civilizations Astrology went hand-in-hand with religion and medicine, earlier astrologers were, on the whole, too fatalistic. A person was born to glory or doom, a destiny handed out by inscrutable Fates or gods working their will through the planets and Signs. Although there were astrologers in all ages who used their knowledge with depth, most of the accounts handed down to us deal with disasters and triumphs prophesied and fulfilled. This attitude—that divided planetary placements and aspects into black and white categories either fortunate or unfortunate—has persisted in astrological interpretation up to the present.

Now that the Aquarian Age is upon us, or *almost* upon us, (there are differences of opinion as to its timing), we are entering the age of Man the Individual, in which even the ordinary person is beginning to look upon his life as unique, with a pattern differing from any other. The thoughtful person is no longer satisfied with authoritarian teachings to be accepted on faith alone, nor is he willing to accept the premise that his character and destiny is stamped on him according to the hour of his birth for better or worse. This seems to make a mockery of free will. Above all he is looking for a pattern and purpose to his life which can provide *meaning* to all things that happen to him as well as a guide to material and spiritual betterment. But it must be something that can be proved through personal observation and first hand experience.

Astrology *can* prove that there is a pattern and plan to the universe encompassing all life, human life included. Once the individual is convinced that Astrology "works" in his own life,* surely the next step will be to search for the *reason* that it works and the *purpose* for which it works. If this purpose can be found, then why not change one's life and character as much as possible in order to harmonize with that purpose? It is here that Theosophy (that Ancient Wisdom which to many of us is found in its most satisfying and comprehensive form in Theosophy),

*It has worked well enough to convince 32 million Americans, according to a recent Gallup poll.

can give depth of meaning to all Astrology and open the personality to the illumination of the Higher Self, or Soul within.

Of course, neither Astrology, Theosophy, nor any other philosophy, religion, or science is a magic formula to success, happiness, or spirituality. There is always a big gap between picturing what needs to be done with one's self and making it a reality. Nevertheless, it is a great help to have even a glimpse of that picture. Opening the door to the Soul means looking at the personality and one's life from the standpoint of the Soul as much as possible. It means the acceptance of certain principles, with all their implications, at least as a working hypothesis. These principles are: reincarnation, karma, and the One Life of which each of us and everything in the universe is an expression. It means a willingness to acknowledge that what may be of great importance to the personality may be of little importance to the Soul. That entity takes the long range view over many lifetimes, always working toward ultimate integration and perfection.

Expert knowledge of Astrology is not essential to understanding the ideas presented in this book, but elementary knowledge of the Signs, Houses, and Planets of Astrology is helpful so a few diagrams and tables have been included, as well as a list of books on Astrology and other related subjects for further study.

Throughout this book I have used the masculine, in a generic sense, to avoid the cumbersome repetition of "his or her", even though most statements apply equally to both sexes. The Soul has no gender, no sex as we think of it. I hope any feminists who take exception to this will understand that it is not due to any bias on my part.

Because this book is devoted to horoscope interpretation, I have not attempted to give instruction on the computation of a chart. There are many excellent books for that purpose (see list at end of book). For those who wish to avoid the labor of learning to set up a chart, I would recommend applying to a good astrological computing firm. The computer does all the mathematical work, but you have to do the interpretation. When using such a service, be certain that you send all the required birth data—day, month, year, time, and place (the nearest city if the place is small or remote). The fee is usually around three dollars to obtain a Natal chart.

I

THE HOROSCOPE: GENESIS DIAGRAM AND MANDALA

The One is the unbroken Circle with no circumference, for it is nowhere and everywhere; the One is the boundless plane of the Circle, manifesting a diameter only during the manvantaric periods; the One is the indivisible point found nowhere, perceived everywhere during those periods; it is the Vertical and the Horizontal, the Father and the Mother, the summit and base of the Father, the two extremities of the Mother . . . Father-Mother spin a web whose upper end is fastened to Spirit, the light of the one Darkness, and the lower one to Matter its (the Spirit's) shadowy end . . .

The Secret Doctrine

This formula for the birth of a universe described with such mysterious and thrilling symbology in The Secret Doctrine is the same as the formula for the descent into physical incarnation of a human being: "As above, so below". In all ages this formula and the entity manifesting, be it God or man, has been variously diagrammed. To me, an astrologer-theosophist, the horoscope is the most meaningful diagram of the Divine in human incarnation. The natal horoscope symbolizes the genesis of the individual incarnation containing the blueprint for that individual's potentialities in character and destiny; the results of his actions, emotions, and thinking in past incarnations.

"THE ONE IS THE UNBROKEN CIRCLE WITH NO CIRCUMFERENCE FOR IT IS NOWHERE AND EVERYWHERE . . ." We are all sparks of the one flame, inseparable parts of a tremendous Being who is everywhere and to be found in no separate defined location. This implies that there is no real separation between ourselves and the other selves who have emanated from the same Being.

"MANIFESTING A DIAMETER ONLY DURING THE MANVANTARIC PERIODS:"[1] As that Being from time to time descends or "breathes out" into periods of manifestation on the lower planes of matter so we "breathe out" from our innermost Center into incarnation from time to time, drawing the Circle—the Ring-pass-not—around our personality. This is diagrammed by the circle of the 360° of the Zodiac encompassing the Natal horoscope.

"THE ONE IS THE INDIVISIBLE POINT FOUND NOWHERE, PER-CEIVED EVERYWHERE DURING THOSE PERIODS:" Always within the Circle is the Center—the Point that is found nowhere and perceived everywhere because it is formless and yet the fountain head of our very life and existence. The personality, which so many mistake for the whole self, is only a partial and as yet very imperfect expression of that Center-point. It is as if that Higher Self, Soul, or Center puts a finger down into the lower planes of manifestation for the purpose of experience and growth.[2]

"IT IS THE VERTICAL AND THE HORIZONTAL, THE FATHER AND THE MOTHER, THE SUMMIT AND BASE OF THE FATHER, THE TWO EXTREMITIES OF THE MOTHER . . ." In the Natal horoscope the vertical line descending from the Midheaven to the Nadir symbolizes the Father—the positive pole: Yang, power, objectivity. The horizontal line stretching from the Ascendant to the Descendant symbolizes the Mother—the negative pole: Yin receptivity, consciousness. All manifested life expresses through these two polarities: the Father diagrammed in the horoscope by the creative descent of the positive power starting from the Midheaven, (the highest point symbolizing our career; public or social life; how we integrate ourselves with the world) to the Nadir, Cusp of the Fourth House, which rules our home, parents, ancestry, growth of psychic roots, the base upon which we build the temple of our life and character.

The vertical descent of the Father impregnates the horizontal receptive Mother but to speak of the creative power of the Father starting at the Midheaven and the consciousness-receptivity of the Mother starting at the Ascendant and stretching to the Descendant gives a misleading two-dimensional picture. In reality there is no upper-lower, East to West but everything emanates from the formless Center.

"FATHER-MOTHER SPIN A WEB WHOSE UPPER END IS FASTENED TO SPIRIT, THE LIGHT OF THE ONE DARKNESS, AND THE LOWER ONE TO MATTER ITS (THE SPIRIT'S) SHADOWY END . . ." This is diagrammed in the horoscope as the twelve Houses and/or Signs raying out from the Center, which encompasses all possible areas of experience for the evolving soul. It is our Web of life in which we are held, not like captive flies caught in some spider's web but supported, protected and provided with all the material we need to eventually become gods in our own right.

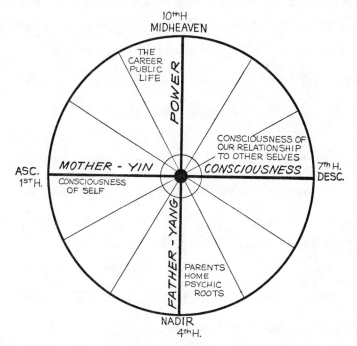

Considering the simplicity of the structure of the astrological horoscope we cannot fail to be impressed by the profundity of its symbolism. A Center, a Cross, 12 radiating Spokes in all, surrounded by a Circle. That is all—and yet it serves as a diagram of a universe ... or a human being.

The horoscope is also a mandala. The mandala is a very ancient symbol of individuation. The word itself is a Hindu term for a circle—that perfect symbol of unity. Mandalas are found all over the Orient and are always used as a means towards contemplation and concentration: as an aid in inducing certain mental states and in encouraging the spirit to move forward along its path of evolution from the realm of material involvement to the spiritual life. The mandala has been incorporated into the designs of buildings and temples such as Borubadur in Java, and carvings, such as the great Mexican Calendar Stone. Mazes, labyrinths, clock faces, sun dials, and the horoscope are mandala forms.

The mandala is a synthesis of a traditional structure plus free interpretation. Its basic components are various elements always enclosed in a square or a circle. This is a vast and complex subject; it is enough to say that the mandala, with all its variety of forms, has functioned as a powerful symbol, an abstract design used as a focus for concentration and meditation when approached from a philosophical or spiritual viewpoint. It can be read as depicting the genesis of incarnated life whatever the scale and also as the formula or pattern for man's return to his Center from the outer confusions of material life. Carl Jung, the great Swiss psychologist, relates that when his patients are nearing integration in their treatment, their dreams often take some form of a mandala although they may never have heard the word or its concept. So it would seem irrefutable that the mandala is one of those eternal symbols imbedded in the deepest consciousness of Man through which the Inner Self can speak and guide the personality.

The horoscope is a mandala—a mandala for the individual. The Circle symbolizing wholeness, the psychic and material circumference of the incarnation: the Center—the Inner, higher Self; the Cross—Spirit crucified or immersed in Matter; the twelve Spokes or parts radiating from the center—the qualities (Signs) and fields (Houses) of experience through which Man must pass in order to realize the Center. The peculiar distribution of the planets throughout the horoscope makes it a unique pattern for a particular individual and shows the karma of character, relationships, and destiny that has been made in the past and with which he must work in this incarnation. If you understand your horoscope you have a mandala that speaks to you, a veritable guide to lead you from the confusions of your life to inner spiritual illumination.

There are many levels of astrological interpretation but the simplistic interpretations cannot be enough for those who are seeking to understand the mystery of their own life and self. The individual horoscope must be plumbed with the aid of the higher intuitive mind—the "eye of the soul". That intuition can be developed through meditation, constant use and an openness to whatever comes "through", whether pleasing to the desires and fears of the personality or not. The scriptures of all religions say in their various ways, "Ask and you will be answered, seek and you will find". But only too often our prayers and questions are colored by selfishness, prejudice, and our set preconditions of what we will accept. The horoscope shows the obstacles, dangers, weaknesses, strengths, joys, and successes that the personality must encounter and learn from on the way to perfection. If one's intuition is particularly unclouded, it can indicate the unique part the Inner Self is endeavoring to play in the universal scheme throughout all its incarnations. That Self's dominant note may be that of Artist, Builder, Scientist, or Leader, and in many lives and many roles as man or woman, slave or king, it sounds that archetypal note.

Astrology deals with the mythos of the sky. The elements it uses are archetypal. This archetypal symbology, or mythos, acts like a projection screen in drawing out the insight. It is the objective pole necessary for calling forth the subjective processes of the consciousness which is a legitimate and healthy exercise of the imagination—a process that goes on all the time in art and science. Imagination must never be despised. "It's just my imagination" is an expression often used to invalidate any subjective perception. Yet no work of art nor scientific breakthrough, and actually very little of anything could be accomplished without use of the imagination. And so it is with Astrology and the astrologer. The essence of Astrology is not something worked out with charts, tables, ephemerides, etc., like a chemist mixing various elements hoping to achieve a usable product. As the astrologer works with the ancient symbology giving it interpretation more suitable to this age, it becomes an active entering-into, a deep participation with those symbols and the personality/Self of the "horoscopee", to coin a word. When that participation is achieved there is a breakthrough. The astrologer can be taken out of his personality inward to realization. Like a lightning flash that reveals a whole landscape formerly in darkness, insight suddenly illuminates the horoscope giving pattern and meaning to what was hitherto just a collection of symbols with stereotyped keywords. A door opens to communication with the Inner Self, whether your own or that of the person whose horoscope is being studied. It does not

matter what approach or method or part of the process gives you
that "door". As Stephen Arroyo says in his book, *Astrology,
Karma and Transformation:*[3]

> If you understand one factor in the chart *thoroughly*, it will
> lead you to the center from which all emanates. In other
> words, just start talking about something you *do* under-
> stand, relate it to the person's personal experience and
> understanding, and then let it flow by itself. As Albert
> Einstein remarked, if you penetrate to the core of anything,
> you will eventually encounter the deepest reality and truth.

All true symbols can work in this manner for the intuitive
person. The symbol acts as a catalyst, a point of focus for that
person to break through to the Real. The original root meaning of
the word "symbol" is "drawing together" (Greek: *sym*, together;
ballein, to throw). We are drawn by that symbol to the truth lying
behind it. The antonym of symbolic is "diabolic" which means
"pulling apart". All religions and philosophies have used symbology. Astrology is rich in symbology, the language of the Inner
Self is symbology and our task is to understand the symbols that
speak to us.

Symbology can be confusing when it seems to conflict with
natural law. In the horoscope diagram, Astrology places the
Earth in the center of the chart with the planets, Sun, and Moon
all seemingly revolving about the Earth. This, we know, is con-
trary to fact and has been a point of ridicule from scientists and
skeptics. They claim that Astrology is still back in the Middle
Ages when men believed the Sun moved about the Earth as did
the planets and, therefore the whole basis of Astrology was and
is erroneous.

There is reason to believe that the ancients knew that the Sun
was the center of our system with Earth and planets circling it
but that this was lost sight of in later centuries. We still move the
Sun about and calculate it in terms of the horoscope as if it were a
planet, but that is just a matter of convenience. Actually, placing
the Earth in the center of the horoscope is not far from the
symbolic truth for Earth is still the *center* for the bulk of humanity. We are still centered in our material desires, fears, hates, and
feelings: very much of the "earth-earthy". The horoscope ideally
should show the Sun in the center. The Sun in Astrology symbolizes the core-center of our being, the basic I AM and his
characteristic is illumination. If the Sun were placed in the

center of our horoscope in realization as well as diagrammatically then we would be living in the Sun consciousness, in unity with and illuminated by our Inner Self. This would be Adepthood for an Adept or perfected Master determines experiences by radiation from his own center not influenced by the conditions and people surrounding him. He is truly a Creator living in his Sun consciousness.

Someday there will be a new system of Astrology with the Sun as the center of the horoscope and the Earth circling the Sun as one of the planets. The Earth will probably be given rulership of the Sign Taurus where now Venus is at present acting as Regent for her child, Earth, doubling as ruler of both Taurus and Libra. We are told in *The Secret Doctrine* and other ancient teachings[4] that the Lords of the Flame from Venus came bearing the gifts and teachings that brought civilization to the infant humanity. When humanity matures, Earth will take over rulership of Taurus.

Even if that system of Sun-centered Astrology is not yet evolved we can still begin to put our Inner Selves, the Sun, the source of our personalities, in the center of our lives. We can begin to view our life and character from the viewpoint of that eternal Self with Its perspective of many lives and unlimited opportunity for growth. Already a number of professional astrologers draw up these heliocentric (Sun-centered) charts to use in conjunction with the more familiar horoscope with Earth at its center. In time, this form may become more widely known and popular.

There is still another aspect to the horoscope. The construction and interpretation of the horoscope is a *ritual,* carrying a magic dimension. All ritual, all magic embodies certain steps of circumscribing the area of work, the words, chant, or hymn setting the stage for the manifestation of power or acquisition of knowledge. Setting up the horoscope is the ritual that puts the astrologer in tune with the individual to be studied. But what about the use of the computer to calculate the positions of Signs, planets and Houses? I do *not* mean those computer printouts that calculate and *interpret* the horoscope but only those that do the donkey work of mathematical calculation. I must admit it took me forty years before the pressure of too much work and too little time forced me to use an astrological computer service. But I still take the information provided by the computer and put it around a chart of my own. I find that chart easier to "read" than the computerized chart or perhaps I need that "ritual" of setting up the horoscope in order to get started.[5]

When it comes to the person whose horoscope is being interpreted, there is also an element of ritual magic in the sense that he is able to see, laid out objectively before him, his faults, powers, fears, blocks and potentialities. Since they are presented in the context of his larger span of eternal life offering him more than one short life in which to grow and achieve, it should work as a psychological expansion, a release from the narrow prison of one personality and one life.

A number of eminent scientists a few years ago issued a joint statement condemning Astrology as "based on magic". Astrology is a form of magic: *all of life is magic!* Religion through the ages has proclaimed that man can achieve some magical transformation of himself and Astrology can show how this may be achieved.

It has always been more convenient to assume that our fates were controlled by outside forces such as angels, devils, demons, gods, and the like. Most educated people today are not so prone to blame their fates on God or the Devil but they still do blame their "bad luck" on other people—rarely themselves. If the horoscope is rightly interpreted, that person can see how the pattern of his character and his life are integrated. He himself and no one else is the cause—and the cure—of his present character and life. If he accepts the fact that Astrology can be a valid means of interpreting his life pattern, then he can set about changing those things in himself and his life that block his growth and live cheerfully with those things in his circumstances that cannot be changed, knowing that all things eventually work together for his good.

NOTES

[1]Manvantaric Periods are periods of Evolution alternating with periods of *Pralaya* or Dissolution. The Breath of the One which is eternal exhales and expands manifesting in the myriad forms of a universe for a certain length of time called a Day of *Brahma* or *Manvantara*. When the Breath inhales, the forms disappear and all life as we know it ceases for a period of *Pralaya* or Night of *Brahma*. *See* H. P. Blavatsky, *An Abridge-*

ment of The Secret Doctrine (Wheaton: Theosophical Publishing House, 1973), p. 9.

[2]There are Seven Planes in our Solar system starting with ADI—the formless One and "descending" into ever-coarsening matter until the Seventh Plane, the physical. It is not the *same* personality that incarnates life after life but it is the *same* Inner Self or Soul that puts down a fragment of itself into a new personality. *See* E. Norman Pearson, *Space, Time and Self* (Wheaton: Theosophical Publishing House, 1967).

[3]Stephen Arroyo, *Astrology, Karma and Transformation: The Inner Dimensions of the Birthchart* (Vancouver, Washington: CRCS Publications, 1978).

[4]Annie Besant and C. W. Leadbeater, *Man: Whence, How and Whither* (Wheaton: Theosophical Publishing House, 1947); A. E. Powell, *The Solar System* (London: Theosophical Publishing House, 1971) and H. P. Blavatsky, *The Secret Doctrine*, 6 Vols. (Adyar, India: Theosophical Publishing House, 1971).

[5]I use Neil Michelsen's Astro Computing Services, P.O. Box 16297, San Diego, California 92116.

II

REINCARNATION AND KARMA IN THE HOROSCOPE

Why look into past lives? Once one accepts reincarnation as the logical answer to so many of life's inequities and mysteries there is a natural curiosity to find out who we were and what happened in our past lives. It is a merciful thing that most of us can recall very little of that past before we are ready for it, otherwise we might spend our present energies daydreaming of past glories or brooding over long dead horrors. I have known people who used memories of past life relationships and wrongs to justify unethical actions in this life such as pressing claims for financial support "because you robbed me of my inheritance in that other life." Whatever we may have done in the past or may do in future lives, this present life is the important one where we should be focussing all our efforts.

From my point of view, there are two positive reasons for some recall of past lives, both reasons rooted in the belief that such recall can be of help in this life. The first reason is that a convincing recollection cannot help but expand one's vision and perspective, giving at least a strong subjective proof of continuous life. Death ceases to be a feared "end-to-everything", and the knowledge that one has eternity to achieve one's goals removes a major source of pressure and frustration. The second reason is that it can take the sting, tte injustice, out of things that happen in this life. It can remove the rebellion and dilute the bitterness of difficult relationships when you can recall something of a past life situation in which you dealt out such treatment to another which they are now returning in this life. The best attitude to have, of course, is a strong faith that whether the details can be recalled or not, all that comes to you is just and, rightly used, can become a stepping stone to greater strength and opportunity. But, being human, it does *help* to be able to fit past and present together.

Some people fear they will uncover all sorts of atrocities for which they would live in fear of karmic retribution in this life. So many recollections of past lives seem to dwell on bad karma but in truth our karma from past lives is nearly always a mixed bag. As C. W. Leadbeater remarked, "There is no reason to believe that we did badly in every life." In his three small volumes which make up *The Soul's Growth Through Reincarnation*, a number of souls were traced back through many incarnations clairvoyantly[1], it was shown that the tenor and tempo of the lives is an individual thing and varies from soul to soul. One soul seemed to move peacefully through life after life with rarely any spectacular events or conditions while another seemed to have one horrendous life of tragedy and violence after another. There is nothing arbitrary about this, it was the Inner Self's *choice* to learn and grow in that manner.

For those who question the veracity of any, or most, past life recollections, I can only insist that it is perfectly possible since the Inner Self remembers *all* lives and, as we are a living part of that Self, it is only a matter of opening up the line of communication with that Self. To give personal testimony, I have recalled several past lives in great detail and convincing episodes in others and it is very much like recalling the events of previous years in *this* life. Memory, even in the present, is arbitrary; certain things stand out in high relief while others, possibly more important, drop out altogether. I have also found it possible to go "through" most horoscopes into past lives recapturing certain episodes and relationships that have relevance to the present life.

I had been an astrologer for many years before even looking into the theory and practice of reading past (or future) lives from the present natal horoscope. It seemed obvious to me that the horoscope would show the general pattern of karma to be worked out in this life, the result of past life actions, emotions, attitudes, and aspirations. But I could not see, in practical terms, how one could get more than a very general picture. When I was preparing a series of lectures, I thought of presenting the theory (or theories, since there are several methods used by astrologers) of reading past lives through the horoscope, mainly with the idea of saying, "Here is what some astrologers believe—but I don't think it can be done." Like many skeptics who take up Astrology in order to prove it nonsense I found that it did *work* and could be useful in counseling people. Such eminent as-

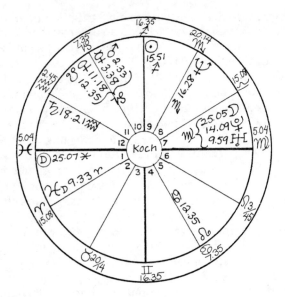

Harold I—Natal chart

trologers as Noel Tyl, Manly P. Hall, Elman Bacher, Stephen Arroyo, and Raymond Merriman used it seriously in books and lectures as well as counseling which impressed me also. As to *proof* of accuracy, that must lie in one's own life and the inner response to a past life recall. Does it "ring a bell" within you? Does it seem to fit or explain certain things in the present life or throw new light on situations, character traits, and relationships? Above all, does it help you deal with your present problems more successfully or with greater understanding? It is not often that we can find ancient records to verify a past life memory such as Dr. Arthur Guirdham was able to do as reported in his fascinating book, *The Cathars and Reincarnation*,[2] or as Dr. Ian Stevenson has done in his *Twenty Cases Suggestive of Reincarnation*.[3] Such verification will increase as records are better kept and belief in reincarnation grows in the West.

A case in point is that of Harold, a young boy who died suddenly at the age of ten. He was taken ill with what appeared to be flu, but after two days he had to be rushed to the hospital where he died in a matter of minutes. The cause of death was never satisfactorily determined by the doctors.

His birth chart shown here is designated as Harold I. You can see in his Natal chart that Neptune, ruler of his Ascendant (Pisces) was placed in Scorpio in the 8th House, closely squaring Saturn in the 12th House.

The horoscope cast for the time of death shows the sudden and unexpected death—Uranus posited in the 8th House in close square aspect to Venus, ruler of the 8th. The Death chart Ascendant is 11° 08 (11° Pisces): the Natal chart Ascendant is 5° 04 (5° Pisces).[4] In Harold I's Natal chart, his Moon is in *exact* opposition to the Part of Death[5] in the 1st House.

Much more could be written analyzing the two charts but, on the whole, neither of the two charts points unmistakably to an early, sudden death.

Nola and Jerry Williams, who have made a special study of death in Astrology, state that a death is shown more clearly in

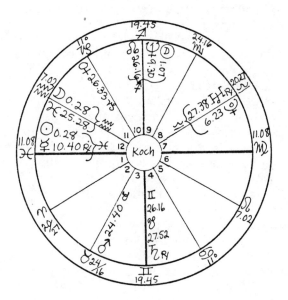

Harold I—Death Chart

the horoscopes of those *close* to the dying person than it is shown in the chart of the person himself! This seems to show that death is not the all-important, awesome event to the one experiencing it as it is to his loved ones. The Williamses found that Jupiter was the most active planet in all charts at the time of death. This might be expected (though the progressed aspects in Harold's chart are not outstanding in this respect) for Jupiter is the agency by which spiritual forces are made manifest to earth consciousness; he is the "go-between" twixt the transcendent and material worlds. The symbol of the teacher, priest, or spiritual father, Jupiter's role in death must be one of benevolence and as the principle of expansion, improvement, and opportunity he opens the way for the personality to escape the confines of incarnation.

In Harold I's Natal chart, Jupiter and Uranus were in quincunx aspect (150°) at birth. Uranus was still in orb of that quincunx while Jupiter had progressed to just a few minutes of exactitude, making it a double aspect. Progressed Mars was separating from a square to Jupiter. In the Death chart, Jupiter is much more active, moving to a grand trine involving Uranus and Saturn—a most fortunate configuration, one would say. Yet, that was the time of death. Uranus was in the 8th House (death, rebirth, transformation), Saturn in the 4th House (the end of any matter), and Jupiter and Sun were in the 12th House (serious illness, the needed redemption that impelled the present incarnation, karma). My reading of this grand trine is that Harold I's Inner Self had chosen incarnation for this short life to work off a particular karma (obesity was one problem—Jupiter in the 1st House) and death came as a welcome release so that he could return with a better body, or for some other reason.

His family was devastated, as any close family would be, over the loss of a young child. Shortly after his death they began to experience mysterious rappings throughout the house, tunes whistled as Harold used to whistle, his particular body scent, and other odd phenomena. His mother and sisters had vivid dreams in which he told them not to be unhappy because he would return to them. There was also the evidence provided by the noted British clairvoyant, Margaret Flavell Tweddell who received further communication from Harold. She told Harold's mother that she would become pregnant shortly and Harold would be reborn to her. Nineteen months after Harold's death she gave birth to a son.

If this were a true case of reincarnation there should be a relationship between all three charts. There is much more that could be said but I will point out only a few interesting points, calling the incarnations Harold I and Harold II, and designating the Death chart as DC.

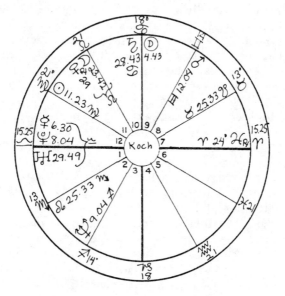

Harold II—Rebirth Chart

Harold II's Sun is exactly opposite the DC Ascendant and only 6° away from opposition to Harold I's natal Ascendant. His Mercury conjuncts the DC Pluto. Harold II's Sun is conjunct to both Uranus and Pluto in Harold I's chart at the midpoint between those two higher octave planets that have so much to do with death, rebirth, and transformation.

Another interesting point is that Harold II's Ascendant is the exact degree (minus only 17 minutes) conjuncting the 8th House Cusp of Harold I's Natal chart! It is possible that the 8th House is the *Door* through which the soul exits from an incarnation and when it enters a new body through a new Ascendant there is still a close connection between the exit door of the previous incarnation and the entrance door of the new one.

Harold II is now three years old; a very bright, *slender*, healthy boy. He claims Harold I's 10-year-old baseball clothing and equipment as his own and recalls people and events from his previous life as if they were a memory of this present life. He has an unusually large vocabulary for one so young and from time to time surprises his family by recounting incidents that happened to Harold I which no one has told him about or discussed in his presence. Such as, "This is where that boy on his bicycle ran into me." Upon hearing that a former neighbor was coming to visit announced, "Oh, that's the lady that used to yell at me!"

The foregoing is a fortunate case of being on the spot and being able to obtain accurate birth and death times as well as much other useful information. But with the average Natal chart how does an astrologer "read" past lives and the karma brought over to be worked out in the present life? First, and foremost, the *whole* horoscope tells the story. But there are special factors that seem to have particular bearing on the past. Most astrologers who work with past lives emphasize the 12th House, the Sign on its Cusp, its ruler, and any planets posited therein. It seems to have a special significance relating to the last *important* life: stillborn births and brief lives do not count. One of the definitions of the 12th House is "the House of Self-undoing" which is identical in meaning with negative karma. It is the House of "secret enemies" and, as it rules our subconscious, it is easy to see why our own subconscious is frequently our secret enemy distorting our character and ordering our lives in accordance with its unrecognized desires and aversions. These are the things most frequently brought over from our past lives.

Some astrologers hold that the Sign on the 12th House Cusp was the Ascending Sign of the last significant life and if the chart is tilted so that the present 12th House becomes the 1st House, the present 1st House becomes the 2nd and so forth until you have the general horoscope of the last life. I find that this does work for me, though I am uncertain how much of it is simply intuition and an empathy with the whole chart that brings through a convincing picture of the past.

Many astrologers hold that we progress through the twelve Signs in order as Ascendants and as Sun Signs. If you had

Taurus on your Ascendant and your Sun in Virgo in this life, according to that theory you would have had Aries on your Ascendant and Sun in Leo in the last life and in your next life you will have Gemini on the Ascendant and Libra as the Sun Sign.

Suppose one has the same Sign for the Ascendant and Sun Sign, does that mean the soul marches in lock step with a double dose of a Sign every incarnation for thousands or millions of years? My feeling is that there is still so little known, except in a general way, about the laws governing reincarnation that we cannot make hard and fast rules. There is probably a general pattern the soul follows with flexibility as the circumstances demand.

The 12th House signifies the heaviest karma made in the past. The Moon represents a general reflection of what we have been in the past—an image assimilated past experience and behavior patterns. The Moon symbolizes, especially according to its Sign position, the particular mental and emotional karmic patterns which either inhibit or help us. Raymond Merriman[6] maintains that the last planet conjuncted by the Moon prior to birth[7] is the one that affects the behavior the most because the qualities of that planet can be used as the main *tool* in dealing with the challenges of this life. The planet that the Moon conjuncts immediately *after* birth—the one toward which the Moon is progressing—shows the experiences and people we need to meet and the nature of the lessons we are to learn in this life. So the progressing Moon points toward the development of the new tools, new experiences, and new people who will help us. Supposing the Sun is the first planet the Moon will conjunct after birth. The Sun then represents the types of people and experiences you are to work upon and with in this incarnation. You will meet leaders, because you are to become a leader and through them learn to deal with attention directed upon yourself. You will learn to develop self-assurance, leadership, optimism, and get rid of all self-negation. The Moon's Nodes and the Signs in which they are deposited can give added information concerning the past as well as the future.[8] David Railey has made a special study of the Nodes and he likens them to a bridge. The South Node shows what we bring into this life with us from the past, and the North Node shows our destination, what we are going to carry on with us.

The South Node traditionally is of the nature of Saturn and shows the karmic past life patterns and the North Node traditionally is of the nature of Jupiter. Like crossing any bridge, both ends are important and we should not lose sight of either. Railey considers the Signs and Houses in which the Nodes are placed, the condition of the rulers of those Signs and their aspects, as well as aspects to the Nodes themselves.

Any planet within 18° of an Angle, shows the function you have developed prior to this incarnation. The Angles, in Astrology, are the Cusps of the 1st, 4th, 7th and 10th Houses, which form the Ascendant, Nadir, Descendant, and Midheaven of your chart. For example, Mercury near an angle shows that you have developed the quality of *perception* in past lives in which you have been working on acquiring knowledge and mental skills.

Uranus, Neptune, and Pluto near an angle show people who from early childhood seem to have a sense of purpose, a sense of mission.

If you have no planets near the angles, then it indicates that you haven't been concentrating on any tool or power but have been a 'jack-of-all-trades'.

The major configurations in a horoscope show where the "action" is going to be in your inner and outer worlds; these show clearly where the *causes* lie in the past. Further, these same patterns show you how and where in this life you are going to meet the effects of those causes.

The horoscope naturally divides into quadrants: 1st, 2nd, and 3rd Houses are the First Quadrant. Houses 4, 5, and 6 make up the Second Quadrant. The Third Quadrant, then, contains Houses 7, 8, and 9; and the last consists of 10th, 11th, and 12th. Note that the Angles divide these quadrants.

The First Quadrant (1, 2, and 3) concerns our essential being and self-awareness, our personal affairs, possessions, and attitudes.

Quadrant Two (Houses 4, 5, and 6) reflects the soul moving out into larger interests such as the family, home, creativity, risk, service, and employment.

The Third Quadrant, which includes 7th, 8th, and 9th Houses, is often the most difficult when the soul must learn to cope with the outer world, people and situations, life, death, sex, socializing, and understanding reality. A concentration of planets in this area, or many aspects that lead into one or more planets in this area, show that the principal lessons in this incarnation will lie in these matters (perhaps because they were avoided or abused in the past).

The Quadrant Four—Houses 10, 11, and 12—reveal your ability and capacity to express yourself in society at large, to make your mark on the world, and to influence others.

These are the factors that the astrologer should take into consideration to get a picture of past incarnations; to form an idea of what, in karmic assets and debits, the person has brought into this life. It is only part of the picture. We cannot do much about the past, but we always have choice and free will in our present and future actions and reactions. We can change our characters and change our lives by making difficult karma work for us. Astrology is a means of clarifying the stages of development when applied to the individual life. It is a tool for gaining a perspective on the constant changes, cycles, growth and decay periods. Like Theosophy, its purpose is the ultimate transformation of the individual.

In considering the individual horoscope, there is always the factor of the *age* of the soul; though one cannot tell precisely from a chart whether a person is an "old" or "young" soul. Is a mere astrologer, with his full share of prejudices and shortcomings, to judge *that* in another? Nonetheless, it is worse than useless to talk of many lives, spiritual growth, and goals, etc., to one who is totally involved in getting as many material gains for the personality as soon as possible. And there are those who just want to talk about the "spiritual" when their lives and horoscopes scream for close attention to their mundane responsibilities as the true field of spiritual growth for them. One cannot be dogmatic, because at this stage of evolution most of us are so uneven in development that only a Master could tell whether one is a case of an evolved soul working off karma in difficult personality and circumstances or a young soul behaving in a way natural to this stage of development. The astrologer can only try to sense what counseling would be most helpful to the particular personality—to reach him where he "lives". He must avoid being judgmental. As Dane Rudhyar remarked, "No astrologer or psychoanalyst can interpret a life and destiny at a higher level than that at which he himself functions." Stephen Arroyo adds, "The quality of any astrological dialogue depends more than anything upon the purity of mind, depth of concentration and the specific life ideals of the counselor."⁹ Which should keep all astrologers humble!

The *Secret Doctrine* and other occult or religious writings and traditions indicate that on the long pilgrimage of evolution we did not start our rounds of incarnations at the same time. Many "older" souls who started earlier (and/or exerted themselves more) such as Jesus Christ, Gautama Buddha, and the Masters of Theosophy have already passed out of the human kingdom into the superhuman. If they retain their links with us it is in order to help and guide us and is done out of compassion and love, not necessity. Other souls are still in primitive stages of savagery. The vast majority of mankind ranges in between. Even looking about us in the immediate social environment we can note a great difference between those who are brilliant intellectually, morally, and spiritually and those who, whatever their station in life, respond to their fellows and circumstances with stupidity, selfishness, and violence.

The age of the soul is an important factor in karma. What is the natural—even good—action for the savage making war on a neighbor would bring negligible karma, perhaps building in that young soul courage, resourcefulness, and endurance. Whereas the same action in an older soul would bring with it much more activity on the emotional and mental levels and therefore incur a more far-reaching karma. By then he should have put aside to a large degree the cruder desires and negative urges to lust, violence and greed and their effect on his more sensitive, complicated being is much more injurious than to the younger soul whose learning requires the strong impact of violent desires and actions. The terrible wars and group aggressions of this century are a sad commentary on the spiritual evolutionary stage of mankind as a whole. We are as yet "barbarians".

After stating that we must not judge the age of the soul, I am going to contradict myself and say that it is not nearly so easy to analyze the character or to predict the life pattern of a more evolved, spiritual person because they can and do change themselves and therefore change their lives. This person is much more sensitive to the influences of the higher octave planets—Uranus, Neptune and Pluto—whereas the majority still react negatively to those subtler influences. For example, an aspect of Neptune will register in a more evolved personality as *spiritual idealism,* a greater realization of unity with the universe. In a younger personality, it may bring a time of self-deceit, delusion, and confusion. An evolved soul will turn the "hard" aspects—squares, oppositions, and some conjunctions—into steppingstones to a better, stronger character where the younger one will still be a battlefield of warring desires and fears to the end of his life.

NOTES

[1]C. Jinarajadasa, ed., *The Soul's Growth Through Incarnation,* Vols. I–III.

[2]Arthur Guirdham, *The Cathars and Reincarnation,* (Wheaton: Theosophical Publishing House, 1978).

[3]Ian Stevenson, *Twenty Cases Suggestive of Reincarnation,* (N.Y.: ASPR, 1966).

[4]I use the Koch House system as giving the greatest accuracy in House Cusp Degrees. There are at least seven House Systems; the most commonly used being the Placidian. *See* Dr. Walter A. Koch and Elizabeth Schaeck, *The Birthplace Tables of Houses for Northern Latitudes 0 to 60,* (N.Y.: ASI Publishers, 1975).

[5]The Arabic Part of Death is found by adding the Ascendant to the 8th House Cusp and subtracting the Moon's position.

[6]Richard Merriman, *Journey of the Soul Through the Horoscope* (Rochester, MI: Seek-It Publishing).

[7]The Moon progresses counter-clockwise around the horoscope, for example, with Moon in Virgo at birth and Mars in Leo, Mars would be the last planet conjunct by Moon prior to birth.

[8]*See* Chapter XIII.

[9]Stephen Arroyo, *Astrology, Karma and Transformation: The Inner Dimensions of the Birthchart* (Vancouver, Washington: CRCS Publications, 1978), p. xii.

III

REINCARNATION AND KARMA IN THE SIGNS

The descent and reascent of the monad or Soul cannot be disconnected from the Zodiacal signs . . . [H. P. Blavatsy, *The Secret Doctrine*, Vol. II (Adyar Edition, 1938), p. 396.]

The twelve Signs of the Zodiac have been called archetypal patterns, universal principles, and energy fields. They are all those and much more even beyond our concept, but at present we can only concern ourselves with what we can understand of life in ourselves and those around us.

Each Sign springs from, or embodies, a combination of one of the four **Elements**—Fire, Earth, Air, and Water—*plus* one of the three **Modes** of vibration or operation—Cardinal, Fixed, and Mutable.

The four Elements of Astrology are the basic building blocks of our universe. All four are in each of us, though we are more attuned to one or two of these Elements than we are to the others. They are archetypal because they are the embodiment, at a level incomprehensible to our finite minds, of an ultimate perfection: Ideas of the One Being. They ceaselessly mold all life, drawing each entity whether mineral, plant, animal, or human onward toward perfection of their particular kind. The ultimate archetype of Aries or Virgo may be beyond our present imagination, but we can see certain characteristics peculiar to Aries or Virgo all through the evolutionary chain of life.[1]

To understand the SIGNS of the zodiac, we must first understand the ELEMENTS and the MODE, or vibration, through which each Sign operates.

The **Cardinal Mode** of vibration or operation—through Aries, Libra, Cancer, and Capricorn—is *centrifugal*, that is, outward radiating energy. They are the first of the triplicities as the name, Cardinal, suggests. Activity and leadership are the Cardinal notes.

4 ELEMENTS

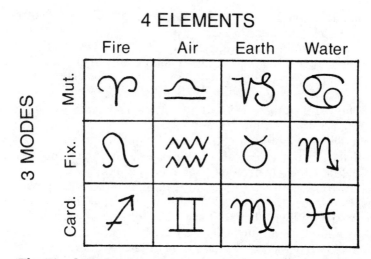

The **Fixed Mode** of operation or vibration—through Taurus, Scorpio, Leo and Aquarius—is *centripetal*: energy radiating inward toward a center. Their qualities of stability, perseverance, and concentration explain why these Signs are the key symbols of the major initiations of the soul because that concentration and perseverance ultimately give those qualities strongly under Fixed Signs the depth and power for the transformation of initiation. Fixity and organization are the notes of the Fixed Mode.

The **Mutable Mode** of vibration or operation—through Virgo, Pisces, Gemini, and Sagittarius—is *spiralic*, revolving toward the past (through Pisces and Virgo) and toward the future (through Gemini and Sagittarius).[2] They strive for harmony through adaptability and reaction, the notes of the Mutable Mode.

The **Element of Fire** expresses in three ways, in energy thrust, inspiration, and impulse. It is said that the Fire Signs—Aries, Leo and Sagittarius—are born to learn to love, and I would add, to learn to handle power rightly.[3]

The **Element of Earth** expresses in concentration of force and practicality. It is said that the Earth Signs—Taurus, Virgo, and Capricorn—are born to learn the lesson of service.

The **Element of Air** expresses in unification, intellect and versatility. The Air Signs—Gemini, Libra, and Aquarius—are born to learn the lesson of brotherhood.

The **Element of Water** expresses in strong emotions, instincts, sympathies, and feelings. The Water Signs—Cancer, Scorpio, and Pisces—are born to learn peace.

For a real understanding of the twelve Signs of the Zodiac, it is essential to understand the four Elements and the three Modes of operation. Their various combinations form the twelve primary patterns of energy which are called the zodiacal Signs.

The Signs of the **Fire Element**—Aries, Leo and Sagittarius—radiate an energy which is excitable, enthusiastic and spontaneous. Those persons with Fire Signs dominant in their charts are self-starters with great faith in themselves and the future. With the impetuousness of their Element, they often strike other Signs as overpowering and insensitive, impatiently brushing others aside as they rush into action. Their natural warmth is often mistaken for love when they are actually rather impersonal and self-centered. Fire can be destructive or constructive: only love, and learning the many lessons love teaches, can eventually transform the dynamic energy of the Fire Signs into spiritually constructive channels.

Aries combines the **Fire** Element with the **Cardinal** Mode of operation making those born with their Sun, Ascendant, or many planets in Aries ardent, keen, energetic, extraordinarily active, impatient and always ready to start new projects. The unevolved Aries is completely self-oriented, reckless, passionate, always rushing in where angels fear to tread. A strong will and talent for leadership marks Aries at any stage of evolution but the evolved, spiritual Aries learns to temper his will to the likeness of a fine sword, used only on behalf of others: for love of God and Man—"Thy Will, not mine, be done!" When they learn to forget themselves for love of those in their care, those who look to them for leadership, the archetypal Aries will indeed shine forth.

Leo combines the **Fire** Element with the **Fixed** Mode. This stabilizes the fiery, impulsive energy of the Element giving it a more practical, enduring expression. Leos like to do things in a royal way as befits the King of the Beast—even unevolved Leos are generous, kind, and given to dramatic gestures. Their faults lie in pride and the desire to dominate. Even when all the cruder manifestations of pride have been conquered there remains the far subtler but more dangerous one of *spiritual* pride to conquer.

In the unevolved Leo, the "I" is prominent. He yearns for love and adulation. That kind of attention is the breath of life to him.

If he does not obtain it (and he often feels unappreciated), or if he feels he has been made a fool of (there is nothing more damaging to the Leo's pride), he can behave very childishly. Manly P. Hall states that the unbalanced Leo types frequently suffer from some form of obsession due to the psychism of Cancer in the previous life.[4] The obsession may range from a divinity complex to an infallibility complex. Leo people sometimes feel that they are not as other mortals, peculiarly endowed with semidivine attributes and they love to reform other people or institutions. The Leo is not self-sufficient like his opposite number, the Aquarian. But eventually the Leo's yearning for love and appreciation teaches him that in order to receive love from others one must first give love—and not with the attitude of "I'll love you as long as you love me!" The warmth of the Fire Element is always present and it draws others like a magnet; they seem to gather instinctively around a Leo to warm their coldness and fill their emptiness. Leo is naturally generous, and in time it becomes an outpouring of genuine, selfless love for all.

Sagittarius combines the **Fire** Element with the **Mutable** Mode. This "mutability" makes him more adaptable and self-sufficient than either Aries or Leo. Intellectual as well as intelligent, the Sagittarian's Fire often turns to matters of religion or philosophy. His tendency for constant movement urges him to take many journeys, exploring both physically and mentally and, in the evolved Sagittarian, spiritually. The symbol for Sagittarius, the Archer, with his bow and arrow ever ready to shoot afar, gives rise to the observation that Sagittarians often seem more interested in *shooting* their arrows than in the *destination* of the arrow. Their arrows of speech can often wound through tactlessness, though they would call it "being open and above board." All the Fire Signs are enthusiastic, the direction or object of their enthusiasm depends on other factors in the horoscope. Because Sagittarius is combined with the Mutable Mode (with its urge to adapt and change to fit the circumstances), his enthusiasms tend to change whether in love, work or activities. Above all he wants to be free to explore, to be on the move, either physically or mentally, into new, intriguing areas. His faults can make him over-expansive, over-boisterous, extravagant and careless. Jupiter, ruler of Sagittarius, when afflicted seems to give too much of a good thing. His high spirits and joviality can become crude horseplay. Sagittarians, whether evolved or unevolved, are attracted to religion and philosophy and they often choose the priesthood or some kind of ministry as a vocation, learning the lesson of love in seeking the well-being of others.

All of the Fire Signs are generally more fortunate in life than the other Signs. Perhaps because their enthusiasm, optimism, urge to activity, and self-confident "push" are more likely to attract the favorable attention of others in material matters rather than any special alignment with Dame Fortune. Fire Signs express the radiating, energizing, warming principle which can manifest as enthusiasm and love, or as egotism. In simple words, *Light On The Path*[5] states the needed lesson for the Fire Signs:

> REGARD MOST EARNESTLY YOUR OWN HEART. For through your own heart comes the one light which can illuminate life and make it clear to your eyes. Study the hearts of men, that you may know what is that world in which you live and of which you will to be a part. Regard the constantly changing and moving life which surrounds you, for it is formed by the hearts of men; and as you learn to understand their constitution and meaning, you will by degrees be able to read the larger word of life.

The Signs of the **Earth Element**—Taurus, Virgo and Capricorn—seem born to learn the lessons of service and to hold possessions rightly. They have a natural attunement with the physical plane and a practical ability to utilize its forms. No one is all "Fire" or all "Earth", but those in whom the Earth Element Signs are dominant have in common traits of solid, dependable practicality. They are careful with possessions or finance: money and *things* matter more to them than to other Signs. Their faults often lie in too much emphasis on material goals, a narrowness of outlook, and an addiction to order and routine.

Taurus combines the **Earth** Element with the **Fixed** Mode and of all the three Earth Signs is the most "earthy": slow to change, persevering, stubborn, and possessive. Ruled by Venus, the Taurean often has great charm and sociability but he also can be very sensual and body-concerned. Desire for sex or possessions can inflict them with an inner restlessness even after they have obtained the object of their desires. The greatest fault of Taurus is possessiveness and stubbornness but in the evolved Taurean the stubbornness becomes the ability to persist against great odds over a long period for some altruistic cause. For all Earth Signs, those instructions given to the aspiring disciple in *Light*

On The Path apply with particular force:

> DESIRE POSSESSIONS ABOVE ALL. But those possessions must
> belong to the pure soul only, and be possessed therefore by
> all pure souls equally, and thus be the especial property of
> the whole only when united. Hunger for such possession as
> can be held by the pure soul, that you may accumulate
> wealth for that united spirit which is your only true Self.

Under Taurus the young soul seeks possessions for his little
self, but as he evolves those possessions are considered in the
light of stewardship and are held—and freely given—in the
service of others.

Virgo combines the **Earth** Element with the **Mutable** Mode
and therefore is the most adaptable and changeable of the Earth
Signs. This Sign naturally rules Service, and in service the Virgo
finds his greatest satisfaction and eventually his true Self. Essentially a worker, the Virgo is neat, precise, and careful of detail.
His faults lie in his over-critical attitudes, analyzing and criticizing the very life out of a thing or a person by dissecting it to
pieces. Like all the Earth Signs the question of values enters all
phases of their life. Where Taurus seeks to establish his value to
himself and the world through the acquisition of possessions,
Virgo seeks to make himself indispensable through his work or
service, and Capricorn values are sought through the acquisition
of power. There always seems to be an element of insecurity in
Earth Sign people which they seek to overcome consciously or
subconsciously by acquiring something they hold valuable. It is
very hard for them to realize that material things, whether
money, position, or power, do not give real security. A Virgo
incarnation is apt to be one of limitation and financial problems.
He tends to restrict his service to those whom, in his critical
opinion, he considers 'worthy' and he measures his service with
a careful eye on an equal return. When the evolved Virgo learns
the lesson of giving service to all without measuring the worth of
the recipient or the return to himself he becomes the selfless
servant of all.

Capricorn combines the **Earth** Element with the **Cardinal**
Mode of operation, which makes him less fixed than Taurus and
not as changeable as Virgo. Being of the Cardinal Mode the
Capricorn welcomes responsibility and is ambitious to rise.
Where Taurus seeks security in possessions and Virgo in work,

Capricorn seeks it through his activities in the outer world. This great desire for security often causes them to overvalue position, possessions and man-made laws. They tend to use people and love things instead of loving people and using things. The Capricorn's vision of power and position often makes his present life seem cramped and limited. Though the limitations are mostly self-imposed, the Capricorn can always see others who have more or have done better than themselves.

The Capricorns I have counseled or known surpass all the Signs in making "heavy weather" out of everything. It is no good pointing out their many blessings for they cannot seem to keep from feeling miserable, apprehensive, and worried. Their lesson is to learn that only through service to others in some form will their intrinsic worth and security be established. Through sharing they will discover warmth and joy.

In human life it seems a truth and a karmic law that the things we *value* the most, and the things we *fear* the most, hold for us the greatest lessons which, when fully understood and fulfilled, become the essential steps in spiritual growth.

The Signs of the **Air Element**—Gemini, Libra, and Aquarius—are intellectual and communicative. They tend to value mind above heart. They love intellectual pursuits, reason, and working in the realm of ideas. Their faults can be a lack of deep emotion and a tendency to occupy themselves with schemes and theories. *"A lot of hot air"* is an expression that describes an Air Sign extreme. Placing such high value on the mind, they feel superior to their fellows who may not be so articulate or intellectual, though they may well be very intelligent. Brotherhood seems to be the lesson to be learned by those dominated by Air and to one under an Air Sign who sets his feet upon the Path these words from the *Light On The Path* have particular application:

> KILL OUT ALL SENSE OF SEPARATENESS. Do not fancy you can stand aside from the bad man or the foolish man. They are yourself, though in a less degree than your friend or your Master. But if you allow the idea of separateness from any evil thing or person to grow up within you, by so doing you create karma which will bind you to that thing or person until your soul recognizes that it cannot be isolated . . .

Gemini combines the **Air** Element with the **Mutable** Mode. The typical Gemini likes to be constantly on the move physically and mentally—contacting, associating, co-ordinating. To his logical mind ideas and their relationships to each other are of fundamental importance. His task lies in comprehending the simple basis underlying the enormous varieties and complexities with which he tends to pre-occupy himself. Being Mutable *and* Air he is more changeable and adaptable than the other two Air Signs. This can make him more superficial, skimming the surface of ideas and relationships rather than probing to any depth. The evolved Gemini learns in time to value others even if their approach is not as quick or as intellectual as his, for then he can appreciate all men and women as facets of the same diamond Self.

Libra combines the **Air** Element with the **Cardinal** Mode. Libra is the natural Sign of partnership, the public, and relationships with others in general, so it might be thought that Libra would certainly know the meaning of brotherhood. But they dislike disagreeableness and confrontations of any kind and prefer to live free of any contact with the seamier facts of life, comfortable with a few select associates who suit their fastidious tastes. The admonition from *Light On The Path* to the disciple to kill out all sense of separateness continues with fitting words for Libra:

> Remember that the sin and shame of the world are your sin and shame; for you are a part of it; your karma is inextricably interwoven with the great Karma. And before you can attain knowledge you must have passed through all places, foul and clean alike. Therefore, remember that the soiled garment you shrink from touching may have been yours yesterday, may be yours tomorrow. And if you turn with horror from it, when it is flung upon your shoulders, it will cling the more closely to you.

Libras are often attractive people in appearance and gracious socially. They are tactful, well-balanced,[6] especially the male Libra. He sees both sides of the question which makes him an excellent arbitrator but it can lead to indecisiveness and vacillation when he has to make a personal decision. He has the tendency to overvalue intellectual and aesthetic matters, looking down on those who do not measure up to his standards—they are weighed in Libra's scales and found wanting! They are often climbers, striving to rise above the proletariat.

Aquarius combines the **Air** Element with the **Fixed** Mode.

This member of the Air Triplicity certainly should be brother-hood personified, for is not Aquarius the Sign of Man—"Mr. Brotherhood" himself? The sign Aquarius is ruled by Uranus the Awakener and Rebel. The Aquarian Age, in which all men will be equal, is upon us we are told. In the forefront, presumably, will be the children of Aquarius, happy to lead a revolution so that all men may be equal and free. But the difficulty comes in the matter of freedom—for the Aquarian cannot bear to have his *own* freedom threatened. When Universal Brotherhood is achieved there still must be rules and limitations so that the free actions of one individual or group does not infringe upon that of another, and *that* is what the Aquarian will resent. Brotherhood can only become a reality to the Aquarian when he desires his brother's freedom more than his own; when his own freedom is surrendered for the good of all. Oddly enough, although Aquarius is the Sign par excellence of humanity, Aquarians can be the most detached and "inhuman" of humans! Part of it is their desire to maintain their freedom by avoiding involvement and part of it is the cool detachment natural to the Air Element—head rules the heart. They find it difficult to mingle in a happy, warm way with others. Aquarians have few close friends—not because people don't like them but because they cannot penetrate the Aquarian aura of super-individuality. There is a joke among astrologers that the only way to get warm with an Aquarian is to be cremated with him! "Kill out all sense of separateness" is the instruction the Aquarian should take to heart if he is to lead us into the New Age.

The Signs of the **Water Element** are generally described by the words "emotional, unstable, and sensitive." Those under the dominance of a Water sign—Cancer, Scorpio, and Pisces—have strong emotions, instincts, sympathies, and feelings. Where those under the other three Elements have lessons to learn in their need to relate to others, the Water Signs are already far too concerned with other people. They have to learn detachment, to find that inner peace that others cannot disturb; only then can they be of real help to those they love. Their strong emotions and need of others cause them to be pulled this way and that. The life of even a mature Water Sign tends to be one emotional upheaval after another. In this they are not alone, of course. With most of humanity at this stage of evolution, the emotions and desires are the great field of battle where control must be won before any real spiritual progress can be made. *Light On The Path* puts it thus:

> DESIRE PEACE FERVENTLY. But the peace you shall desire is that sacred peace which nothing can disturb, and in which the soul grows as does the holy flower upon the still lagoons.

First, the Water Sign person desires peace around him, that others treat him with the love and harmony he so desperately desires. All that is needed for peace and harmony, he feels, is that *others* behave themselves—it is *they* who ruffle his emotional waters. But in time he comes to realize that the peace he wants must first be established within his own heart before it can be reflected in others about him. Peace is the lesson for the Water Signs.

Cancer combines the **Water** Element with the **Cardinal** Mode. Like its symbol, the Crab, Cancer loves his home, his family, his shell. He is protective, supportive, devoted to his own family. He is a great collector who finds it hard to throw anything away and that extends to his relationships. He tends to hang on to a relationship be it friendship, romance, or a job, long after the life or usefulness of it has gone. He never seems to know when, or be able, to "let go". He is often emotionally insecure and seeks that security in his domestic, personal life. The Cancer person is easily offended and moody, but good in business because of the innate protectiveness that makes him cautious and economical. Hurts sink deep and are brooded over. All Signs have strengths and weaknesses; there are no "good" or "bad" Signs. Control of the emotions and imagination is needed with Cancer. They should practice using their imaginations creatively instead of negatively. The evolved Cancerian eventually expands the maternal urges beyond his immediate family giving that tender, compassionate love to every living creature.

Scorpio combines the **Water** Element with the **Fixed** Mode. This much maligned member of the Water triplicity has two symbols—the Scorpion crawling in the dust with the poisonous sting in its tail, and the Eagle soaring in the sky. These symbols aptly describe the lowest and highest type of Scorpio person. The Sign Scorpio is associated with the 8th House which rules death, regeneration, rebirth, and the basic concerns of life such as sex and other people's money. These things are as necessary to the evolution of material and spiritual life as any life-producing and life-preserving factors ruled by the other Signs. The mature Scorpio realizes this and attempts to plumb the depths beneath these facts of life. Intense, passionate, and ambitious, with the staying power inherent in the Fixed Mode of operation, Scorpio's great problem is controlling the emotions and desires. His ideas of justice often become entangled in emotional reflexes or he suffers from an exaggerated sense of being unjustly judged or dealt with by others, leading to much resentment and brooding. Once he turns from the real or fancied injustices to the reformation of his own character his progress is swift, he becomes the soaring eagle. In the words of *Light On The Path:*

> But to learn is impossible until the first great battle (i.e. control of the emotions and desires) has been won. The mind may recognize truth, but the spirit cannot receive it. Once having passed through the storm and attained the peace, it is always possible to learn, even though the disciple waver, hesitate, and turn aside.

Although this battle for control of the emotions and desires (which so distorts every Sign's perception of truth) must be fought—over and over—until that final triumph is attained, the eventual victory is certain. Then, as the *Light On The Path* describes it:

> The peace you shall desire is that sacred peace which nothing can disturb, and in which the soul grows as does the holy flower upon the still lagoons.

Thus, those of the Water Element will find the inner peace in the unruffled waters of their emotions and desires by first controlling and then transcending them.

Pisces combines the **Water** Element with the **Mutable** Mode. Of all the twelve Signs the natives of Pisces seem to have the most difficult lives. They are subject to all the instability, strong sympathies and feelings, sensitivity to hurt and tendency to brood which are intrinsic qualities of the Water Element. Without Cancer's dynamic expression through Cardinal Mode activity and leadership or Scorpio's Fixed Mode stability and power of organization, Pisces fluctuates like the tides. The flexibility of the Mutable Mode makes Pisces the most fluid of the three Water Signs, pulled this way and that by every current. The Pisces symbol, two fish swimming in opposite directions, is very descriptive. It is also the last Sign of the Zodiac which began with Aries, bringing to an end one evolutionary cycle in which all the loose ends of unfinished business must be gathered up and disposed of before starting another cycle. It is, in a sense, the weakest of the Signs in *material* accomplishment because it represents the end of a cycle of experience. The first few or last few degrees in any Sign often indicates weakness or confusion affecting the planet or Ascendant so placed because they are not established firmly in the Sign they are beginning or leaving. Thus it seems to be with Pisces as the last of the twelve Signs but it is a necessary process of karmic law, necessary for the health and progress of the whole and not to be considered by any means an *inferior* part of the cycle. Many people view old age with horror—the decline and fall of any person, culture, or era—as terribly sad and depressing after the strength and glory that had preceded it. This is the limited, personality view of a stage in the life cycle Man would just as soon do without. The Inner Self's viewpoint—which we are trying to make our own—sees the larger picture stretching over the eons with all stages of life as equally necessary to growth.

The Water of Pisces is the water of the sea—boundless, infinitely deep with many hidden currents. It is the Sign of the Savior, the last crucifixion before transformation into the superhuman kingdom.

The evolved Piscean is capable of devoted selfless service for others, of a deep universal vision and mystic at-one-ment with all living creatures which they show at all stages of evolution in their tenderness for animals and plants. The Piscean is the most sensitive of all Water Signs, depending on others for support. The danger lies in the more forcefully expressed opinions and defined personalities of others confusing and distorting their own unique selves. A Piscean must learn to move from self-pity, indecision, and feelings of inadequacy (which sometimes lead to the escapism of alcoholism or drugs or daydreaming) to practical uses of imagination and idealism in the arts, religion, selfless service, and healing.

In most charts there is a mixture of Elements, with perhaps an emphasis on one or two. No one is all Air or all Water, or at least that is a very rare occurrence. Even the Sun Sign can be misleading. So often a person will say, "I have my Sun in Capricorn but my character doesn't fit the description of Capricorn!" He may have Sun in Capricorn (an Earth Sign) but have his Moon and Ascendant in Aries and five planets in Leo—all these latter are ruled by the Fire Element. Capricorn and Saturn may color his basic nature, but the outgoing, enthusiastic, expansive qualities of the Fire Element will predominate.

The Element of the Ascendant Sign's ruling planet is of vital importance in assessing the primary motivating urges of the individual—unless that ruling planet is Uranus, Neptune, or Pluto. They rule Aquarius, Pisces, and Scorpio respectively. The Elements of those three planets affect more the unconscious factors motivating the generation to which the individual belongs rather than his personal or individual consciousness. In the case of Pisces on the ascendant, one would consider the Element in which Jupiter was placed rather than Neptune. With an Aquarius rising, the Element of Saturn instead of Uranus would be used. And if the Sign of Scorpio is the sign on the ascendant, instead of studying Pluto, one would consider the Element of the planet Mars.

The balance or imbalance of the Elements in a chart is important. One should always bear in mind that an imbalance—too many or too few planets in any one Element—can be offset or compensated for, by some other factor in the chart. For example, a chart with no planets in Water signs, but having the Moon and Neptune both in the First House gives the native the qualities of sympathy, sensitivity, and emotion by the nature of those two planets.

With too little emphasis in Fire Signs, energy, enthusiasm, and joy in life may be lacking or the faith and optimism may be low. Too much Fire emphasis in the chart tends to make persons hyperactive, restless, "pushy" and very insensitive to the feelings of others.

With too little emphasis on the Earth Element in a chart, the person always seems to be at a loss in dealing with the material world. The practical business of earning a living or making a home, or even coping with bodily needs such as food, rest, and hygiene, is so difficult or unsatisfying that the person often tries to escape into a world of imagination or spirit. Too much emphasis in Earth Signs, on the other hand, can give extraordinary strength and practicality; yet, material concerns can become so overvalued that the person becomes blinded to ethical and spiritual principles.

Persons with not enough emphasis in Air Elements often lack perspective or even perception of the ramifications arising from their actions. They may exhibit a resistance to new ideas and a distrust of intellectual people. They can rarely be detached enough to view anything and anyone—especially themselves—objectively. Too much Air produces an overactive mind which can run away with the person making him at times brilliant and articulate or at other times out of touch with practical considerations.

People with too little emphasis in Water signs have great difficulty appreciating the feelings of others, or even understanding their own emotional needs. They lack sympathy and understanding of others so their relationships are sterile or troubled. These arid persons also suffer from a variety of psychological, emotional, and physical problems for the Water Element is a much needed cleansing, healing energy without which the subtle bodies[7], as well as the physical body, becomes clogged. Too much Water emphasis gives a nature too sensitive to any experience; the person over-reacts to every trifle. They can be compared to people adrift on a storm-tossed sea, but the waves and wind that toss them are within themselves. They are often psychic, but it is usually a negative psychism that leaves them open to every influence whether helpful or not, unless aided by other positive elements in the chart.

Usually when there is little emphasis in one Element, there will be an over-emphasis in another Element. Richard Ideman has done much work on what he terms "the missing or inferior function" (none or only one planet in an Element or Mode, the Ascendant and Midheaven are not counted) and the "dominant function" (in which five or more planets are found in one Element or Mode).[8] In brief, his thesis is that areas in a chart with a concentration of energy (many planets therein) constitute a dominant function and they are the areas that seem easiest for us in expression. Areas most psychologically potent are those with *less* emphasis—few or no planets where we must *work* for expression. It is an area in ourselves and in life about us that is *different*, which completely mystifies. For example, a person with little emphasis in Water Signs is mystified by the emotions of others and confused by his *own* emotions. A person with an inferior function in his chart can unconsciously repress it, overcompensate for its lack, or even project it onto another.

If they repress the function psychically or psychologically it will eventually surface in some physical illness. Overcompensation produces such examples as a person who, with his inferior function in Earth Signs, becomes obsessed with sex, money, food and the body. Or they may project that missing function onto someone else—"I can't do it, you do it!" I have a friend with eight planets in Air Signs, none in Water, who seeks out for personal relationships people with very strong emotional natures (obviously those with *many* planets in Water Signs) to supply what he lacks.

The seeds of greatest creativity come out of the inferior function because we try harder to compensate in that area. But naturally, one cannot change one's emphasis or imbalance in the Elements or Modes simply through analysis but recognition of that lack can be a help in understanding ourselves and others. We can become more whole, less lopsided in character when we recognize our tendency to overvalue certain factors and devalue others. We should be aware that there are fields of activity and types of people who can teach us in areas where we are lacking.

Instead of interpreting the twelve Signs of the zodiac as twelve separate bundles with characteristics peculiar to each, it can be seen that putting the emphasis upon the four Elements and three Modes gives a much deeper meaning to the interpretation of astrological charts and to the understanding of oneself because one is then dealing with the basic universal energies at work *through* the Signs.

NOTES

[1] The Four Elements can be divided into the basic divisions of Chinese philosophy: Water and Earth being Yin, and Air and Fire being Yang.

[2] For a detailed analysis, *see* Stephen Arroyo, *Astrology, Psychology and the Four Elements* (Vancouver, Washington: CRCS Publications, 1975).

[3] Joan Hodgson, *Wisdom in the Stars* (White Eagle Publ.).

[4] Manly P. Hall in *Astrology and Reincarnation* (Los Angeles: Philosophical Research Society, Inc.) makes a good case for the theory that the soul incarnates from one Sign to the next in orderly procession. A Leo Ascendant or Sun in the present life would mean the previous life was under a Cancer Ascendant or Sun. The next life would be under Virgo.

[5]*Light On The Path* (Wheaton: Theosophical Publishing House, 1970). This classic of Eastern Wisdom offers guidance and instruction to those who aspire to tread the path of spiritual unfoldment. Its sources are very ancient but its message is timeless.

[6]Recent astrological research involving thousands of people has shown that male Libras were outstanding for their stability, which is basically a matter of balance: the very essence of Libra's symbol of the Scales.

[7]Theosophical and many Eastern teachings maintain that Man has seven bodies or "sheaths" in which his Inner Self is clothed of which the physical body is but the coarsest, most visible to our eyes.

[8]Richard Ideman has a book exploring these ideas coming out soon but the title has not been decided upon.

IV

THE TWELVE HOUSES: FIELDS OF EXPERIENCE

The 360 degrees of the Zodiac of the horoscope are divided into twelve "Houses" representing the environment, the fields of experience, the Web of life in which we are provided with all the material we need for growth. Moving counter-clockwise around the horoscope beginning with the 1st House and ending with the 12th we have a picture of the journey of a person through one lifetime. It can be viewed with deeper symbology as the soul's journey from primitive, self-involved man in the 1st House to the spiritual, Self-evolved man in the 12th House ready to sacrifice himself for all living creatures. During that long journey the soul has worked to acquire those skills and abilities necessary for survival. In the process of doing this he has created all sorts of karma and maya[1], both necessary for the first half of his evolution. Most of us have passed the halfway mark and achieved success in acquiring those skills and abilities, but we find it isn't enough, it doesn't bring the hoped for happiness and completion. So we start the journey back home resolving the karma and transcending the *maya* we have created.

While the primary energies of the horoscope are always shown by the placement of the Signs and planets, there is a sympathetic correlation between the twelve Signs and the twelve Houses. No matter where Aries falls in the chart there is always a relationship between that Sign and the 1st House, between Taurus and the 2nd House and so forth. However, the Signs and Houses should always be seen as distinct and separate factors in interpreting the chart.

The **Angular Houses**—1st, 4th, 7th and 10th—correspond with the Cardinal Signs Aries, Cancer, Libra and Capricorn. They are the beginning, initiating, focussing Houses like the Cardinal Signs, and their mode of expression is *action*. If the planetary emphasis in a horoscope lies in these Houses that person is likely to be an activist: energetically striving to make

THE TWELVE HOUSES

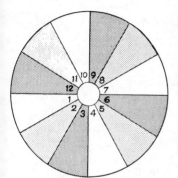

The Angular Houses: 1, 4, 7, and 10
Powerful, active, and initiatory.

The Succedent Houses: 2, 5, 8, and 11
Consolidating that began in Angular Houses.

The Cadent Houses: 3, 6, 9, and 12
Learning and communicating and dispersion of ideas and energies.

1st House:	The primary self in action, physical characteristics, personal concerns.
2nd House:	Finances, possessions, resources, material values.
3rd House:	Brothers and sisters, close relations, neighbors, mental activities, all kinds of communications whether by speech, writing, learning, visiting, short journeys, etc.
4th House:	The family, parents, psychic roots, early environment, latter part of life, the foundation of one's self regard.
5th House:	Children, creativity, pleasure, love affairs, risk, speculation, hobbies, sports, love given.
6th House:	Work, service, health, hygiene, employees, fellow workers, and the working conditions.
7th House:	Marriage, partnership, enemies, the public, groups, unions.
8th House:	Finances and resources of others, inheritances, emotional values, death, regeneration, sex, beginnings and endings.
9th House:	Expansion of self through spiritual, mental, or physical exploration, philosophy, the law, religion, publishing, travel, foreign lands.
10th House:	The career, reputation, highest achievement in life, one of the parents, government.
11th House:	Friends and acquaintances, group affiliations, long-term objectives, love received.
12th House:	The subconscious, that which is hidden, self-undoing, the service which is sacrificial, the psychic, serious states of ill health, large institutions, enclosure in hospital, prison, monastery, etc.

his mark in the world. His life is full of action and events.

The **1st House** is where consciousness begins, the primary stage of the self, the most natural inherent tendencies, the window through which the self views the world, the personality— which means literally the "mask of the Self." Emphasis in the 1st House (many planets or dominant planets) shows that personal problems and affairs occupy an unusual amount of concern.

The **4th House** rules the early crystallization of the self in the home, with the parents and family. It also rules the latter part of life which is really the summing up of one life and the preparation for the next. The early childhood has much to do with the foundation of selfhood for the entire life: like the building of any structure if the foundation is poorly laid—all that is raised later will be out of plumb or in danger of collapse. The 4th House shows how the person views himself—with self-confidence or lack of it. The Cusp of the 4th—the Nadir or I.C.—is the *transformation* point of the chart. It marks the accumulation of impressions from the past. If you want to know what you truly are: what you have come into incarnation for—study the Sign and the planet on the Nadir.

The **7th House** rules the relationship with others, the concept of sharing and above all partnership. The business partner, the marriage partner, one's equals and the public at large. Planets here show the ease or difficulty one has in relating to those associates and the public and the *kind* of people we attract into those relationships with ourselves. For example, Saturn in the 7th House indicates our partners in marriage or business are likely to be older, more serious. Marriage may be delayed until later in life, even denied, while public recognition will come slowly and only after much hard work.

The **10th House** rules one's profession, career and public honor. If the 4th House shows how the person sees himself, the 10th House shows how the world sees the person. It shows the highest projection of the person in the world; his most visible public image. The condition of planets in this House shows the *kind* of recognition he will get—whether fame or notoriety.

The **Succedent Houses** (2nd, 5th, 8th, and 11th) correspond with the Fixed Signs—Taurus, Leo, Scorpio, and Aquarius. They consolidate and structure what the Angular/Cardinal Houses began, motivated by the need for *security*.

The **2nd House** shows how the personality strives to acquire

money and possessions to ensure his security financially and
also because possessions for most of humanity are the measure
of self-worth. It shows what the person *values*, for we put our
money where our heart is. It shows our *sense* of values: whether
we give value for value received in our dealings. An afflicted
Sun in 2nd House can indicate a person who feels the world
owes him a living without any effort on his part. One of the laws
of karma is that each one must pay his way in life, for all the
things given him in nourishment, shelter, opportunity, protection and emotional relationships (to name a few). We must repay
in whatever coin we have available. This means more than
money, buying and selling. In the evolved man it means nothing
less than the sum total of what he *is* poured out in universal
giving. In a "young" soul and average person it means giving an
honest day's work for his income and never seeking to take that
which is not rightly his.

The **5th House**   Here the personality strives for security in a
more creative sense—creating children of the mind, talents, or
body. It is also the House ruling amusements, hobbies, sports,
the avocation, pleasures, love affairs, speculation, and gambling. It is interesting that the House of speculation, gambling, risk
should be the same as that concerned with creativity and bearing
children. But bearing and raising children carries risk; one never
knows what kind of soul one will attract; some of the heaviest
karmic links seem to be worked out between parent and child.
Every artist or musician knows the risk of daring new tech-
niques, new inspirations. The 5th House shows the ability to
give love—as the 11th House shows the ability to *receive* love: to
love someone or something makes one vulnerable and that is a
risk many will not take but no real growth is accomplished
without love.

The **8th House** shows how the personality strives to find
emotional and soul security. It is the House of life's mysteries:
the experiences this House brings are like initiations opening
our eyes to deeper realizations. Death, sex and other people's
money have a deep effect on the person's emotional security.
The sexuality associated with the 8th House has its roots in the
need to feel at-one with another, less alone, less insecure. The
8th House is one of the occult Houses and sexual practices were
often a part of Black Magic. There is a mystery and a power to the
sexual act which has never been fully understood. People with

an 8th House emphasis are often involved with thoughts of death, the afterlife, legacies, and spiritualistic activities. It is the House of death but also of rebirth and regeneration: the destruction of forms is necessary and productive: some part of ourself whether physical, emotional, mental, or in attitudes or relationships is always in process of dying and being reborn in a new form. As remarked in Chapter II, the 8th House is the Door to the next life or the new life.[2] By trying to plumb the mysteries of life, death, and sex the person seeks both emotional and soul security: to know that there is continuity to life and in the deepest relationships.

The **11th House**   In this House the personality seeks to expand his security in his relationships with friends and with groups joined together for altruistic purposes. His larger goals are shown here and his ability to gain and receive love from others. The efforts and action of the 10th House—the career—are consolidated in the 11th House. The planets here show the kind of people attracted as friends and how they help or harm one. It represents the search for social and intellectual security.

The Cadent Houses (3rd, 6th, 9th and 12th) correspond with the Mutable Signs: Gemini, Virgo, Sagittarius and Pisces. As the Angular Houses are associated with action, with initiation of ventures, the Succedent Houses are concerned with the consolidation of those actions, the things we desire and want to control and manage, motivated by our need for security. So, the Cadent Houses are concerned with *learning and dissemination* of what we have learned from the experience in the preceding Angular and Succedent Houses. The flow of life experience from beginning, consolidation through dissemination, and beginning again is the cycle of spiritual and material evolution in which we all participate. Our individual horoscopes show the phase or phases in the cycle which are dominant in this particular incarnation. It used to be considered by astrologers that the Angular Houses were the Houses of prime importance—persons with many planets in Angular Houses were considered to be those who would make their mark in the world. Angular planets were considered very strong by position. By implication those persons were stronger, more effective than their lesser brethren with more planets in Succedent or Cadent Houses. Planets in Cadent Houses were decidedly "weak" and the most their owners could hope for was a rich, subjective life but an ineffective role in the world! This was a case, in my opinion, of mistakenly equating the usual visability before the world of people with emphasis in Angular Houses with their greater importance in the scheme of things. Three or four planets in Angular Houses were supposed to give one a good chance of fame and recognition. Astrological thinking has changed considerably and most astrologers now recognize that the work and qualities of the Succedent and Cadent Houses is of equal if different importance. Each phase is of absolute necessity to the individual in his one life and his span of many lives as it is to the universal economy.

The **3rd House**   In this cadent House, the personality moves out from the basic "I" and "Mine" of the 1st and 2nd Houses into the world of the mind; it has to do with such areas as brothers and sisters, neighbors, writing, elementary education, short journeys, and the sense of humor. Here the person learns not only from his studies but from the experiences of his 1st and 2nd Houses and communication with those near him. What he has assimilated and learned, he now communicates to others and they with him. The 3rd House is concerned with the lower, concrete mind; its opposite—the 9th House—rules the higher, abstract mind.

The **6th House**   In this House the personality begins to move from the self-involvement of the first five Houses to a wider participation through work and service. This House rules health and sickness; employment; employees—both those working with you and for you; and the environment of your work. The 6th House and its opposite—the 12th—seem to be most karmically-bound of all areas in the horoscope, because these two Houses are most often concerned with the karmic debts we owe to others. That is, they are concerned with the obligations we subconsciously or consciously feel to serve, nurse, or care for others. The illnesses and handicaps we suffer (shown in either House) are the last working out in the physical body of causes originating in the emotional or mental bodies.

If we work long hours for poor pay or under bad conditions for a harsh employer, be sure that in another life we meted that same treatment out to him when he was our employee or slave. Or else we shirked our duties while drawing full pay for work not done. Remember, karmic laws are inescapable and for all that is given or paid to us we are expected to repay in some manner. We can resolve that karma by serving that same employer with patience until the day another job opens, with the attitude that we are eliminating an old debt while helping fellow workers with happy companionship. Planetary emphasis in the 6th and 12th Houses shows the kind of bondage, the 6th House especially shows where we failed to serve—or where we served well and faithfully. It is here that the personality first learns to serve others and eventually become a Servant of all using the skills and qualities he has developed in the previous Houses.

The **9th House**   In this House the personality moves yet deeper into the fields of learning and communication of what he has learned. This is the House of the higher, abstract mind;[3] higher education; the law; religion; philosophy; long journeys;[4] and foreign countries or lands far from the place of birth. The journeys need not only be physical ones, but also those of exploration into uncharted regions through our dreams, visions and mental speculations. That which is concrete, objective form in the 3rd House becomes abstract and formless in the 9th. It shows the kind of religion or philosophy to which he is attracted, the kind of teacher or guru he needs, and the difficulty or ease with which he finds spiritual nourishment. In this House it is learning, communication, and dissemination in higher, more abstract and less personal matters.

The **12th House**   Here the personality expands his vision and learning into universal consciousness, identifying himself with the inclusive Self of all instead of the exclusive self of the 1st House. This usually does not happen in depth until his spiritual evolution is well along. Before that he experiences this House as the place where he meets all that is hidden, repressed, or avoided in order to resolve those blocks to his progress. It rules confinement whether voluntary (in a monastery or convent) or involuntary (in a hospital, prison, or asylum). Interestingly enough, astrologers find it also seems to rule other large institutions such as educational and financial institutions. It rules large animals (the opposite 6th House rules small animals) and serious illnesses, (chronic and less serious illness are 6th House concerns) hidden enemies and "self-undoing." This is appropriate as the 12th House is the House most directly linked with the past incarnation and the subconscious.

The phobias, neurotic aversions, compulsions, and other

"hang-ups" that are rooted in the past are real "hidden enemies" that become secret, undermining enemies within our own gates, so to speak. Often these things accomplish our self-undoing if we do not recognize them and deal with them. There may be hidden enemies without as well, of course. It is here that the personality assimilates all that he has experienced in the preceding eleven Houses and learns his final lessons by tying up and resolving all the loose ends of karma. A concentration of planets in this House can give a life in which the personality feels frustrated and confined, his life cramped by handicaps, duties, guilts, and obligations. All is not negative though, for there are hidden strengths and secret friends and helpers to be found. He learns to purge the residue of the past so that he can express himself clearly and actively when he starts the next cycle in the 1st House. Only those who have suffered and understand the causes of their suffering can truly help others. From the learning fields of the 12th House spring the great Saviors of the world who willingly sacrifice themselves out of love and compassion for others.

Signs as Rulers of the Houses

Wherever the natural ruler of a House is placed, there is an empathy between things ruled by the two Houses. For example, if Taurus, natural ruler of 2nd House is placed on the 7th House there will always be a relationship between one's possessions—personal money and values—with marriage, partnership, and the public. If Taurus is on the 11th one may gain or lose money through friends, join altruistic Groups for mercenary reasons, or contribute money or possessions to them.

The first six Houses are more concerned with personal matters, with everything viewed more or less from a self-centered viewpoint. The big change comes when the personality in one incarnation or in the larger span of lives crosses the line from the 6th to the 7th House and enters into that phase where he must learn to deal with his equals, such as partners in marriage or business, and with the public. Dealing with equals is much more difficult than with those above you or below you. He must learn to give to others, balance his rights with theirs, enlarge his interests so that their interests become as important to him as his own. The Scales, symbol of Libra, aptly describes the balancing point between the personal and the larger impersonal.

There is another classification of Houses which astrologers find helpful, that is, dividing them according to the Elements associated with those Houses.

The **Water Houses** are the 4th, 8th and 12th. Cancer is associated with the 4th House; Scorpio, with the 8th; and Pisces, with the 12th. The dynamic energies of the Water Element express in these Houses through instincts, desires, and emotions relating to the past. Cancer and the 4th House are often involved with family tradition, psychic roots, and antiques. Scorpio and the 8th House are concerned with reincarnation, contact with those dead and their possessions, legacies, and occult studies or ancient mysteries. Pisces and the 12th deal with karmic bondage of past life relationships, subconscious obsessions, fears resulting from deeds committed and avoided in past lives. These three Water Houses are termed the occult, hidden Houses where the soul, yearning for emotional peace, eventually resolves the results of past life experiences and responsibilities. The Water Houses are concerned with *inner development*.

The **Earth Houses** are the 2nd, 6th and 10th. Taurus rules the 2nd House; Virgo, the 6th; and in the 10th, Capricorn. The dynamic energies of the Earth Element express in these Houses through material, practical forms—our needs for survival such as money, possessions, jobs, reputation, and health. We acquire security by working to consolidate, control, and manage things and people.

The **Fire Houses** include Aries in the 1st House, Leo in the 5th, and Sagittarius in the 9th. The dynamic energies of the Fire Element express through these Houses with fiery, driving, self Will. Aries and the 1st House are propelled toward action, self-assertion. The "I" with its personal affairs and the need to be first are always prominent in an emphasized 1st House. Leo and the 5th House extend the "I" to include children; children are often looked upon as extensions of their parents. The creative activities of the 5th House, as mental offspring, are likewise a matter for pride—that outstanding characteristic of Leo. Last are Sagittarius and the 9th House. Here, the Fire Element fuels that "Divine discontent" that propels men and women to exploration of the unknown, higher mind and ideals. Its zeal makes a saint or a fanatic, an explorer in the jungle or in space, or an ever-restless "rolling stone".

The **Air Houses** are Gemini and the 3rd, Libra and the 7th, and Aquarius and the 11th. The dynamic energies of the Air Element express in these Houses through social, intellectual means. Gemini and the 3rd House are involved with the lower mind activities—learning and communication—which cover everything from talking, writing and traveling to exchanging ideas in every form. Libra and the 7th House are involved with partnerships—in business or marriage. Incidentally, the horoscope does not show the marriage license: any one-to-one relationship entered into with thoughts of permanency such as "common law" marriage, even a homosexual "marriage" will show as a 7th House partnership. I have had a number of people consult me who were involved in heterosexual or homosexual relationships that they considered as firm a partnership as any legal marriage. People with emphasis in the 7th House are often arbitrators, diplomats, consultants, and counselors because of their intellectual competence and even-balanced judgment. When they deal with the public their ideas find easy acceptance. The social, intellectual urges find ready expression with Aquarius and the 11th House in friendships, group associations, and systems of thought. The give-and-take of those more impersonal relationships appeals to all Air Signs who are truly "in their element" exchanging ideas and working for some political, scientific, metaphysical, or humanitarian cause with others.

The **Empty Houses**—Sometimes one or more Houses in a chart will be empty of planets. Most astrologers interpret this to mean a lack of interest, or only a passive interest in the things ruled by that House. My personal experience agrees with that to a certain extent, except when the planet ruling the Sign on the Cusp is very important in the horoscope.

Intercepted Signs It is not unusual to find a Sign "intercepted" in a House; that is, totally contained within the House and yet with the preceding Sign of the cusp of that House. [For example, Pisces on the cusp of the 4th House and Taurus on the 5th House cusp with Aries *intercepted* in the 4th.] Interpretations vary. Some feel that there is always some bother with the problems of that House with an intercepted Sign; they tend to preoccupy us, even if subconsciously. Others feel that the qualities of that Sign are somehow *inhibited* by interception and are not able to express freely until, by progression, they reach the Cusp of the House.

Two House Cusps Occupied by the Same Sign   There are times when one Sign stretches across two-House areas. The influence of that Sign, the Element and Mode it manifests, as well as the planet that rules the Sign are active over the matters ruled by *two* Houses instead of one. Those matters ruled by the two Houses will be linked or related in some manner. For example, if the same Sign spreads over the 1st and 2nd Houses: the personality will have a closer than normal identification with his money, possessions, and values. They will seem like a veritable *extension* of himself.

The Overall Pattern of Planetary Placement in the Houses Students are urged to read *The Guide to Horoscope Interpretation* by Marc Edmund Jones,[5] for his detailed analysis of planetary patterns and what they mean. He maintains there are seven basic patterns: the **Splash type** where the planets are scattered all over the chart. This indicates the person has a wide, even universal range of interest, or negatively, one who dissipates his energies by scattering them over too many interests and activities. The **Bundle type** showing most of the planets bunched together indicates one who concentrates his interests and energies on only one or two things. This can make for tremendous drive and accomplishment in a selected field but it also can mean a very limited person with an obsession or one who puts all his eggs in one basket, so to speak. When something happens to that basket he is in real trouble! The **Bowl type** has most of the planets in one-half of the horoscope and that person has something to give his fellows, whether for good or ill. The **See-saw type,** where the planets are in two groups roughly opposite each other in the chart exemplifies a person with the ability to see both sides of any matter, but often has great difficulty in making decisions or taking decisive steps because he keeps seeing both sides—pro and con—to a proposed action. The **Locomotive type,** with planets in two-thirds of the chart with one-third empty, shows one who senses a strong lack or need, or has a problem to be solved related to that empty section, either for himself or in the social and intellectual world about him. He is a self-driving individual and it is termed "locomotive" because the leading planet (of the string in the occupied two-thirds) dominates and pulls the other planets along behind it. The **Bucket type** is like the Bowl but with a handle. The handle (formed by one or two planets) opposite the bowl formation (all the other planets) indicates a special capacity or gift for some particularly effective kind of activity. The **Splay type** with planets placed in strong aggregations at irregular points in the chart indicates a highly individual or purposeful emphasis in the life—a rugged individualist who refuses to be pigeonholed in any category.

NOTES

[1]*Maya* is a Hindu word describing the powerful force that creates the cosmic illusion that the phenomenal world is real. Reality is a relative thing: the further from the One Source and Center, the more clothed with illusion and transitory phenomena our world becomes. One of the best books on this subject is Alice A. Bailey, *Glamour: A World Problem* (N.Y.: Lucis Publishing Co., 1967).

[2]Chapter II, page 15.

[3]In the mental body (and mental plane), that subtle vehicle of thought, there is a division between the concrete, objective, empirical thinking and learning and the more abstract, intuitive, higher reasoning. This corresponds to what is termed in Theosophical parlance as the "lower" and "higher" mind and in Astrology to the 3rd and 9th Houses, Gemini and Sagittarius. See E. Norman Pearson, *Space, Time and Self* (Wheaton: Theosophical Publishing House, 1967).

[4]Up to the present era, the astrological terms of long journeys—9th House and short journeys—3rd House were appropriate, but now with air travel the distinction is no longer so clear. An example was given recently of driving a friend 30 miles to the airport to catch a plane to Chicago—a distance of almost a thousand miles. The round trip from home to airport and back with road traffic took over three hours while the friend flew from New York City to Chicago in *two* hours. Which one took the short journey (3rd House) and which one took the long journey (9th House)? Should it be measured in miles, time or how the person *experienced* the journey?

[5]Marc Edmond Jones, *The Guide to Horoscope Interpretation* (Wheaton: Theosophical Publishing House, 1975).

V

ASPECTS: DYNAMIC RELATIONSHIPS

I once showed some horoscopes to a psychic friend who knew little about Astrology. She remarked that to her they gave the appearance of a pattern of different colored lines running from one brilliant center to another—the whole, pulsating with movement and color. When astrologer Rose Elliot studies a horoscope, she feels the planetary forces playing upon her like the rays of a sun, but they are colored rays. Where two planets are in aspect, she sees the rays blending and the color of the planetary ray is tinted by the Sign through which it is working.[1]

This certainly indicates that the horoscope is more than an exercise in symbols and degrees on paper but a door to direct realization of the energy pattern peculiar to each chart. The planets are also said to sound their individual and distinctive notes—"The music of the spheres"—which vary as they relate to one another by aspect. It should be possible for one with the gift of clairaudience[2] to *hear* the theme or themes sounded by the horoscope. The pattern of the birth chart is similar to a piece of music, various themes, or perhaps one dominating theme, sounding again and again with variations as the planets progress, aspecting each other and their natal positions. The transitting planets making their aspects would also add to this "music of the spheres."[3]

An aspect is the relationship measured in zodiacal degrees between planets or between a planet and an important point in the horoscope such as the Midheaven, Ascendant, House Cusps, the Moon's Nodes, etc. For example, if Jupiter is 10° Cancer and Saturn is 10° Libra, the two planets are 90 zodiacal degrees or three Signs apart. They are in a **square** aspect to one another. If Saturn were 10° Scorpio the distance between would be 120° and a trine aspect would be formed between the two.

The energy flow (with its influence on the individual's psyche and circumstances), from Jupiter or from Saturn called forth by any aspect is always characteristic of them, but the particular aspect between them decides the *type* of expression from each planet. When there is a square aspect between Jupiter and Saturn, their qualities express in a dynamic, stressful, and challenging manner. Jupiter's characteristic expansiveness and benevolence are likely to be extravagance, over-optimism, lack of commonsense; his benevolence becomes false pride and conceit. Saturn's characteristic ambition, conservatism, and power of organization are likely to become a drive for power regardless of the cost to others, or in materialism and excessive attention to routine and order. Jupiter and Saturn are opposites in character and effect yet linked as a pair in the evolution of man.

If there is a **trine** aspect between the two, then the more positive qualities of each are likely to express. The expansiveness, enthusiasm and wisdom of Jupiter will work harmoniously with Saturn's ambition, carefulness with planning, and hard work to accomplish constructive ends. This does not mean that a square aspect is always unfortunate or that a trine aspect is always fortunate. Often a square is most productive in stirring the individual to action and effort. In overcoming obstacles, he develops his character and achieves success. A trine, because it does bring an ease of working, "lucky breaks", and an apparently comfortable road to success, often means laziness and lost opportunities.

There are five major aspects: the **conjunction** (0°), the **sextile** (60°), the **square** (90°), the **trine** (120°) and the **opposition** (180°). Also, there are a number of minor aspects. The ones usually considered are: the semisextile (30°), the semisquare (45°), the quintile (72°), the sesquiquadrate (135°), the biquintile (144°), and the quincunx or inconjunct (150°). I personally only use the major aspects plus the semisextile, semisquare, and inconjunct. There is also the **parallel** which is not an aspect in longitude like the aspects named above. The planets have a second measure of position called declination—the measurement north or south from the equator toward the nearest pole. When planets have the same degree of declination north or south, they are said to be in parallel of declination.[4]

Orb of aspect: Each aspect has a certain range of effectiveness called the orb of influence. The aspect is said to be "exact", when the two planets occupy the same degree in the same Sign or in different Signs. For example, if Saturn is in 10° Libra and Jupiter in 10° Cancer, they are in an exact square: 90° or three Signs apart. A planet enters or leaves an aspect when it reaches the arc of its orb of influence. The orb of the square aspect is usually 8°, though some astrologers differ on the extent of orbs the modern tendency is toward smaller orbs of influence than in the past. Using the above example, we remember that the orb of influence is 8° and know that until Jupiter reaches 2° of Cancer the aspect is not in effect. By the time Jupiter reaches 18°, it has reached the limit of orb of influence—that is, it is out of the square aspect.[5]

In the past astrologers generally divided the aspects and their influences into good or bad, fortunate or unfortunate. The modern approach takes into consideration advances in psychology; it stresses a positive rather than a fatalistic view. The view of the higher Self must be that there is nothing either good or bad; every experience that comes to us is for our ultimate and even immediate good. That attitude is very hard to maintain when one is struggling with a bereavement or major injustice done to one. It is cold comfort to be told it is doing our character a world of good! Life is often difficult and painful, but it is possible, with effort and with the right attitude, to make something constructive out of any experience. It may seem that astrologers dwell more upon the difficult squares, oppositions, and some conjunctions but that is because those aspects so often bring a major life crisis; they reveal where one is being challenged to make a change in some basic way and to grow through concentrated experience. The square and opposition are often destructive to *form*, the karmic structures built in the past which block the individual's growth. The harmonious and easy "flowing" aspects such as the trines, sextiles and some conjunctions show the fortunate abilities, talents, and characteristics upon which one is able to draw in dealing with obstacles and difficulties. They, too, are karmic structures built in the past.

Squares, oppositions, some conjunctions (depending on the planets involved), quincunxes, semi-squares, and sesquiquadrates I categorize as difficult, stressful, but also dynamic and challenging. Easy flowing, harmonious, more flowing aspects are the trine, sextile, some conjunctions (depending on the planets involved), and the semi-sextile. The quintile (72°), is said to be strengthening to the mind when Mercury is one of the planets involved, and the biquintile (144°), is said to be slightly helpful. But neither of the latter two aspects is used by most astrologers.

Conjunction: 0° with an orb of 11° for Sun and Moon, 8° for the planets. The conjunction is the most powerful aspect in astrology. It can be either harmonious, difficult, or a mixture—depending on which planets form the aspect. When two planets—or a planet and an important position in the chart (such as the Midheaven or the Ascendant), are within 8° of each other, it indicates an intense merging and interaction between the energies, characteristics, and things ruled by the two aspecting planets. In the Natal chart, it indicates a quality or factor in the individual's character and life that will be consistently expressed in significant ways. There will be an intense focus on the qualities of the two planets, colored or modified by the Sign and the Element in which the conjunction takes place. The affairs ruled by the House in which the planets merge are profoundly affected. For example, a conjunction of Sun and Mars in the 1st House gives both the personality (Ascendant), and the core character, vitality, and self-regard (Sun), an infusion of the driving, dynamic energy of Mars. With this aspect often comes the fiery temper, the impatience, and accident-prone qualities of Mars.

With a Sun-Neptune conjunction, the core character is infused with a larger, more universal vision—humanitarian, artistic, psychic, or spiritual—than normal. With this can come a tendency to self-delusion, a difficulty in seeing oneself objectively. Remember that a conjunction always indicates a focus of important karma which affects character and circumstances.

Trine—120° with an orb of 8°, or 11° for Sun and Moon. The trine is the strongest of the fortunate, flowing aspects giving an ease of working with the world and with oneself. This aspect indicates the psychological assets, talents, and abilities which the individual expresses spontaneously, or which can be easily developed. The trine shows the "good" karma made in past lives—such things as the unselfish deeds, emotions, desires, and aspirations or the hard work, even for a selfish purpose and motive, done to develop some skill or talent. A natural talent for music or mathematics is often spoken of as a "gift", but there is no such thing as a "gift" in karmic law. Every natural talent or ability has been worked for and *earned* at some time, perhaps developed over many, many lives.

In *The Soul's Growth Through Reincarnation*[6], the past lives of British artist, John Varley, were traced by clairvoyace. He was given the star name, *Erato*, to avoid confusion in the changing personalities and sexes. It was noted that whenever there was an opportunity, Erato was drawn to some form of art.

> In this last British life he was a landscape painter; in the brief one preceding, he was an etcher and engraver; in Athens he was a sculptor: In Ancient Egypt he was once an architect: In Peru as a girl Erato took eagerly to painting. In a life in Japan as a woman, we find Erato's artistic tendency manifesting itself in the painting of kakemonos (pictures or writing on silk or paper suitable for hanging). In a life in Etruria, where civilization was backward, the artistic tendency was cramped, and could only express itself in the combination of colors in the weaving of cloths and carpets.

The obvious effects of a trine are often called "good luck". One individual is "lucky" in the circumstances into which he was born. He has good luck or gets "lucky breaks" as he progresses through life. His ventures and relationships prosper in spite of no apparent wizardry on his part. Another individual with perhaps more brains, ability, and hard work may fail. This should not be interpreted to mean that the first individual was necessarily more virtuous and hardworking in past lives than the second person. No one, other than an Adept, understands the mysteries of karma and reincarnation; but one can venture a guess that the first person *may* be enjoying an "easy" life after several difficult ones, and the second one may be confronting in this life certain difficult karma from the past; perhaps he is being challenged to basically change himself and to grow through concentrated experience.

Sextile—60° aspect with an orb of influence of 4°. The sextile is much like the trine but weaker. Its characteristics give mutual support of the planets involved. The sextile acts as a modifier and brings opportunities. Stephen Arroyo remarks that "the sextile is an aspect of openness to the new: new people, new ideas, new attitudes; and it symbolizes the potential for making new connections with either people or ideas which can ultimately lead to new learning. The sextile is chiefly an aspect of flexibility and potential understanding and it tends to be a mental aspect, although the planets involved in such an angle have to be taken into consideration. Perhaps most importantly, the sextile shows an area of life where one can cultivate not only a new level of understanding but also a greater degree of objectivity which can lead to a feeling of great freedom."[7]

Semi-sextile—30° aspect with an orb of 2°. Semi-sextile, that is *half* a sextile, has the nature of a sextile but is weaker in its effect.

Parallel—0° declination with an orb of only 1½°. When the parallel involves two or more planets with the same direction, whether north or south, it has the nature of a conjunction but its effect is not as dramatic as a conjunction between planets in longitudinal aspect. Its significance is subtler, more like a background emphasis. When the parallel takes place with one planet north and the other south, the effect resembles the opposition aspect. The most important function of the parallel is when it relates two planets not in any longitudinal aspect, or when it supports a strong aspect such as a square.

Square—90° aspect with an orb of 11° for the Sun and Moon, and 8° for all planets. This is the most dynamic, energizing, and difficult of all the aspects. Squares in the Natal chart indicate conflict within the individual which eventually produce conflict in and with his environment. The inward self and outer circumstances and relationships cannot be separated; they are sides of the same coin. Throughout life there is a constant interaction with the original impetus coming from *within* the individual. Or, to put it simply but in another way, *if you want to change your fate, change yourself.*

Under a progressed square aspect or a heavy transit of the same nature,[8] the individual feels more aggressive, independent, out of harmony with himself and with his environment. This discomfort drives him to change, and break away from old patterns in order to construct new patterns. Squares show conflicts in past lives that were not resolved and now must be met and resolved in this life. Otherwise, the individual will meet the same difficult situations and relationships repeatedly until he does resolve the matter constructively, in effect turning a square into a trine or sextile.

In a square aspect, the qualities of the planets involved tend to clash with conflicting or contradictory motives and urges, both seeking expression and both interfering with each other. The square can lead to great creativity and awareness. It is usually the inner conflict—that "divine discontent of the soul"—that drives great artists to compose, paint, or write. The horoscopes of those who accomplish things in life are often studded with square and opposition aspects.

Opposition—180° aspect with an orb of 8° for planets, 11° for

the Sun and Moon. Two planets on opposite sides of the horoscope or a planet opposite an important position, such as the
Ascendant or the Midheaven, set up a polarity which often
indicates over-stimulation in the separate energies of the two
planets, manifesting as difficulty in the area of personal relationships. A great tension is set up between the two planets and
between the two Houses in which they are placed. For example,
an opposition between planets in 1st and 7th Houses can involve
a tension/conflict between one's personal independence and the
demands of a partnership, marriage, or other people in general.
In a deeper sense, there is no separation between "I" and "You",
the one and the many. An opposition calls forth an awareness
(we are rarely awakened to awareness of anything except
through discomfort), of this fundamental truth of unity.

The opposition aspect shows where we have ignored the
needs and rights of others in the past and draws our attention to
such blind self-centeredness by difficult tensions in personal
relationships. The little self struggles to gain for himself advan-
tages against the pressures of his other selves and his own higher
Self.

There is often a marked lack of objectivity. Often the individual feels he is forced to choose between two equally desirable
things, such as the 1st House personal independence and the
closeness and support of 7th House marriage, and he will continue to feel this until he realizes the illusion of separateness as
well as the mistaken conviction that his needs should be given
priority over the needs of others.

Quincunx (or Inconjunct)—150° aspect with an orb of 2°. This
minor aspect is often related to compulsive—and guilt-
motivated—behavior patterns which produce strain. It can indicate major personality problems since there is a constant irritation and annoying compulsiveness that interferes with the expression of the planets' energies. Some astrologers attribute a
measure of fatefulness to the quincunx and it often seems to be
connected with death. Compulsive and guilt-motivated behavior patterns stem from ingrained habits formed in the past;
they call for a conscious effort of discrimination and discipline
to resolve the largely unconscious reactions. Discrimination
implies an awareness first of the problem and then a sensible
adjustment rather than a radical repression which only tends to
drive the trouble into some other form of expression.

Semi-Square—45° aspect with an orb of 2°. This is a minor aspect which makes for difficulties, often in the nature of friction. It partakes of the nature of the square.

Sesquiquadrate—135° aspect with an orb of 2°. The sesquiquadrate is difficult and has the nature of the square to a minor degree. It produces minor upsets.

Leaving aside moderating influences in other parts of the horoscope, the great "X", that unknown quality which is not shown in the horoscope is what the individual's attitude and reaction to a given aspect may be. Some people meet every handicap or obstacle as a challenge, it brings out their best in courage, effort, and ingenuity. Others react negatively, blaming everyone and everything except themselves for their problems. A planetary configuration only shows the *potential* within the individual's pattern, not a predetermined characteristic or event. What he does with it is where the divine gift of free will comes in to the picture.

Most people reflect their horoscopes fairly well and general estimations of future events and character changes prove reasonably accurate. But with spiritually evolved people—at least spiritually evolved to my admittedly limited perception—it is very difficult to predict with accuracy. The astrologer does not know for a certainty what a client has made of his Natal potential in the intervening years between birth and the visit. This fact should make every astrologer very cautious about judging another's stage of evolution. Nevertheless, there are those persons whose character and accomplishments are known and whose very presence carries conviction of spiritual stature. With these individuals I can tell from their horoscopes with what potentials they began life, but present and future analysis can be difficult and uncertain. I leave the "rules" of Astrology to one side and lean on my intuition in these cases. My feeling is that these individuals have consciously grasped their character and, therefore, their destiny with the power of their higher Self—the "warrior that fights within," as Annie Besant put it. No longer blown here and there by their planetary configurations and aspects, they use their potential to the full whether the aspects are favorable or adverse.

A case in point is that of a close friend. Every year I would give her an update on the coming year's progressions and transits. One year the aspects looked particularly strong and fortunate.

She had already held high positions in both worldly and spiritual organizations and the year ahead seemed to promise even greater opportunities. There was little in her chart to indicate a health problem but intuition made me urge her to have a checkup. She did so and after a thorough physical examination with all tests, the doctor pronounced her in perfect health. But within the year she was dead of cancer after a brief illness.

Astrologers are very good at finding the cause of just about any event *after* it occurs but in this case, except for some minor things[9] I searched in vain. It became my conviction that for reasons best known to her higher Self she chose at that time to leave her physical body. Death does not necessarily show as an unfortunate event in a chart; sometimes it is a welcome release. In my friend's case it may have been an opportunity for greater work on higher planes.

The word karma in Sanskrit literally means *action*. All action springs from desire, desire for those things to which we are attached. Both the harmonious and difficult aspects in the horoscope show what our deepest attachments and mental emotional patterns are, karmically brought over from past lives. The planets and Houses involved indicate the area of our attachments and with the aspect show whether those attachments are benign, destructive, or excessive. For example, the Sun involved in a configuration may show an attachment to being the boss; which can mean the urge to genuine leadership or to dictatorship. The Moon involved shows attachment to the mother, family, home, tradition, and the past. Mercury involved indicates attachment to intellectual and communicative accomplishment. Venus denotes attachment to physical and emotional satisfactions, aesthetic values, social life, and other people in general. Mars, on the other hand, points out attachment to action, aggressive tactics, and achievement of desires. Jupiter can signify attachment to religious forms, a high opinion of oneself, or doing things in a lavish manner. Saturn involved shows attachment to the structured life, "law and order", power, and reputation.

All of these things and many more can be virtues or faults if carried to extremes or if done with ruthlessly selfish motivation. They are all necessary in the earlier stages of the Soul's long journey to perfection. But there comes a time when even good karma, attachment to *anything* for the little self, no matter how praiseworthy in the eyes of the world is seen as a block, a bondage, preventing complete spiritual freedom.

There is a marvelous passage on karma from *Light On The Path* which points the way to those who have reached that stage:

> He who desires to form good karma will meet with many confusions, and in the effort to sow rich seed for his own harvesting may plant a thousand weeds, and among them the giant.[10] Desire to sow no seed for your own harvesting, desire only to sow that seed the fruit of which shall feed the world. You are a part of the world; in giving it food you feed yourself. . . . Learn now that there is no cure for desire, no cure for love of reward, no cure for the misery of longing, save in the fixing of the sight and hearing upon that which is invisible and soundless. . . . Live in the eternal.

NOTES

[1]An article, "Astrology and the Psychic Faculty", in the British quarterly, *The Astrological Journal,* Autumn, 1974.

[2]Clairvoyance means literally "clear sight", the ability to see objectively or in the "mind's eye" things in the subtler worlds. Clairaudience means "clear hearing", the ability to hear voices and sounds from the subtler worlds.

[3]For those new to Astrology, the *Natal* or *radical* planets are those planetary positions at the moment of birth. Thereafter, the planets are progressed at the rate of one sidereal day to one year of an individual's life. The *transits* or *transitting planets* refers to actual daily movement of the planets.

[4]The degrees of declination for each planet are listed in the Ephemeris under the abbreviation "Dec." on the same page or opposite the longitudinal degree positions. One must be careful not to read Lat. or latitude for Dec. or declination. Latitude is a very different measure of planetary position.

[5]This applies to orbs in the Natal chart only. In secondary progressions and transits the planet moves into orb of an aspect when it reaches and leaves 1° from exactitude though usually the Sun and Moon in progressions are given 1½° orbs.

[6]Edited by C. Jinarajadasa from C. W. Leadbeater's writings of his clairvoyant investigations.

[7]Stephen Arroyo, *Astrology, Karma and Transformation: The Inner Dimensions of the Birthchart,* (Vancouver, Washington: CRCS Publications, 1978), p. 113.

[8]The transitting Sun, Moon, Mercury, Venus and Mars move so swiftly that their influence is rarely important. Not so with the slower moving Saturn, Jupiter, Uranus, Neptune and Pluto. Their transits, often moving back and forth over the same few degrees can have a marked effect.

[9]The only indications of death I could find were the progressed Moon moving through the 8th House in trine to her natal Jupiter in the 12th House. Jupiter was also ruler of Sagittarius on the Cusp of the 8th House. By transit, Neptune was within 2° of conjunction with the natal Moon in the 7th House. Neptune and Jupiter are often connected with death. None of this, to my mind, was enough to explain astrologically her sudden and unexpected death in the prime of life.

[10]The "giant weed" is the sense of separateness from which springs all selfishness.

VI

SUN AND MOON: FATHER AND MOTHER

The old sexist connotations in astrological symbology have long been unsatisfactory. Two thousand years of emphasis in our Western culture on a patriarchical Godhead from the Old Testament have buried the true and natural expression of the feminine principle. The Christian Church, grappling with the polarities, came to symbolize Woman and the feminine as evil, beginning with Eve. They equated Male and Female with positive and *negative*, light and *dark*, good and *evil*. Man was espoused as the positive symbol of reason, leadership, and spiritual aspiration, relegating Woman to the negative symbol of emotion, inferiority, and her aspirations restricted to home, children, and kitchen. The astrologers carried this into their Astrology, the Moon shining only by virtue of reflected light from her lord and master, the Sun, symbolic of Woman's role in the world.

With the advance of Science and the knowledge of the law of polarity, a law in which neither positive is superior, nor negative inferior, but each is essential to the action of the other, one would have supposed a more objective, less chauvinistic attitude would have come into being in Astrology. It is only in the last few years that a change in interpretation has begun regarding the positive and negative, masculine and feminine, lights and planets in Astrology.

Those familiar with Eastern teachings and theosophical divisions of the planes of the universe recognize that our universe is septenary in nature. There are seven planes beginning with *Âdi*, the first plane, the One without differentiation. The atomic structure of that plane is so fine that it is without form. The second plane is *Anupâdaka*, the Monadic plane, where the atomic structure is coarser but still formless. The third plane is that of *Âtma*, the spiritual Will, followed by the fourth plane of Buddhi, intuition and infinite love. The fifth or Mental Plane is divided into Higher Manas, the world of the abstract Mind, and Lower Manas, the world of the concrete Mind where thoughts take on forms objective to our consciousness. Still lower on the scale and coarser in atomic structure is *Kâma Loka*, the astral or emotional plane, where the emotions rule and appear in every color, shape, and force. Lowest and coarsest in atomic structure is the physical plane, *Sthûla* in Hindu terminology.[1] It must not be thought that these seven planes of our universe are like steps on a ladder or skins of an onion because they all exist and interpenetrate at the same "time" and in the same "place".

It seems futile to speculate on the nature of the higher, formless planes since our conceptions are so confined to those of material form. However little our present consciousnesses can grasp the subtleties of the abstract planes, we can reason that the universal law of positive and negative polarity may apply.

- The first plane is the One, the Creator, "masculine" and positive. From It emanates the Divine Sparks, the Life Waves, everything in essence.
- Descending to the Monadic plane, the peculiar vibration would be, then, negative, feminine, though not in the way in which we usually think of male or female.
- The next plane is that of *Âtma*, the spiritual Will, with the vibration of masculine-positive.
- The Buddhic plane, the plane of the intuition and infinite love, is again negative-feminine.
- The plane of *Manas*, the Mind, of both abstract and concrete thought, would be positive.
- The plane of *Kâma Loka*, the emotions and desires, would be negative.
- Last, the plane of the Physical would be positive.

The Monad, our very highest Self, exists on the formless Monadic plane and is without sex as we know it. So, too, is that extension of the Monad called the Ego (in theosophical terminology) which exists on the higher, formless level of the Manasic or Mental plane. It is only when the Ego extends itself into the lower planes for purposes of reincarnation, taking on bodies composed of matter peculiar to those planes, that we become male and female, sexually polarized, so to speak.

A soul or entity inhabiting the body of a male is positive on the physical plane, negative on the emotional plane, positive on the mental plane and negative on the Buddhic. A soul inhabiting a female body is negatively polarized on the physical plane, positive on the emotional plane, negative on the mental plane and

ÂDI	Positive-Masc.	ONE		1
MONADIC Plane	Negative-Fem.	●	☽	2
ATMIC Plane	Positive-Masc. (Will)	☉	☽	3
BUDDHIC Plane	Negative-Fem. (Intuition/Love)	●	☽	4
MANASIC Plane	Positive-Masc. (Abstract Mind Concrete Mind)	☉	☽	5
ASTRAL Plane	Negative-Fem. (Emotion/Desires)	●	☽	6
PHYSICAL Plane	Positive-Masc.	☉	☽	7

positive on the Buddhic. This is not to be taken literally, that a man is always positive in the physical world, negative on the emotional, etc., or that a woman is always negative on the physical, positive on the emotional, etc. It is a matter of the dominant vibration on each plane to which the soul, whether inhabiting a male or female body, responds and which it uses in an infinite variety of ways. Perhaps it is somewhat easier when incarnated in a female body to be positive and dynamic on the emotional/ desire and intuitional/Buddhic planes; while, in a male body, the soul may find it easier to express positively on the physical and mental planes. It is difficult to know how much of our conception of this symbology is true to universal law or just cultural conditioning.

All this is not meant as a digression into esoteric fields but an effort to take our thinking out of the rut regarding the usually implied "male and female" connotations and characteristics and their place in the universe when we come to consider the Sun, Moon, and the planets, but particularly the Sun and Moon.

☉ The Sun

The circle without a dot in the center symbolizes spirit un-manifested; *with* the dot, it shows manifestation, like the nucleus of life within the egg and all cellular formations which will manifest when the time and conditions are ripe. The circle also *encloses*, which shows the extent of the Soul's limitation as differentiated from the Cosmos. Like the confines of the circle, the soul is a being without beginning or end. In the horoscope the circle with a dot symbolizes the more basic, relatively un-changing characteristics, the core character. The Sun's qualities, like the qualities of the planets and Moon, have to be mastered and brought into the unity of the whole person. It governs the Power urges. Its characteristic is to illuminate, to shine forth, to rule. In whatever House of the horoscope the Sun is found those matters ruled by that House are infused with vitality. It symbolizes authority, the male sex, the father, employer, the government or ruler. A Sun-dominated person has an active, assertive, dominating approach to the world.

The condition of the Sun in a person's chart (whether weak or strong by position of Sign, afflicted or favored by aspects to planets and the Moon), tells how that person used his authority in past lives. The power urges take many forms of expression and everyone has some degree of power in some area. If you have misused power in the past, your karma in this life may take the form of difficulty from those in authority over you in this life. You may experience what it is to suffer the tyranny or thought-less whims of your superiors. Our present use of power and authority over those subservient to us and our reaction to those over us is creating the power circumstances of the future in this life and the next. The use of really enormous power is one of the most difficult tests a soul has to face. We may *think* we would be righteous and kind in such a position but would we do any better than the multitude of tyrants in the past and present?

Leo and the 5th House

The Sun cannot be considered without also considering the Sign and House it rules. The Fifth House ruled in the natural order of the Signs by Leo (*see* Chapter IV, p. 46) is one of the three Fire Houses, 1st, 5th and 9th. This triangle represents a pattern of energy flow which in many cases verges on the transcendent.

Stephen Arroyo gives a dramatic account of a dream which brought this realization to him. He had been studying the charts of about a dozen spiritual masters, trying to discover the common factors in their charts. The only thing that was regularly emphasized in the majority of those charts was the emphasis of planets in the Fire Houses. After struggling with this factor without success, he had a vivid dream in which he was shown a flow of fiery energy circling around the triangle formed by the Ascendant and the Fifth and Ninth Houses. He commented:

> The fire Houses deal with pure being and becoming.
> The purity of self-expression represented by them can, in some cases, be accurately classified as spiritual (mainly in those cases where the person has ceased to identify his ego with the creative forces flowing through him and instead sees himself only as a channel for the manifestation of a greater power).[2]

The Fifth House has been trivialized by emphasizing its connection with children, gambling, love affairs, and other pleasures but that House with its rulers Leo and the Sun denotes the *tremendous creative power* of love that every Soul can tap. It has been said that the Fifth House shows either the power of love or the love of power for the Sun rules the power urges as well. It shows the capacity for love, that greatest creative force for spiritual transformation and so from a spiritual standpoint can be considered the most important House after the Ascendant.

The Solar Chart   When the time of birth is unknown many astrologers set up a chart with the Sun's longitudinal degree as the cusp of the First House, with other cusps placed at 30° intervals. If the Sun on the day of birth is in 23° Taurus, the Ascendant degree is placed at 23° Taurus, the 2nd House cusp at 23° Gemini and so on, with the planets falling into their appropriate places according to the ephemeris for that day. This is actually a sunrise chart with equal Houses.[3] This is the system used in most of the popular magazine and newspaper forecasts except that they relate the daily *transitting* planets to the position of only your Sun at birth. Obviously they cannot take into consideration the infinite variety of planetary positions over the years whereas the Sun is in the same position annually. If you were born on February 3, 1970, your Sun is in approximately the same degree and Sign as one born on that day in 1920, so the popular forecasters can give a general forecast applicable to all born around that date regardless of the year.

The Sun's Aspects

The Sun is the very heart of our solar system and the heart of the horoscope. C. E. O. Carter, in his *Foundations of Astrology*, refers to the Sun as the "élan vital," life itself, with a predominantly emotional bias, masculine and positive, bold and adventurous, and, with faith, controlling the chief decisions, outstanding events, and eminent achievements of life. For the Sun's manner of expression we look to the Mode and Element; for the area of life it dominates we look to the Houses it rules by position and Sign. As to whether our Sun shines freely or is obscured by clouds, we look to the aspects it makes.

SUN AND MOON   One of the first steps in interpreting a chart is to evaluate the relative compatibility of the Sun and the Moon, the two primary polarities. In Jungian terminology, the Sun is symbolic of the principal archetypal *animus* (Mars and Saturn are the other two), the masculine side within a woman's personality. The Moon is the principal symbol of the archetypal *anima* in a man's psyche (the other two are Venus and Neptune). A square or opposition aspect between the Sun and the Moon, especially if they are placed in inharmonious Elements, produces conflict in self-expression because the subconscious needs (Moon) inhibit or conflict with the conscious desires and objectives (Sun) resulting in an inner struggle. An example of this inharmonious placement would be Moon in Scorpio-Water and Sun in Aquarius-Air. In effect, it is two personality patterns striving against each other for dominance. When the Sun and Moon are posited in harmonious Elements, the conflict is not so intense, but there is still difficulty in self-expression and in dealing with the opposite sex since the Sun represents the masculine sex in a woman's chart and the Moon represents the feminine sex in a man's chart. The Sun-Moon aspects have a great effect upon the popularity in general, for the Sun rules influence and honor, and the Moon represents the public and public opinion.

All aspects to or from the Sun, not only from the Moon, affect one's self-respect. This is understandable when one realizes that the Sun rules one's sense of identity and the manner of creative expression. If the Sun were afflicted by Saturn, for example, one might feel acutely the gap between one's ambitions and inherent abilities—a fear that one lacked the power to rule one's life.

There would be periods of depression, feelings of failure and of inferiority. A more fortunate aspect, from Jupiter, would give added enthusiasm, an expansion of self-confidence, and a forward-looking, aspiring approach to one's future.

SUN-MERCURY The conjunction is the only aspect possible between the Sun and Mercury because Mercury is never more than 28° away from the Sun. Any planet aspected by the Sun is strengthened and vitalized so a conjunction between these two would affect the Sign and House in which the conjunction takes place. Mercury symbolizes intelligence and communication and transmits the light of the Sun through the mind. When Mercury is positioned ahead of the Sun (greater longitude) the mental energy has more eagerness, the person more apt to act first and consider afterwards. Positioned following the Sun, the person acts with greater deliberation.

SUN-VENUS The only aspects possible are the conjunction, the semi-sextile and the semi-square because Venus is never more than 48° away from the Sun. Venus carries the light of the Sun into self-expression through beauty, emotion, and harmony when they are in aspect. It is my experience that the gentler qualities of Venus tend to be burned up or overpowered by the dominance of the Sun in a conjunction. Venus expresses through the affections, art, and in gentle ways. In men the conjunction can give effeminancy. The semi-sextile is mildly favorable and the semi-square produces friction in matters of the affections.

SUN-MARS Both Sun and Mars are alike in their masculine, aggressive, assertive, dominating approach to the world. This can make one bold, strong, forceful, and hardworking with the conjunction but it can also make one hot-tempered and reckless. Much depends on the rest of the horoscope as to whether the accelerated energy and dominance of this combination will be under control. Difficult aspects increase the danger of overstrain, impatience, anger, and recklessness while the more fortunate, "flowing" aspects give the same qualities as the conjunction but they are more likely to be expressed constructively and without annoyance to others.

SUN-JUPITER Jupiter symbolizes expansiveness, enthusiasm, knowledge, honor, and opportunity and is often called the "Greater Fortune", Venus being the "Lesser Fortune". An aspect between Jupiter and Sun expands the scope of reward and opportunity. The person feels cheerful and "lucky" in his dealings. With the square or opposition Jupiter's excess becomes a problem in some form, often accompanied by an excessively high opinion of oneself and one's judgment. When Jupiter afflicts it is always through too much of a good thing so the individual has to learn discipline, efficiency, and moderation.

SUN-SATURN This combination is always very powerful. As Saturn is one of the symbols of the father, the conjunction, opposition, or square can show limitation, loss or coldness connected with that parent. The motif of Saturn is self-perfection which is why its position and aspects show where the individual feels the greatest lack in himself and his life. With the Sun in aspect the result can be wisdom or it can be arrogance and difficulty with men particularly when Sun squares Saturn in a female chart. With the difficult aspects there is often a fear of expressing the true Self, fear of criticism, or of being inadequate which curtails initiative. The nature of the Sun is to shine forth, illuminate. Saturn constricts, but only because we are attempting to pass on without facing the things we have left undone in the past. With the opposition the person frequently projects his fears and failings onto others. The lesson to be learned is that of taking responsibility for oneself and learning to take some risks in self-expression in order to realize fully and deeply what one is capable of doing.

SUN-URANUS Uranus has been called the "Awakener" and, indeed, revolutionary change is an outstanding characteristic of Uranian aspects. Any Uranian aspect with the Sun often brings periodic radical change into the life so that it is like the closing of one volume and the opening of another. The difference between the difficult and the more fortunate aspects seems to be that with the latter the person may make radical changes in the life but has the ability to build the new attitudes and life situations upon the foundations of the old, whereas the person with difficult aspects feels urged to wipe out all remnants of the old in order to be completely independent and free to enjoy the new experiences. Originality, inventiveness, and individuality are particularly strong with the conjunction and characteristic of the other aspects also. The difficult aspects tend to produce more willfulness and eccentricity, and, unless there are moderating factors in the chart, the individual can become so brusque, independent, and unconventional that his personal and business relationships suffer.

SUN-NEPTUNE Aspects between these two are common in the charts of astrologers, artists, humanitarians, and visionaries in political and spiritual fields, those whose lives are guided by a larger vision than normal. The negative side of Neptune often gives self-delusion and, especially with the difficult aspects, an unrealistic perspective of oneself; the person has difficulty in seeing himself objectively. Whatever the aspect there is always great sensitivity, intuition, and compassion. Often extreme idealization of one or both parents, and men, especially, have difficulty in finding a mate who can live up to their unrealistic expectations. This applies to both sexes especially when Neptune is in Virgo.

SUN-PLUTO Both Sun and Pluto are concerned with the urge to power so that any strong aspect between them—particularly the conjunction, square, and opposition—introduces an extra ruthlessness. Pluto always symbolizes a form of extremely concentrated power with many of the qualities usually associated with Sun in Scorpio—the urge to remold the self (and others!), willfulness, and intensity. Pluto rules all eliminative processes and an aspect with the Sun indicates the areas in the character that are ready for elimination. Usually these areas are connected with past abuse of power and authority. Stephen Arroyo comments[4] that a Sun-Pluto aspect often indicates separation from the father that leaves deep psychological scars. The separation may be caused by the father's departure, death, or because he simply disappeared without a trace. In men's charts there is often an extra close tie with a woman, often the mother. In women's charts, it seems to correlate with experiences of great difficulty with the father and usually with other men as well. With both sexes the opposition makes them prone to make unreasonable, though often unconscious, demads on those with whom they are intimately involved. Severe disappointments in close relationships is often observed with Sun-Pluto aspects.

The positive side of Sun-Pluto aspects gives the power for the transformation of one's inner powers and resources, particularly the mind and will power. But anyone with difficult aspects between Pluto and the Sun, Moon, Venus, or the Ascendant should strive for an objective comprehension of all his major relationships, particularly those involving the parents.

Disregarding any aspects made to other planets, if the Sun has few or no planets within 30° of its position, it is considered "isolated". A person with an isolated Sun is able to stand back from his own behavior and see it objectively. A person with his Sun crowded by several planets (the closer by degree, the more dominant the effect), cannot do this for he is more totally involved in whatever he is doing.

A serious actor or comedian tends to have a chart with an isolated Sun. He is consciously playing a part and often has a number of parts that he plays, whereas a person whose Sun is crowded by planets nearby tends to behave in a more natural and spontaneous way. This person cannot easily separate his consciousness from his behavior or see his actions objectively.

The ability to separate consciousness from behavior would seem to be a very desirable quality to one striving to transcend the confusions of the personality, because a person cannot be truly awake to the directives of the soul or identify himself with that higher Self until that stage of detachment is attained and sustained, at least most of the time. Why, therefore, does it distress some people? Perhaps because they feel that there is a split in themselves—two or more people in one skin—and they may not feel certain which one is "the real me." The higher Self is the real "me", of course, and the illusions produced by incarnated life on the lower planes only makes the personality and its acquired behaviorisms seem to be the real Self. Until the person is integrated with the higher Self there could be periods of identity uncertainty.

When the Sun is unaspected the person may feel disconnected from the rest of the character, but this feeling of disconnection is only felt in its fullest form if the Sun is both isolated and unaspected. A case in point is that of Queen Elizabeth II whose Sun is extremely isolated and almost entirely unaspected; she keeps her real self entirely hidden while playing a part before the world and, perhaps, even amongst her friends and family does not reveal her true self.

These matters of isolation, crowding, or lack of aspects are not necessarily unfortunate or difficult things. They are factors which must be taken into consideration in order to understand oneself and others. One very fortunate result of isolation of the Sun is that it tends to make for a more creative person, at least in the cases of actors and writers. Who can say about Queens?

☽ The Moon

The Moon, in astrology, is the feminine polarity; the archetypal feminine principle, the *anima* or feminine side of his psyche in a man; the mother or mother substitute; the women in one's life, particularly in a man's chart; and women in general. The Moon also rules that part of the personality, which results from tendencies inherited from past lives, parents, ancestry, and environmental conditioning in the present life. The Moon has a great deal to do with one's feelings about oneself—how comfortable one is with the self and one's relationship to other human beings. It rules maternity but also, in a deeper sense, the care and protection of all the young and helpless. The affairs governed by the House in which the Moon is placed are subject to fluctuation and many small changes.

The placement of the Moon in the chart and its aspects show how the individual behaved *as* a woman or *to* women in the past life. A man with an afflicted Moon in his horoscope will reap in this life the karma accrued from the mistreatment he gave to women in past lives. If he was in a female body, that still applies, for many women treat other women badly. The Moon's condition shows how, in the past, one used the role of mother, wife, or daughter and as a woman in the community. The planets and aspects with which the Moon is involved give a general picture of the particular type of karma. The Houses involved show the department of life affected. To give one illustration, Moon in aspect to Sun indicates that the maternal urges may have been in some way identified with the power urges. Afflicted, it may mean that as a woman you used your position as wife, mother or mistress to wield power over others in an oppressive way. A favorable aspect may mean you used your position as a woman in power in a beneficent way, protecting and nurturing the young and weak.

Too much attachment to the past, to family, and to racial background can also be indicated by the negative aspects. These traits are often most difficult to deal with for they are so deeply entrenched and subtly pervasive, having been such dominating features in human life for ages. Pride of family, home, race, religion, sex, and culture has been, and still is, influencing us from birth—life after life. This was necessary and beneficial in earlier stages of evolution but now it too often produces prejudice, cruelty, discrimination, and war because it is essentially separative, since attitudinally, it sets the individual and his group apart from or above his fellows.

How often we feel that we would be better people, less "hung up" in certain areas, altogether happier and more successful if our mothers or fathers had been less dominating, more supportive, more understanding, and less involved with their own "ego trips"! Since modern psychology gained popularity, that kind of thinking has been the great excuse for all our weaknesses and mistakes—blame our parents. Those who believe in Astrology but not reincarnation could blame their planets as well!

But why did you *choose* your parents? That seems a puzzling and provocative question, for a baby seems quite innocent of choice. It is a very profound question. To my way of thinking, individuals are drawn into homes and to parents where the needed negative and positive experiences for their growth will be provided. We must remember that the Sun and Moon are the primary symbols for our personal father and mother. Saturn or Jupiter can also symbolize the father and Pluto the mother. The Sun symbolizes the archetypal Father and the Moon the archetypal Mother so we experience in our relationship with our parents a complex blend of the personal and impersonal. Our father is the parent but is also the image of the archetypal Father and all authority figures whose approval we must win or earn. Our mother is the other parent but she is also the image of the archetypal Mother, the eternal feminine, the supportive, nurturing one who loves us just as we are no matter what we do. In evaluating the relationship of the individual to his parents and the effect they have on the character and life, look to the aspect between Sun and Moon first. It shows the harmony or disharmony between the parents and how it affects the child. I have frequently prepared the charts of siblings whose parents were unhappy together, divorcing after some years. Two of the children may show square or opposition aspects between their Sun and Moon: the third a trine. The first two felt the parental inharmony and divorce markedly and the third was barely affected. One can only conclude that the experience of parental inharmony was not *needed* by the latter child and perhaps his relationship with both parents was so warm that he was not affected by their personal relationship with each other.

In another case, that of three sisters with a dominating and irrational mother, "A" had her Moon as part of a T-Cross; Pluto in the 8th House in opposition to Venus in the 2nd House, both of them squared by the Moon from its 11th House position. There is a compulsive quality to Plutonian aspects and, combined with the Moon, traditional symbol of the Mother, it often produces the dominating super-mother nurturing her children with one hand while destroying them with the other. Pluto in this case was in Cancer, the Moon's Sign. With the 2nd and 8th Houses involved, the most destructive effect seemed to be upon the woman's valuation of herself and intimate relationships. She never earned the salary her artistic talent and other abilities should bring, nor did she have the self-confidence to develop her originality. Her aspirations and long-term goals (11th House) were thus thwarted. "B" had her Moon in 7th House in close opposition to Jupiter, Mars, and Neptune in 1st House and this gave her a deep problem in relating to other people (7th House), looking for them to respond to her with all-encompassing mother love and understanding missing in her relationship with her mother. When that response was inadequate, her escape became alcoholism. Neptune is often involved with alcohol, drugs, daydreaming, and other forms of escapism. The third sister, "C," had her Moon in the 8th House in exact opposition to Mercury in the 2nd House. Like her sister "A," her self-valuation was profoundly affected especially concerning money and possessions so that her insecurity focussed upon money. She was extremely able in the handling of her own and other people's money but no matter how well she did in those matters, she never felt secure and self-confident. None of the three had any meaningful relationship with the father who died suddenly just as they were emerging from childhood. All three had unhappy marriages which ended in divorce.

The negative relationship with the mother affected the three women differently but the key similarity lies in the opposition aspect figuring in all three horoscopes (see Chapter V, page 56). The opposition aspect shows where we have ignored the needs and rights of others in past lives and draws our attention to that blind self-centeredness by difficult tensions in personal relationships. The opposition calls forth an awareness—and we are rarely awakened to awareness of anything except through discomfort—of the fundamental truth of unity. One should be very hesitant to delineate the exact causes of such karma but the horoscope does give clues which can lead to better understanding of oneself and of difficult personal relationships which so often emanate from our early parent-child relationships. To re-

deem a negative parent-child relationship so that a real transformation in later relationships and self-understanding can
come is a painful process but the freedom that results is worth it.

Moon, Cancer and the 4th House

The Moon cannot be considered without also considering the
Sign and the House it rules. The 4th House, ruled by Cancer, (see
Chapter IV, pp. 40 and 46) is one of the Water Element Houses,
those three Houses are especially concerned with inner development. Cancer, like its opposite Sign Capricorn, is more
concerned with the past than the other two Cardinal Signs, Libra
and Aries. Family, parents, tradition, and early conditioning
stem from past lives where we sowed the seeds of the circumstances into which we are born in this life. As we mature we can
consciously break away from the early pattern, though few do:
the power of the Moon, Cancer and the 4th House is very deep,
like an underground river flowing silently until it surfaces with
surprising power from time to time. Persons with many planets
or important planets in the 4th House often spend their lifetime
trying to escape the conditioning of early childhood and parental influence.

Astrologers disagree over whether the 4th or the 10th House
rules the mother or father. Traditionally Capricorn and Saturn,
the natural Sign ruler of the 10th House, would seem to point to
the father and Cancer/Moon ruling the 4th House would designate the mother. Traditionally it is the father, by his career in the
world, who sets the status and worldly position of the
individual—a 10th House matter. And it is the mother who rules
the home, early environment, and so much of the family life and
tradition: these are 4th House matters. But in today's world
tradition often goes by the wayside when many women work—
frequently as single parents—and their income and earned position sets the status for the individual. Now, men often take more
of a hand in child rearing and home care, expressing many of the
mothering qualities while women in the business world express
many of the traditional masculine qualities. The old rule of 10th
for the father and 4th for the mother no longer can be fixed; an
astrologer simply has to pick the House that fits the particular
parent. However, if there is a problem concerning a parent, it is
nearly always found in the 4th House and the 4th House rules the
parents in general.

The Moon's Aspects

Enough has been said about the Moon's influence on motherhood, the home, and family, expressing through the receptive, negative, feminine, Yin polarity. She is intimately concerned with human relationships which, in the more important relationships, leads into that intermediate realm between sense and spirit. It is the Moon's influence in us that makes us feel comfortable or uncomfortable with others and within ourselves. Regardless of outer manifestations she enables us to *feel* the importance of little words, actions, and gestures; in making or breaking a relationship; or welding a number of disparate members of a group into a family-whole. The Moon's aspects spell out the areas of conflict or harmony within ourselves and others. For example, a chart with the Moon trine Mercury gives intellectual rapport with others, an ease in learning and communication. But the Moon square Venus gives difficulty in expressing and receiving affection with frustration in achieving closeness in our relationships.

MOON-MERCURY The conjunction often gives wit and cleverness but unless confirmed by other factors which lend depth and stability in the chart (such as a strong Saturn or Saturn aspect) it can be superficiality. The trine adds flexibility and curiosity. The square and opposition give the same ability to be articulate and witty but the wit tends to get out of line, annoying others. Any aspect to Mercury increases the intelligence and communicative powers.

MOON-VENUS The conjunction and more fortunate aspects give a gracious, attractive personality, social ease, and material good fortune. The difficult aspects increase tendencies to inferiority feelings, sensitivity to slights, spells of unpopularity, and difficulties with women.

MOON-MARS The conjunction and fortunate aspects give one a robust, courageous manner though a tendency to be overactive at times. An independence of spirit and for women: a charm and magnetism with men. The difficult aspects tend to overwork, overexertion and conflict. An enormous drive to achieve.

MOON-JUPITER The conjunction and fortunate aspects strengthen the social awareness, the ideals of honor, and personal worth, as well as financial assistance from others and good luck. The difficult aspects make up for such qualities as laziness,

over-optimism concerning finances, false pride, religious difficulties and extravagance.

MOON-SATURN   Serious ambition allied to a cool, cautious
manner marks the conjunction. Duty, conscience, and orderli-
ness are of importance. Often shy and timid, especially in youth,
Moon-Saturn conjunctions can also mean early loss through
death or separation of mother or father. The fortunate aspects
give the same good qualities with depth and control often leading, in time and through hard work, to a position of authority.
The square between Moon and Saturn is an extremely powerful
aspect leading to success if there is a willing acceptanre of duty
and responsibility. Experience becomes a good teacher and the
individual is often independent early in life. There is strong
parental influence in evidence. The opposition aspect between
these two intensifies the shyness, the practical is overvalued,
and there can be much worry, delays, and frustration. A severity
of purpose prevents relaxation and easy happiness.

MOON-URANUS   All the aspects between the Moon and
Uranus give great individualism, a desire for the unusual and
unconventional, especially in domestic life, and an inflexibility
and difficulty in adjusting to changes in the life. There are
always periodic, radical changes in the life, starting with early
youth. The character tends to be self-centered, excitable, and
unpredictable—especially when the aspect is a conjunction—
with a lot of moving and restlessness. Men particularly find the
monogamy of marriage too restrictive, for they like to be free to
experiment with new emotional experiences. Many individuals
with this configuration experience name changes during the
lifetime, quite apart from the usual name change women accept
upon marriage. The more fortunate aspects give excellent reflexes enabling the individual to react well to almost any situation and their intuitive insight leads them to right decisions.
Sometimes the trine makes the individual rather lazy. The
square and opposition can make one rebellious and headstrong,
the urge to independence disrupting the status quo and upset-
ting the security. With all aspects the intuition is particularly
strong but discrimination is necessary in order to use it constructively or to discern true intuitive knowledge from emotional
opinions.

MOON-NEPTUNE   All these aspects make the individual
highly imaginative, often creative in some field of the arts,

particularly sensitive, intuitive, and receptive with a strong
tendency to the psychic, the mystical and idealistic. Often there
is a deep devotion to an ideal. In men's charts the conjunction
and difficult aspects give an idealization of women, usually
including the mother. There is a hunger for emotional nourishment, for the ideal, that is difficult to satisfy because no mere
human being could fulfill the totally selfless image Moon-
Neptune people look for! Often there is a deep inner restlessness,
a dissatisfaction with oneself and the world which makes it
difficult for the person to settle down to anything. Even with the
fortunate aspects there is always danger of laziness, escapism,
and self-delusion, especially if the rest of the chart is weak.
Neptune can produce the highest spiritual insights and universal compassion if the individual will exercise relentless objectivity concerning his motives and desires, honestly *living* his
ideals rather than fantasizing about them.

MOON-PLUTO   Give an intense, almost explosive sensitivity
with an urge to remold oneself. There is the ability to destroy for
renewal and this often extends to the self. Periods of intense
emotional turmoil are common. There is a strong psychic attunement with a need to get to the root of things—other people's
motivations, mysteries of life. Along with resourcefulness and
self-discipline there is an urge to break with the taboos established by parents and early upbringing. A "mother complex" is
frequent though sometimes it will be the father who is domineer-
ing. The mother is often symbolized by Pluto and combined with
Moon emphasizes the maternal drive to the point sometimes of
becoming a "super mother" with a strong need to absorb others
or treat them as mere extensions of herself. It can work the other
way around with the individual trying to destroy his separate
identity by being absorbed into the other person. Sometimes the
aspect, particularly if connected with the 8th House, indicates
death in public.

There can, obviously, be no completely accurate listing of the
meaning and effects of the various aspects between the Sun,
Moon, and planets, for no single factor can be taken alone. The
whole horoscope must be considered; the unique pattern of
Modes, Elements, Signs, Houses, Ascendant, Midheaven, Sun,
Moon, planets, and the North and South Nodes, as well as all of
the aspects. At first, the interpretation of all these many factors,
some of them often contradictory, may seem overwhelming to

the beginner. The only course is to become completely familiar with the basic principles of each factor, memorizing a few keywords for each, if that is helpful. In doing as many charts as possible, learning from people's responses to certain configurations, those basic principles will come alive. The characteristic energies of Jupiter, for example, will become distinct from those of Saturn or Venus, and the various relationships will form a picture of character and life potentials.

NOTES

[1] A. E. Powell, The Solar System (London: Theosophical Publishing House, 1971).

[2] Stephen Arroyo, Astrology, Karma and Transformation: The Inner Dimensions of the Birthchart (Vancouver, Washington: CRCS Publications, 1978), pp. 219–220.

[3] Dennis Elwell, whom I consider one of the most astute and readable astrologers today, gives a convincing exposition of this method in his article, "Is There A Solar Chart", in Astrological Journal, Spring, 1975.

[4] Arroyo, Astrology, Karma and Transformation, pp. 135–137.

[5] From article in the Astrological Journal, Winter '76–77 issue.

VII

♀

MERCURY: MIND AND COMMUNICATION

The symbols of the planets use but three symbols: the *circle*, which represents the higher Self, the Soul; the *cross*, which represents the body or immersion in matter; and the *crescent*.

When the crescent is shown on end **)** (as in the usual Moon symbol), it represents a partial side of the Sun, the part that belongs to form—the personality image which has been molded by the mother, father, ancestry, cultural roots, and experiences in past lives. This form is used in the symbols for Saturn ♄ and Jupiter ♃ .

When the crescent is shown lying on its "back" ∪ resembling a cup, it symbolizes the higher octave of love, the Buddhic intuition, inner understanding, and compassionate love that knows no boundaries. This is the form used in the symbols of Mercury ♀ , Neptune ♆ , and Pluto ♇ .¹

The symbol of Mercury first introduces the cross. The cross far antedates Christianity, being found in the symbology of most ancient religions and primitive peoples. We are told it dates to the period of the Third Root Race, the Lemurian Race, which inhabited the great continent of Mu, now beneath the Pacific Ocean. It was during that period that the separation of the sexes first took place.²

The symbol for Mercury has the cross as its base showing that the planet's base is in the worlds of form and matter. The cross rises into the circle, symbolizing the higher Self dwelling in the upper half of the Manasic plane, the plane of the higher, abstract mind. Finally, it is crowned by the crescent Moon lying on its back symbolizing the Buddhic intuition which, in the evolved man or woman, illuminates all thought. The whole is the mind, once purified of selfishness, that acts as a divine messenger of the gods, linking the higher and lower worlds, acting as a guide to Man throughout his long pilgrimage.

Astrologically, the keyword for this planet is *communication* and the condition of Mercury in the horoscope shows the ability to communicate in all forms—talking, writing, traveling, thinking (our thoughts influence others and communicate with them through telepathy), and it has a great deal to do with our intelligence, our conscious perceptions, reason, and all the attributes of the mind.

Mercury rules the capability and urge to learn, to perceive, and to express oneself. By nature, Mercury is androgynous, neuter, being neither male nor female. Its aspects show how we have used or abused our mental and communicative powers in past lives. Abuse can mean neglect, laziness, or use of our quicker wits to take advantage of others. By rationalization, a negative form of reasoning, we deceive ourselves and others; and few of us are free from rationalizing our selfish motives and actions. The karma for such mental deviousness is the inability in this life to perceive the truth when it is presented to us.

Another failing of Mercury is the temptation to use one's wit at the expense of others. The karmic result of such a characteristic is well-illustrated by an account of a British astrologer, Rose Elliot, who uses her ability to look back into past lives of her clients whenever the cause of some traumatic "hang-up" cannot be found in this life. A woman consulted Rose Elliot complaining of a crippling phobia, an absolute terror of speaking in public, and asked how she could overcome it. Nothing in her present life seemed to explain this phobia and her position was such that it was necessary for her to do some public speaking. Pondering on the problem, and using the woman's horoscope as a "door" to her past lives, Mrs. Elliot had a vivid picture of her client as a very witty young Roman male, who could crush others with a few words. The young Roman inspired terror in the hearts of others around him with his sarcasm and they cringed, terrified, at the prospect of becoming the butt of his brilliant wit. So now in this life, this same sharpness of mind, this critical wit is turned inwards and the current personality is trembling in fear of speaking before others, just as others were in fear of her in the past. This explanation helped the woman to understand and accept herself, eventually learning to speak publicly without fear.

In that classic of Eastern Wisdom, *The Voice of the Silence*,[3] the aspirant is instructed to "seek out the rajah of the senses, the Thought-Producer, he who awakes illusion. . . . The Mind is the Great Slayer of the Real. Let the Disciple slay the Slayer."

This does not mean that to be truly spiritual one must become mindless—we would be little more than vegetables then—but that we must control the mind and cleanse it of all the devious rationalizations, falsities, self-deceits, and other illusion-making devices by which our minds (Mercury) delude us, keeping us from recognizing the Real. The mind can indeed be the great deceiver but without it nothing can be accomplished.

Another ancient aphorism puts it, "As a man thinks, so he is." We become that upon which we think, for better or worse, and it is to Mercury's condition in the horoscope that we must look for the revealing clues to the person's mental picture of himself and his world. Mercury's condition, then, is its position in the Signs, Houses, and its aspects to other planets.

We are now entering the Age of Aquarius—an Air Sign. Air Signs are correlated with the mind's sensation, perception, and expression. It seems obvious that the coming centuries will see the powers of the mind—and its dangers—increased beyond present conception. This is underlined by statements in *The Secret Doctrine* and *Man: Whence, How and Whither*[4] to the effect that we are now about a million years into the Fifth Root Race in which the Mind is the faculty to be developed. Each Root Race develops a particular faculty. Mercury, that winged Messenger of the gods, should be our guide to the Real, which at this stage is our higher Self. It can only be that guide when aligned with truth and directed by the Self.

Gemini, Virgo and their Houses

There are only three Signs in the zodiac that have human symbols: Aquarius, the man pouring water; Gemini, the twins; and Virgo, the virgin. This suggests the close connection between humanity and mind. Of these three Aquarius and Gemini are Air Signs and Virgo is an Earth Sign. Virgo presents the mental faculties expressed in a practical manner, in response to practical needs.

Virgo is the natural ruler of the 6th House which concerns the daily work and its environment, fellow workers and employees, service, and health. Mercury is not only ruler *of*, but is "exalted" *in*, Virgo[5] which suggests that the mind and its powers find their best expression ultimately in the service of others.

Gemini and the 3rd House in particular express Mercury's

communicative and mental abilities whether by speech, letter, lecturing, teaching, learning, etc., and also by all sorts of communicatory activities such as walking, motoring, visiting, and short journeys. Also, persons such as brothers and sisters, and neighbors come under the aegis of Gemini and the 3rd House. Mercury and the 3rd House show one's intellectual gifts and the difficulties or blockages to learning and thinking. Both Gemini and Virgo are Mutable Signs. Mutable literally means "changeable" and it is significant that Mercury's mineral is quick-silver, both of which describe the lightening movement and flexibility of thought. Mercury rules, or is correlated with:

☿ Rulership

1. Orators, writers, accountants, teachers, secretaries, interpreters, printers, publishers, clerks, postal and telegraph services, newspapers, all types of local and domestic communication.

2. The nervous system, brain, memory, hearing, lungs, hands, arms, tongue and mouth.

Three of the four Mutable Signs are also dual or double-bodied Signs—Gemini, Sagittarius and Pisces. Persons with one of those Signs on the cusp of the 7th House, for example, are likely to have more than one marriage. The same thing would apply to a Mutable, double-bodied Sign on the 10th House where the native would be apt to have more than one vocation or profession during the life. Afflictions between planets in the Signs of Gemini and Virgo or between the 3rd and 6th Houses often indicate mental or nervous troubles, especially if Mercury is one of the planets involved. It is particularly noticeable when Mercury is in difficult aspect to Mars or Uranus in these two Signs or Houses.

Mercury in the Elements

The Element in which Mercury is placed in any chart shows *how* one thinks and expresses one's thoughts. For example, Mercury in a **Fire Sign** indicates that the type of logic, reasoning, and thinking is influenced by one's enthusiasms and aspirations. If Mercury is in the Fire Sign Aries, the person's expression could be quite opinionated. In Leo, it would be more demonstrative, dramatic, and generous. But in Sagittarius, Mercury becomes voluble, tactless, or philosophical.

Mercury in the **Earth Signs** would show that the person's thinking is influenced by practical needs and is pragmatically expressed. Mercury in Taurus would likely exhibit slowness in reaching decisions and even slower to change, but would be thorough in most things. In Virgo, Mercury would denote precise, painstaking, and critical attention to everything. But in the last of the Earth Signs, Capricorn, Mercury's influence on the thinking shows as structured, able, and given to worry.

In the **Air Signs,** Mercury is very much at home, for the mind can function freely in Air, though there is always danger that the exciting play with large concepts and schemes will become an end in itself—"mind games". Mercury located in Gemini is dilettante and witty, quick, chatty, and, unless there are stabilizing aspects from other planets, superficial. In Libra, Mercury becomes expressive, sociable, diplomatic, and sometimes indecisive. In Aquarius, Mercury displays itself as detached, broad-minded and humane.

With Mercury in the **Water Signs,** the thinking is strongly colored and directed by the emotions and the influences to which the person is subconsciously predisposed. If Mercury is in Cancer, the thinking is sentimental, quick to see slights in another's words, and is very self-protective. In Scorpio, Mercury is reserved, sarcastic and has a long memory for real or fancied wrongs. Mercury in Pisces is compassionate, but can be vague or wooly-headed.

Of course, the foregoing is a superficial sketch of Mercury in the various Signs, always subject to modification by other factors in the chart. The Element in which Mercury is placed gives a strong clue as to understanding between people. If A's Mercury is in favorable aspect to B's Mercury, or their respective Mercurys are in harmonious Signs, then understanding will be practically instantaneous, at least intellectually, no matter how badly the thought is expressed. Whereas if the Mercurys of C and D are in square or opposition or in inharmonious Signs, their exchange of ideas tends to bring misunderstanding regardless of how articulate they may be.

Mercury in the Houses The affairs of the House occupied by Mercury will indicate those to which the mind is largely applied, and there will often be connections between that House and the Houses of Gemini and Virgo in that chart. For example, Mercury posited in the 2nd House with Gemini on the 9th and Virgo on the 12th, involved a man with huge expenses and financial losses (2nd House affairs) caused by a lengthy hospitalization (12th House) while traveling abroad (9th House long journey).

Mercury's Aspects

Being a neutral or androgynous planet, Mercury tends to *take on* color from any planet with which it is in aspect, rather than *giving to* that planet. Traditionally, Mercury is neither fortunate nor unfortunate, positive nor negative, hot nor cold.

MERCURY-VENUS   The affections are related to mental evaluations. Often such aspects give a facility in one or more of the arts though the chart has to be strong with aspects from Uranus, Neptune, or Pluto to give real talent or genius. Idealism and sociability are two strong qualities of the Mercury-Venus aspect.

MERCURY-MARS   Aspects with Mars noticeably invigorate the mentality and communicativeness, though if in difficult aspect the nervous system may suffer from overstrain. As one astrologer remarked, "Mars configured with Mercury can mean an argument, a fire in the wastebasket, nerve inflammation, and many other things!" In the Natal chart, and when "set off" by progressions or transits, it predisposes the person to be argumentative. The square aspect tends to denote explosions of nervous energy and the opposition aspect seems to show up as nervous anxiety and indecision needing a practical application of the energies. The sextile and trine give a quick mind and mental (as well as physical) dexterity. But if the rest of the chart is not strong, even with the favorable trine and sextile aspect, there can be a waste of these easy energies.

MERCURY-JUPITER   The mental attitude is optimistic, direct, and open with these two planets in conjunction; but if Mercury is in a Fixed Sign, it tends to stubbornness perhaps because Jupiter often gives one such a good opinion of oneself and a little pride so that the person is convinced he is always right! The trine gives ease in learning, good luck in educational matters but with a tendency to inflate concepts so that one loses sight of practical consequences. With a square, exaggeration may shade into lies and blur the judgment. Commonsense is often lacking with difficult aspects between Mercury and Jupiter. Both the square and the opposition can bring financial difficulties through lack of objective thinking and through over-optimism.

MERCURY-SATURN Any aspect between Mercury and Saturn increases the seriousness of the mind; this can range from profound wisdom to melancholy. With the conjunction and harmonious aspects, the speech will show confidence and authority. The trine is particularly good, giving balance and strength to all of Mercury's qualities. The square and the opposition tend to signal depression, moodiness and introspection, feelings of frustration, and inadequacy. Even so, the difficult aspects—if rightly understood and correctly used—can lead to deep mental awareness and wisdom.

MERCURY-URANUS The conjunction and harmonious aspects give a brilliant, swift, and an often original mind. The difficult aspects give the same qualities but the difference seems to be that the stability and continuity of effort required to express the mental assets constructively are often lacking. Under the unfavorable aspects there may be much nervous tension, with energies wasted through willfulness and extreme independence. Personal relationships suffer, especially with the opposition. Mercury rules the memory, so with a strong Uranus aspect, either difficult or harmonious, the person may be able to extend his memory to past lives. This applied in my own case, with natal Mercury in close square to Uranus. I was brought into Astrology and Theosophy in my teens (both are ruled by Uranus). But it was not until many years later, when Uranus, by progression, came to an *exact* square to the natal Mercury, that I found I could use the horoscope as a door to past-life recall.

MERCURY-NEPTUNE This relation is often found in the charts of inspired artists and musicians. The conjunction and harmonious aspects give great sensitivity, flexibility, and imagination. With any of the Mercury-Neptune aspects, but particularly the difficult ones, there is extreme bodily and nervous sensitivity to drugs, allergies, and ugliness that offends them deeply. Unless the rest of the chart is strong, or there are modifying factors, the person has a tendency to escape into daydreaming, alcohol, drugs, or simply mental confusion.

MERCURY-PLUTO With this combination, profound powers of concentration are common. There may be a deep interest in the occult, sex, and death when these two planets are in aspect.

Persons with the difficult aspects are especially prone to compulsive talking, opinionated ideas, and using their power to manipulate others. The individual's perspective and will is likely to outrun their capabilities, resulting in a keenly felt sense of personal futility. With the opposition, the perspective can get dangerously out of focus, but when balanced by another aspect, the perspective can become deep, powerful, and persuasive. The trine gives an ethical structure and respect for the mysteries to mental probings and adds a cautious rein to the will.

Mercury Retrograde

Mercury goes from direct motion to retrograde motion at least four times every year. Persons born during one of these retrograde periods will be greatly influenced by that planet. Actually, no planet retrogrades, that is, goes backward;[6] they only appear to do so because of a celestial optical illusion. When you are sitting in a slowly-moving train and another, faster moving train passes you, at that moment it may appear that you are either standing still or going backward. That is what happens when a faster moving planet overtakes a slower moving one. Mercury orbits faster than Earth, and because of our elliptical orbit, the apparent retrograde Mercury occurs four times each full earth-orbit—one year.

Mercury retrograde at birth tends to slow down the learning process, sometimes causing confusion and difficulty in thinking and expressing thought. My experience with retrograde planets is that the same abilities are there as in a forward-moving planet but they are in some way inhibited—the planet's energies are expressed *inwardly* rather than outwardly. The year that Mercury goes direct by progression usually marks a year of change, the person appears to undergo a change of personality—becoming more self-confident and better able to express himself. People with only favorable aspects to the Natal retrograde Mercury may never have any difficulties with learning or communication. In fact, they often become very articulate, creative speakers.

Those with difficult aspects to a Natal retrograde Mercury tend to be more introspective, confused, and inhibited in expressing themselves or in understanding others. Sometimes what learning or thought that has been acquired but unexpressed under a retrograde Mercury is stored until Mercury turns direct when it is released. Many persons with a Natal retrograde Mercury feel they think more clearly and express themselves better when transitting Mercury is in retrograde motion during the year. But for those with a forward-moving Mercury in their Natal charts, the transitting or progressing Mercury when retrograde often brings difficulties and misunderstandings in communication, letters, legal papers, clerical errors, etc. Personally, I try never to write an important letter or sign a legal paper when transitting Mercury is retrograde.

A retrograde Mercury has a greater impact on those with either Ascendant or Sun in Gemini or Virgo. Mercury retrograde in Pisces seems to have less difficulty than in other Signs. A retrograde planet seems to act in a subconscious way. As Pisces rules the subconscious, this may explain why it seems to be a harmonious placement for a retrograde Mercury.

Retrogradation is often thought to be an important consideration in determining karmic meaningfulness in a chart.[7] There does seem to be a stronger and perhaps karmic focus on the functions of those planets which were retrograde at the time of a particular experience than on those planetary functions which were direct.

NOTES

[1]"The Babylonian carving of the Moon in this position compares it with a cup continually filled with and emptied of ambrosial fiery liquids of which sacramental intoxicants are the extracts," Joseph Campbell, *The Mythic Image* (Princeton: Princeton University Press, 1975), p. 88.

[2]There is a vast literature on the two great continents of Atlantis and Mu said to have sunk beneath the Atlantic and Pacific Oceans respectively ages ago. See Annie Besant and C. W. Leadbeater, *Man: Whence, How and Whither* (Wheaton: Theosophical Publishing House, 1947). Humanity was first androgynous. The Genesis account states, "So God created man in his own image, in the image of God created he him; male and female created he them" Gen. 1:27. This creature was told to "Be fruitful, and multiply . . ." so it had the ability to reproduce itself without need of another. It is only later in Gen. 2:22 that God took one of Adam's ribs and made it Woman. This may well be an interpolation or it may refer allegorically to the separation of the sexes. See Geoffrey Hodson, *The Hidden Wisdom in the Holy Bible*, Vol. II (Wheaton: Theosophical Publishing House, 1967), pp. 116–131. Like many such

statements in the Bible, unless taken with a deeper meaning it makes no sense.

[3]H. P. Blavatsky, *The Voice of the Silence*, Fragment I (Wheaton: Theosophical Publishing House, 1970), pp. 17–34.

[4]Theosophy posits that the Plan of the Logos unfolds in humanity through seven Root Races of which we are now in the fifth. Each Root Race (composed of seven sub-races appearing consecutively) develops certain qualities and powers until, at the end of the seventh Root Race Man is complete and passes into the superhuman kingdom. The power to be developed in the fifth Root Race is that of the Mind. The term "Race" used by the Adepts who imparted this knowledge has been much misconstrued by many people. It was used for lack of a better word and is not to be taken as referring to races according to color (like the black, white, or yellow races of modern idiom) or cultural stock (like Negro, Nordic, Aryan, Caucasian, etc.).

[5]The planets are considered *dignified,* i.e., expressing their positive qualities, in the Signs they rule or in which they are "exalted"; but they are weaker in certain other Signs of "detriment" or "fall". For example, the Sun is said to be strong in Leo, its rulership. It is especially strong and well-expressed in its Sign of "exaltation"—Aries. The Sun is considered weakest, its expression of natural qualities most inhibited in Libra its Sign of Fall—opposite Aries. Further, the Sun expresses negatively to a lesser degree in its Sign of "detriment"—Aquarius. Modern astrologers tend to give less importance to the dignities, as these are called.

[6]The Sun and Moon are never retrograde. In the yearly ephemeris, the letter "r" in the column giving a planet's longitude shows that it has turned retrograde in motion on that date. The letter "d" shows the date on which it turns "direct" in motion again.

[7]Elman Bacher, the great Rosicrucian astrologer, states in his series on *Studies in Astrology,* Vol. III (Oceanside, CA: Rosicrucian Fellowship), "Planetary retrogradation, as studied in astrology, is a periodic, rhythmic action which illustrates the great evolutionary principle of *recapitulation* ... it is a pattern or mode by which Nature insures the thoroughness of evolutionary processes. That which was accomplished in one round of a given cycle is recapitulated or reviewed at the resumation of the new activity in order that the complete integrity of organic powers may be established."

VIII

♀

VENUS: LEARNING TO LOVE

The placement of planet Venus in the horoscope shows how one expresses affection, feels appreciated, and gives of oneself. She is one of the three personal feminine principles, Moon being the most important feminine principle and Neptune being the universal, transcendent feminine principle. Venus expresses the qualities of harmony, giving and receiving, sharing, and values. She rules the urges to unity, balance, social relationships, the arts, romance, love, and marriage. Through her rulership of Taurus she has to do with the accumulation and administration of money and possessions which constitute an expression of the karmic law of giving value for value received (see Chapter IV, p. 40 on the 2nd House). As seen in the symbol of Venus, the circle of the spirit takes precedence over the cross of matter; and Venus at her best gives love and works for the comfort and happiness of others with no thought of gain for herself. Her negative expression can be self-indulgence, greed, too many emotional demands, and vanity.

No man is an island unto himself—or herself—and our relationships with others are of prime importance for they are what objectify or "ignite" our own inner states. Through our close relationships—particularly to parents, children, marriage partners, friends, and enemies—we learn many of our most valuable lessons. The most intense karma of love or hate is worked out with those with whom we have close ties. The position and aspects of Venus in the horoscope show how well or how badly you have done in those departments in past lives and therefore what you can expect to meet in this life.

I had a client whose Venus had absolutely no aspects, and even the two Signs she ruled, Taurus and Libra, were empty of planets. When Venus is weak, unaspected, or afflicted by dif-

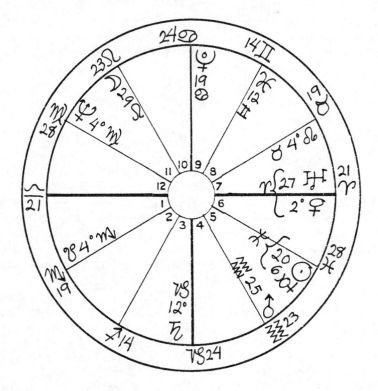

Henry—The problem of an unaspected Venus

ficult aspects, the planets in the Signs Taurus and Libra (ruled by her) can extend her influence into the chart. However, the client's Ascending Sign was Libra. Not surprisingly, the problems about which Henry consulted me were Venus problems. He wanted to know, 1. what he could do to improve his relationship with his son and, 2. whether he should continue living with the woman he had been living with for the past four years. My instinctive response to the last problem was, "If you have reached the stage of asking that question the answer is most likely that you have answered it yourself in the negative."

After studying his chart I gave my opinion that he lacked love and affection in his nature so that if he wished his relationship

with his son and others to improve he must work to foster those
qualities in himself. Henry agreed and told me that his psychologist had told him the same thing. Karmically speaking, his
Venus gave little promise of reward in this life, but if patterns
were established by which impulses for self-isolation were
transmuted into giving or devotion to an ideal or the cultivation
of sympathetic understanding the process would build a happier Venus karma in the future as well as easing things in the
present life.

Henry's Venus was placed in Aries which indicated that he
looked upon love as a form of self-expression, the primal "I"
carrying out the egoistic, dynamic influence of Mars, emphasizing the tendency shown in a sterile Venus to be self-centered and
aggressive in affectional matters. His Moon was in Leo, another
Fire Sign inharmonious to the sensitive, gentle qualities of that
body. His Moon was also in opposition to Mercury and Mars
manifesting as difficulty in the area of personal relationship (see
Chapter V, p. 56). Also, his Moon was conjunct Neptune, so it is
little wonder that his experiences with his mother had been
unfortunate. The Neptune conjunction showed that his attitudes
and relationships with all the women in his life had been fraught
with illusion, fantasy, and frustration. Placed in the analytical
Sign Virgo, it was unlikely that any woman could live up to his
ideals and love withers under such a critical eye. The barren
Venus and afflicted Moon indicated that in his past life or lives,
Henry's treatment of women and his denial of love, affection,
and understanding of others had brought him little happiness in
those areas.

But it is not enough to pinpoint the factors in the horoscope
reflecting the causes in past lives, the astrologer must seek clues
in House and Sign positions and aspects to give the individual
practical avenues through which he can best develop the missing or distorted quality. In Henry's case Venus was posited in the
6th House, the House of service so through service of others,
unselfish work on their behalf, sympathy and concern for those
in his employ and fellow workers, he could begin to develop
Venus qualities. The 6th House is also concerned with health, so
a good place to begin would be with some volunteer work in a
health clinic. A lawyer by profession, his legal training could be
useful in giving guidance to people seeking medical aid at the
same time giving him contact with the troubles of others less

fortunate. The Sun and two planets in the 5th House ruling
children as well as his Leo Moon in the 11th House, the House
which often has to do with children,[1] shows his concern for his
son. Kindness and love of offspring are characteristics of Leo so
he could develop his concern for others through his love for his
son. To improve that relationship he must emphasize a friendship approach (11th House), avoiding the paternalistic or bossy
qualities of that Sign. Leo is a joyous Sign connected with
pleasures, sports, hobbies, etc., and he should make their meet-
ings (the boy lived with his mother) a pleasure by taking the lad
to sporting events, the theater, and other such Leo-ruled activities.

Moon, Venus, and Neptune represent the different aspects of
his inner feminine counterpart (the "anima" in Jungian terminology), as well as the actual women in Henry's life. His Mars
on the cusp of the 5th House, in opposition to Moon in the 11th,
clearly shows that his expressions of love in the past were
aggressive and selfish. It is little wonder that women did not
respond to him with love and evaded him with deception in this
life (Moon conjunct Neptune). He would have to change his
attitudes toward women by trying to see things from their
standpoint, aided by his Sun in Pisces, the most sensitive, receptive Sign in the Zodiac. Pluto in Cancer, in the 9th House was the
highest planet in the chart and trine to his Sun in 5th House,
indicated an extra close tie with a woman (often the mother)—so
close that it may have been the closeness of absorption leaving
no room for true growth. But because the aspect is harmonious
there is good reason to think that the transformative qualities of
Pluto could be brought into play. Pluto's house position shows
the area where one is living out an old pattern of behavior and
where the results of that compulsive urge are often creating pain
and suffering. Pluto in the 9th promises deep spiritual experiences which may serve to change his ideas about God, truth and
the value of human life. Pluto in Cancer also emphasizes that the
karmic lesson of this life lies in the Moon/Cancer ruled areas of
life: women, home, family and the past cultural roots. He could
achieve transformation by getting to the depths of his emotional
nature and integrating his inner feminine counterpart with his
objective masculinity.

Venus is also concerned with values where money and possessions are concerned. Henry viewed women and marriage as a

matter of money paid for value received as indicated by his opening remark concerning the woman he lived with, "I don't want to keep on paying for a dead horse if our relationship is over." The need for harmony and balance and unity with others that a Libra Ascendant demands, requires that he learn to express Moon-Venus qualities constructively. His high intelligence, Pisces Sun, and the powerful transforming Pluto will refuse to let him continue through his life as a male chauvinist.

Taurus, Libra and their Houses

No matter where she is placed, Venus extends her influence through her ruled Signs—Taurus and Libra—and to a lesser extent to the 2nd and 7th Houses over which her Signs have natural rulership. At first glance, there may seem to be little connection between the things ruled by Taurus and the 2nd House or by Libra and the 7th House (see Chapter IV), in spite of the fact that the same planet rules both areas. The connection, to my mind, lies in the fact that possessions (2nd) which reflect our values and marriage (7th) are two of the three most fundamental and lasting factors in humanity's existence; the other factor being, of course, the family which is ruled by Moon and Cancer.

Before the rise of the patriarchal religions, many of the greatest deities were female—the Great Mother reigned supreme.[2] The family and marriage constituted the basic unit and institution, with possessions acquired to ensure their survival. We are told that in time reproduction of the species will be accomplished by the power of the mind and physical mating of male and female will slip into disuse except among primitive peoples. When that time comes, perhaps marriage and the family will give way to new forms of communal relationship.

Libra and the 7th House also rule the relationship between people (other than in marriage), even our "other selves", in opposition or contrast to the personal "I" of the 1st House. Perhaps never in history have human relationships undergone such a shaking—so much re-examination of the long accepted status quo. There have already been many changes, most of which have not yet permeated the vast mass of humanity, but which any thinking person can see will come inevitably.

These changes were set into motion, first, by the transit of Neptune through Libra from 1943 to 1956, followed by Uranus transiting Libra 1968 to 1974, and then, the drastic and transformative Pluto entering Libra in 1972. Neptune first permeated the matters ruled by Libra and the 7th House with its inspiration and idealism, loosening the limitations of form so that there was a greater consciousness of oneness with others. In an effort to break the bonds of the little self, many young people took to drugs and mystical religions and the new cults (all Neptune ruled). But, to quote Stephen Arroyo:

> Unless one has come to terms with the pressures, realities, and obligations of Saturn, one is not sufficiently grounded to handle the intensity and disruption of any of the trans-Saturnian planets. In other words, one has to take the insights and freedom of Uranus, and the inspiration and idealism of Neptune and *make them real* by bringing that awareness down to earth, testing those far-out inclinations, and incorporating them into our everyday life. Failure to work on this integration inwardly with great honesty and diligence will often bring about either a tremendous feeling of discontent or, in some cases, psychological disturbances which can eventually lead to a large scale disintegration of the personality.[3]

Following Neptune's transit through Libra came the electric Uranus which so often manifests as impulses toward independence, rebellion, the unconventional, and the original. And now we have Pluto, which entered Libra in 1972 to stay until 1983, bringing with it the elimination of all that stands in the way of total rebirth.

The far-reaching changes that the trans-Saturnian planets have already brought about and will bring about in Libra will not affect everyone in the same way or to the same extent. Those who will feel it most are those with Natal planets in Libra, especially if they are numerous or importantly aligned with the rest of the chart, or if there are close aspects (particularly the conjunction, square, or opposition) from Saturn to Uranus, Neptune, or Pluto.

Taurus will feel the effect of oppositions from Neptune, Uranus, and Pluto with the passage of those planets through Scorpio. Neptune has already passed through Scorpio from 1956 to 1970 and is now in Sagittarius. Uranus entered Scorpio in 1974 and will oppose Taurus until late 1981. Pluto will enter Scorpio, opposing Taurus, in 1984. The energy crisis (particularly oil, which is Neptune-ruled), and inflation have played havoc with the value of the dollar, goods, and property (all

Taurus-ruled matters). The value of one has plummeted and the value of the others has shot upward. We are not yet at the end of all the changes which the oppositions to Taurus will bring in our economic scene. It is not a comfortable time. The only thing one can do is to take the long view—to the higher Self. The experiences brought by the planets are karmic and necessary for the growth of individuals and larger entities such as groups and nations.

From the foregoing it can be readily seen that Venus and her Signs and Houses are not solely concerned with love and romance! Basically, that planet always works to establish balance and harmony, two qualities that have been very much lacking in world and individual affairs, which is why the turmoil caused by the passages of the trans-Saturnian planets through Libra and then opposing Taurus from Scorpio have caused so much turmoil and pain. The ancient inequalities and inharmonies must be eliminated, at least to some extent, otherwise Man will destroy himself and a good deal of earth with himself.

$$\female$$

Rulership

Some of the people and activities associated with Venus are:
1. Artists, caterers, farmers, financiers, singers, musicians, all occupations connected with art, fashion, home decoration, entertainment, social life, luxuries, money, jewelry, beauty, possessions, diplomacy, romance, marriage, partnerships.
2. The kidneys, thyroid gland, neck, chin, throat, vocal chords, hymen, hemorrhoids, bladder, and hair.[4]

The Element in which Venus is placed at birth colors one's expression of affection, the give-and-take in all human relationships, sensual pleasure and, along with the Moon, has much to do with the emotions.

Venus in a Fire Sign requires affection and close relationships expressed with enthusiastic warmth and grand gestures. In Aries, love can be self-expression in an egotistic, dynamic way.

In Leo, Venus is the arch symbol of romantic love, warmly dramatic. In Sagittarius, she takes on a quality of spirituality and idealism.

Venus in the Earth Signs requires tangible commitments as a convincing demonstration of affection. In Taurus, she will be earthy, sensual, faithful, possessive, and practical in her affections. In Virgo, she is not often at her best because the perfectionism and critical tendencies of that Sign, the Sign of Fall for Venus, interfere with spontaneous loving and giving. Venus in Capricorn tends to be selfish, cold and calculating if afflicted, the affections used to further ambition; or it may indicate marriage to an older, more serious person. It can also show reverse in expressing love.

Venus in an Air Sign requires affection expressed in words, the more articulate the expression the better. Venus in Gemini extends affection particularly to brothers, sisters and relatives, much talkative friendliness and changeableness. Venus in Gemini is a lively companion but not the most faithful lover and is quite able to keep two or more loves going at the same time! Venus in Libra is in her most congenial Sign where she can express her essential urge to balance, harmony, and beauty. In Aquarius, Venus tends to a cool detachment and an avoidance of involvement that might curtail independence, her affection spread among a circle of friends rather than the intensity of a one-to-one relationship.

Venus in a Water Sign requires a great deal of emotional reassurance, sympathetic love feelings expressed frequently. In Cancer, she is home-loving and motherly, easily wounded, jealous, and tends to hang on far too long after a relationship is really over. In Scorpio, Venus is intensely magnetic, passionate, and secretive. A balanced partnership can be threatened by personal desire, and afflictions to Venus in Scorpio can bring sexual difficulties. In evolved persons the intensity and depth of the Sign can transmute love and sex into a truly consecrated devotion. Pisces is the Sign of Venus's "exaltation" and is considered the best Sign for her qualities of love and empathy. In Pisces Venus extends her gifts into idealism, at-one-ment with the individual and the world, and compassion for all who are in need.

Venus in the Houses

The affairs of the House occupied by Venus will be influenced by that planet's urge to harmony, unison and beauty. The House where Venus is posited will be connected in some way with the Houses bearing Taurus and Libra on their cusps. For example, a woman with Venus posited in the 2nd House with Taurus on the 7th House, Libra on the 12th, married several times (7th House) for emotional and financial security (Taurus and the 2nd House) but found that with it came many years of karmic suffering (12th).

Venus Aspects

Venus in any horoscope is the symbol of the aesthetic faculties as well as the love potential. As Elman Bacher puts it: "Rhythm, balance, proportion, and taste are just as evident in cultivated relationships as they are in the qualities of things which we call beautiful."[5]

VENUS-MARS   The conjunction gives extreme attraction to and for the opposite sex. The assertiveness of the self (Mars) transformed through relationship (Venus). In any Venus-Mars aspect the planet which will predominate depends on their relative strength. A planet is considered strong in influence, if placed in an Angular House, or near the cusp of any House, especially the Ascendant and Midheaven, high in the chart; or in major aspect to the Sun, Moon or Mercury; or is ruler of the Sun Sign or Ascendant Sign. A planet is considered weak in influence, when it lacks major aspects; or is in a Cadent House far from the cusp; or in the last or first few degrees of any Sign, and is not ruler of the Sun Sign, Ascendant or Midheaven Signs. If Mars is strong, Venus weak, there will be a predominance of masculinity, self-assertion and sexual urges. With Venus strong, femininity will predominate, the Mars qualities toned down. In some charts this can mean there is little urge toward work and effort. With the sextile or trine, the qualities of Venus would be more apparent as Venus is of the same nature as those aspects. With the square and opposition, the qualities of Mars would be more in evidence for the same reason. The fortunate aspects promise fulfilling sexual and love experiences, a healthy emotional nature, and happy relationships with the opposite sex. The difficult aspects give the same warmth and attraction but also give attendant difficulties.

VENUS-JUPITER The conjunction gives good fortune and idealism. The union of the "Greater Fortune" with the "Lesser Fortune" as Jupiter and Venus are traditionally called, is not as fortunate as one might suppose. Apart from an expansion of luck, gentleness, and benevolence the result can be an emotional placidity and laziness unless there are other more dynamic factors in the chart. This applies also to the sextile and trine. The difficult aspects give an expansive emotional nature that can run to blind love and financial extravagance. The opposition, particularly, can give vacillation, waste of emotions and resources.

VENUS-SATURN This conjunction has been called the aspect of the Poet: a sensitivity to the love and joys of life mingled with sorrow and loss. It usually gives a complex emotional nature with romance or marriage to those very much older or younger than the self. In the harmonious aspects, Venus expresses her love through responsibility, constancy, and fidelity. The difficult aspects often mean joy sacrificed to responsibility, or love constricted by duty or discipline. The conjunction and, even more often, the opposition seem to show an inability to love, as if the person's love nature has been frozen. Usually the cause is early denial of love by a parent. Security is much more important than love, when Venus and Saturn are in a different aspect.

VENUS-URANUS With all the aspects between these two planets there is emphasis on the unusual in relationships, often signifying marriage or love affairs with divorced or married persons, partners much older or younger, or with foreigners. The emotional nature is often so independent and eager for the excitement of new relationships that partnerships and friendships are rarely long-lasting. The conjunction, square, and opposition between Venus and Uranus give a lot of nervous tension; sexual relationships can be unconventional to the extreme, punctuated by unexpected explosions or changes.

VENUS-NEPTUNE "This is pre-eminently the artist's combination and is more nearly related to beauty than to either the moral or scientific spheres."[6] It nearly always gives great aesthetic sensitivity, but it can remain passive or lazy unless there is a square between the two to stimulate effort. The difficult aspects are, in fact, prime indicators of true spiritual and mystical seeking. They are not comfortable aspects to live with for the emotions of Venus combined with the idealism of Neptune often lead to a rejection of mere human love with all its imperfections. There is great compassion and openheartedness making the individual vulnerable to deceit. Sexual relations are often plagued with difficulties, the individual sometimes has a warped attitude toward the physical side of love, considering it gross and unattractive. With certain charts, it can indicate homosexuality, perversion, or life-long celibacy.[7] There is always a lively imagination which can be used constructively or abused.

VENUS-PLUTO Venus and Pluto in conjunction, square, and opposition aspects often indicate the individual will try, in a personal relationship to overpower the will of another person in order to bend or break them to his own personal desires. Or it can mean guilt feelings over breaking social, moral, or familiar taboos, with an inner conviction that such transgressions will have to be paid for sooner or later. Nevertheless, the compulsive willfulness of Pluto pushes the person to break those taboos. Pluto's aspects are often concerned with the destruction and elimination of the old, necessary to make way for the new. For the growth of the individual, certain of his relationships with others must be eliminated or transformed and such drastic changes are often accompanied with guilt feelings. The karmic difficulties of Venus are the results of lack of balance in human relationships. Self-understanding, love, and compassion are needed to bring about right relationships with others. The karmic patterns of these two planets when in aspect can be very strong. With the sextile and trine aspects, the emotional perspective is deepened and expanded. The emotions and love are often directed to a larger group rather than to an individual.

Venus Retrograde

A Venus retrograde in either the Natal or progressed chart indicates that there is to be a period of recapitulation in the matters ruled by Venus. This may mean that those matters will be experienced much more subjectively, rather than objectively. New or fresh ways of expressing the affections, for example, will be inhibited for a time because the person will be going through a process of inward review and digestion. The motion of the planets is a rhythmic one, like all universal life: a time of forward, outward action alternating with a time of inward, germinating action. The year in which the progressed planet changes motion, either from retrograde to direct or from direct to retrograde, marks a change at that time in the method of the planet's expression. With Venus it would mean a change in the person's way of expressing affection, handling relationships or finances, etc. This, of course, would bring about objective changes in relationships and other Venus-ruled matters, for our outer life sooner or later reflects faithfully our inner lives.

NOTES

[1]The births of my three children were signalled by progressions *within the 11th House* while there was only one background aspect to the ruler of my 5th House. The 11th House is the 5th House of the marriage partner and father of the children.

[2]Erich Neumann, *The Great Mother: An Analysis of the Archetype*, tr. R. Manheim (Princeton: Princeton University Press, 1972).

[3]Stephen Arroyo, *Astrology, Karma and Transformation: The Inner Dimensions of the Birthchart* (Vancouver, Washington: CRCS Publications, 1978), p. 43.

[4]A listing of things, persons and vocations ruled by the different planets, Signs and Houses must of necessity be very brief in a book this size. For a much more comprehensive 428-page dictionary, *see* Rex E. Bills, *The Rulership Book*.

[5]Elman Bacher, *Studies in Astrology*, Vol. I (Oceanside, CA: Rosicrucian Fellowship), p. 68.

[6]C. E. O. Carter, *The Astrological Aspects* (Romford, Essex, England: L. N. Fowler & Co., 1977).

[7]This is not meant as passing a moral judgment on homosexuality as perversion, only to indicate that Venus-Neptune aspects often take a form that is out of the usual contemporary expression. By perversion I mean something involving fetishism or sadism where the individual gets his emotional and/or sexual satisfaction out of an object or the giving or receiving of pain.

IX

MARS: PLANET OF SUCCESS

In the symbol of Mars, the cross of matter dominates the orb of the spirit. The cross is usually shown as an arrow, which also demonstrates the outward thrust and the aggressive expression of this planet's influence. Just as the Sun symbolizes the positive-masculine-creative center of all things, so Mars stands for the energy that flows like blood through all manifestations of life and makes possible all forms of growth, sustainment, and progress. Together, the Sun and Mars synergize the masculine polarity. Essentially, the masculine energy is aggressive, but not hostile; it is, rather, an active, assertive, dominating approach to the world. Compared with the Sun, Mars is more egotistical, separative, frictional, and dynamic. His is the voice of 'I am; I want; I will get; I will defend myself; I will defeat my enemies; I must survive.' Mars is the principal maker of karma. There is no need to belabor examples of Mars' action in primitive and average types of humanity; there is all too much of it in individuals, groups, and nations. But a strong Mars is absolutely essential in a horoscope to accomplish anything worthwhile, which is why it has been called the planet of SUCCESS because it seems to be a common denominator in the charts of those who have made their mark in the world. A horoscope with a weak Mars usually indicates a weak, colorless person—a Casper Milquetoast—who accomplishes nothing, either for good or evil. Mars' position in the horoscope by Sign, by House and through aspects shows how strong is the urge to work, to apply effort, to development and self-expression. A weak Mars shows a depletion of urge, a scattering of energy, a lack of courage, and a tendency to knuckle under rather than to carry out one's destiny. An afflicted Mars gives drive and energy, but if uncontrolled and misdirected it

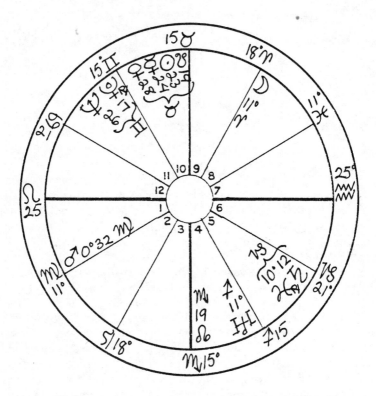

ROBERT—The challenge of an afflicted Mars

gives destructive rather than constructive results. Even the fortunate aspects of Mars have to be controlled to produce constructive results which is why the Sign of Exaltation for Mars is the Saturn-ruled Sign of Capricorn. Capricorn gives caution and careful planning to the energies of Mars.

A friend of mine, Robert K., was the very epitome of a Mars-dominated horoscope (see chart) in appearance, character, and profession. Athletic, strong-muscled, with a heavy, over-hanging brow, he was a building constructor. From humble beginnings he rose to executive status after years of night school and unceasing work. Robert just did not know how to rest or relax. If he went on holiday he always tried to combine it with business. When he bought a house, he knocked down sections and rebuilt them several times. He could not see a tree or shrub without taking an ax or clippers to it, often killing the poor thing in his efforts to improve it. Robert was the same with the people in his employ or with members of his family—ceaselessly criticizing, disciplining, and prodding them on toward *his* idea of perfection. Naturally, many of these objects of his efforts protested so that his relationships were fraught with difficulty. In spite of all this, his great warmth and well-meaning concern for others made him many lasting friends. Some, of course, were alienated; his marriage ended in divorce and his career was hampered by his inability to work harmoniously with others. His chart showed Mars in Virgo conjunct the Ascendant and square Sun, Mercury, and Venus in the 10th House. His Moon's Nodes were the opposite of Henry's (Chapter VIII, the unaspected Venus), with the North Node in Scorpio in the 4th House and the South Node in Taurus in his 10th House. The South Node showed where we start in this incarnation, the load we bring in with us of past life karmic patterns. As Atlanta astrologer David Railey described it, "The South Node in Taurus is like a covered wagon: *really* loaded down with past karma!" This placement also gives a tendency to not listen. Placed in the 10th House close to the Midheaven, it showed that in his last life Robert was very important in some public position. Much of his dissatisfaction in this present incarnation stemmed from the subconscious feeling that nothing he did was important enough, worthwhile enough compared with what he did in his past life.

The North Node indicates what one is hoping to accomplish in this life and, being in the 4th House, often brings fundamental, dynamic changes in the home. Robert began life in a small country village and spent most of his adult life in foreign countries living in every kind of habitation from a mansion with many servants, a prisoner-of-war shack, to a small walk-up apartment. Of course, Uranus placed in the 4th House also gives radical changes in the home.

Looking to the rulers of the Signs in which the Nodes are placed we find the relating aspect between Venus and Mars[1] is a dynamic, challenging square. Along with the emphasis of planets in Taurus, it is indicative of stubbornness and possessiveness. Robert married late in life a much younger, foreign-born woman (Moon trine Uranus, ruler of the 7th House posited in the 4th—latter part of life), and that marriage ended in divorce after some years. In spite of such difficulties and a chart almost wholly filled with hard aspects, He had many friends and these friendships were important to him. The stellium in Venus-ruled Taurus plus the warmth of Mars in 1st House made him very likable when he wasn't impatient or in a temper, characteristic of an afflicted Mars.

Brooding over this horoscope one day, the intuition came that Robert's Archetype and path was that of the Cosmic Builders, those superhuman entities who construct and develop worlds and universes. This life was a necessary stage of learning for Robert, uncomfortable as it might be for some of those near him. Mars is the destroyer and the builder, and as disturbing and even self-defeating as it may seem, this was *right* for him at this stage of his evolution. Astrologers and others who are endeavoring to see their fellows with true perspective must try to see them in the light of their many lives and probable archetypes. They must try to intuit what the Self is attempting to learn and develop in themselves on their particular path leading to their unique destiny.

Late in his life, Robert turned his energies to working with the handicapped and nursing sick friends. Thus, he expressed caring, compassionate, nurturing qualities of his Moon trine Uranus, using *constructive* energies of Mars. In so doing, he was finally able to tame to a great extent the more abrasive side of his Mars-dominated nature.

Mars (and Pluto on a deeper or higher level), is the prime symbol of the sex impulse, the basic creative motivation of life. In the primitive and average man that expression is largely selfish. All persons on the path of conscious evolution are tested in terms of the use of their sexual energies. And a time always comes for the transformation and refinement of those energies. This testing, initiation, and transformation in the mysteries of sex are under the higher octave ruler of Scorpio—Pluto. (Chapter XII)

Signs and Houses Ruled by Mars

No matter where Mars is placed, by Sign or House, he extends his influence through the Signs of Aries and Scorpio and, to a lesser degree, the 1st and 8th Houses over which those Signs have natural rulership. Since Mars is the first planet we've examined who holds joint rulership, this is a logical place to delve into this co-ruler subject.

Joint Rulerships Most astrologers give Pluto rulership of Scorpio, with Mars as a part ruler. In like manner, Jupiter shares the rulership of Pisces with Neptune, and Saturn shares the rulership of Aquarius with Uranus. This may seem confusing, especially in the case of Aquarius where Saturn exemplifies the structured, disciplined, slow, and materialistic while Uranus exemplifies the original, revolutionary, quick-witted, and humanitarian, to mention but a few of the contrasts. My feeling is that it is a matter of lower- and higher-octave planets.

The Sun, Moon, Mercury, Venus, and Mars are the basic, *personal* planets; they characterize the more obvious personality traits and urges in the person as well as having a more obvious, direct effect on the environment and events. Jupiter and Saturn are related to the deeper motivational and collective factors and are the planets which mediate between the higher/ impersonal planes and the lower/personal planes of manifestation.

Uranus, Neptune, and Pluto symbolize the most profound sources of change and transformation. In judging the effect of a joint rulership of a Sign, much depends on the stage of evolution of the particular individual whose horoscope is being studied. In the character and life of the average person, the influence of higher-octave planets, such as Uranus, Neptune, and Pluto is likely to be so subtle that its material effect is unnoticeable or negative. For example, in Pisces the rulership of Neptune may manifest as muddled emotionalism or a self-destructive escapism into alcohol, drugs, daydreaming or evasion of responsibility. In a more spiritually evolved individual there can be the highest kind of all-encompassing compassion and idealism; Jupiter's religious aspirations, benevolence, and expansion of goals carried to selfless heights by Neptune. In Aquarius, Uranus may manifest as willfulness, rebellion, and a restless need for excitement and change in the average person but in the evolved person there can be enhanced intuition, originality, and an attunement to truth replacing the insistence on personal freedom. The characteristics of Uranus seem almost like a revolt in Aquarius against the discipline, self-restriction, and acceptance of responsibility of Saturn. People with Sun, Ascendant, or many planets in that Sign experience this conflict in themselves and as we are entering the Age of Aquarius this conflict can be observed on all levels of society. It is my feeling that Uranus and Saturn need the qualities of the other and there must eventually be a marriage of the best qualities so that the discipline and responsibility of Saturn will make possible the material and spiritual manifestation of the humanitarian concepts of Uranus.

At first, Pluto's rulership of Scorpio may express negatively in neurotic compulsions, and a misuse of power. The negative expression of Mars has always been resentment, revengefulness, and violence. But as the individual evolves, his passion can be directed into healing channels, using Scorpio's persistence and desire to penetrate below the surfaces to plumb the mysteries of life and death and regeneration. Eventually Mars' dauntless courage, initiative, and dynamic energy is lifted from the pursuit of power for selfish ends to be concentrated upon one's own transformation which is the highest expression of Pluto.

Mars in the Houses and Signs

The 8th House is one of the three Water Houses—4th, 8th, and 12th. (See Chapter IV) They represent the trinity of emotional and soul experience concerned with inner development. As Scorpio's natural House, the 8th has been called the House of sacrifice, death, and rebirth. Why sacrifice? And what would the connection of Mars be with sacrifice? Sacrifice has acquired an aura of unfortunate and painful "giving up of something desired", but we sacrifice desirable things frequently for some goal which has become necessary. It is the courage and energy of Mars which impels us to make the sacrifice so that we can grow and progress.

Mars gives us the courage to sacrifice the lesser for the greater, to die to outworn habits, conditions, relationships, desires, so that we may be born anew, moving ever forward toward higher goals. This is what is embodied in Scorpio and the 8th House, through which Mars partly expresses.

In Aries, a Fire Sign, the energies of Mars express in a one-pointed drive toward action and self-assertion—'to be the first with the most.' The qualities of Mars in Aries and the 1st House appear in their purest form, uncomplicated by the subtleties and questioning of Scorpio. The fiery nature of the planet harmonizes with the Fire Element of Aries, whereas in the Water Sign Scorpio his energies are directed more into emotional channels. But in Aries, Martian energies find their highest expression in leadership where his qualities of courage and initiative are essential ingredients.

♂ Rulership

Some of the people, vocations, and things associated with Mars are:

1. Military men, surgeons, chemists, metal workers (particularly with iron and steel), dentists, butchers, barbers, engineers, and builders.
2. Fever, inflammation, headaches, the skull, face, arteries, external sex organs, muscular tissue, motor nerves, excretory organs, red corpuscles of the blood.

Mars in the Modes, Elements and Signs

The dynamic energy and self-assertive urges of Mars will vary in expression according to the Mode, Element, and Sign in which he is placed. In **Cardinal Signs,** his qualities of activity and leadership will be more evident. In the **Fixed Signs,** the Martian qualities of organization and building are most evident. In **Mutable Signs** Mars' energies tend to be expended in a variety of interests which are changed rather often.

The Element in which Mars is found shows the particular channel through which his energies and urges will express. People with **Mars in Fire Signs** prefer direct physical action; they are very enthusiastic but get impatient unless there is movement—action—in whatever they are engaged.

People with **Mars in an Air Sign** will try to assert themselves through ideas and some form of communication such as speaking, writing, or traveling. With **Mars in Water Signs,** the desires and emotions are particularly strong and forceful, a difficult placement. When **Mars is in Earth Signs** the energies and desires will be expressed through practical, concrete achievement and interests.

Mars in the Signs

It is difficult to condense the significance of Mars in each zodiacal Sign. The application of his energy depends upon the whole of the character. An Aries will use Mars energy differently than will a Piscean, for example. Generally speaking, in **Aries,** the energy is ardent, projected with courage and initiative, though somewhat recklessly. Unless self-control is used, the person may be too aggressive, belligerent, and militaristic. In **Taurus** the energies are expressed with patience and persever-ance which spring from a steady urge to acquire security and/or with obstinacy. When Mars is in **Gemini,** the energy expresses on the mental plane. There is a great deal of "nervous energy" which often makes the person restless and changeable.

In **Cancer**—the Sign of Fall for Mars—there is a kind of intro-version which expresses through emotional channels. Cancer seems to focus the Mars energy upon security (emotional or financial), and the home. Women with this Mars position are often demon housekeepers and become family-ruling mat-riarchs. Under Cancer's emotional influence, the Mars temper is quick to flare in defensiveness or flash forth over some imagined slight.

In **Leo** Mars exudes warmth in the royal manner, tending to arrogance, if there are not modifying factors in the chart. The energies are bent toward making the self important. In **Virgo,** the energy is concentrated upon details and the critical ability can be very constructive, or it can be very destructive if expended in fault-finding. Mars in **Virgo** can be extremely critical of others but rarely can take any criticism directed to himself.

Libra is the Sign of Mars' detriment, so his natural expression is impeded. The eagerness for harmony and balance, for seeing both sides of the question, can hamper the natural forcefulness of Mars. In **Scorpio,** the Mars energy is channeled to a wide spectrum of emotions, increasing their intensity. If Mars in this Sign is well-aspected, regeneration can be stimulated by deep analysis. There is great magnetism but self-discipline is needed to direct it constructively rather than selfishly.

In **Sagittarius,** athletics and outdoor activities are a good outlet for Mars' energies. There is a tendency to over-extend, over-exert, act in haste. A long-term application of energy to-ward some goal is difficult to maintain because enthusiasm bounds from one thing to another.

Mars is exalted in **Capricorn** and his energy there is applied with discipline, caution, and good timing—the latter, a quality often lacking with Mars. Control, strategy, and materialism aid in the acquisition of position and possessions.

The Martian energies in **Aquarius** express through the intellect and ideas. Friendship, group activities, and humanitarianism are infused with energetic interest and activity. The individual can express himself with originality or eccentricity.

The forcefulness of Mars is diluted or confused by the emotions in the Water Sign, **Pisces.** Energy has difficulty materializing in some positive action unless there is an impelling inspiration.

Mars in the Houses

Keywords for Mars are energy, heat, activation, and initiatory force. The affairs of any House occupied by Mars will show the sphere in which the type of keyword-actions will be expressed or experienced from others. It often happens that the exertion of energy and force evokes opposition and reflex from others so that strife and struggle are frequently found in the House that Mars occupies.

Mars Aspects

Mars acts like a catalyst in aspect with other planets, his energies stirring their principles, urges, and needs to active expression. A square aspect, the most energizing of all aspects, may increase the energy to the point of possible disruption. Too much Mars vitality and thrust can cause accidents and strife, over-exertion, etc. Any aspect between Mars and the Sun or Moon increases the vitality.

MARS-VENUS Mars is the prime symbol of the sex impulse, the creative motivation of life. In primitive and in average man that expression is largely selfish, so a Mars-Venus affliction particularly shows karma of sexual selfishness and possibly violence from former lives. Gradually, Mars is redeemed through Venus into higher expressions of love and sex. Any aspect between these two planets warms the emotions with passion.

MARS-JUPITER The energy and thrust of Mars often seems to enlarge the expansiveness of Jupiter to excess, even with the more fortunate aspects. The conjunction gives an abundance of energy, enthusiasm, and love of life. The square stimulates the urge to gamble with an expansive over-confidence that requires careful moderation. There may be legal problems and extravagance. The square between Mars and Jupiter is one of the most difficult aspects in the spectrum of planetary relationships. The sextile and trine can bring wealth, or luck in gambling even in the stock market or speculative business. The opposition often means loss through gambling, a lack of commonsense, and ineffective preparation and planning. There can be conflict with others due to one's conceit and excesses.

MARS-SATURN The "hard" aspects between Mars and Saturn show frustrations in expressing the self or one's emotions; and with the conjunction, especially, it is like an irresistible force meeting an immovable object. The conservatism of Saturn frustrates the driving energy of Mars with resultant unhappiness. The square is an aspect denoting bad judgment; one's dynamic drive (Mars) and caution (Saturn) clash, with impulse and passion causing trouble. Rebellion against authority is an example of this combination of planets. With the trine and sextile, the drive of Mars is aligned with the control and power of organization (Saturn). The opposition shows conflict, frustration, and loss—particularly in relationship with others.

MARS-URANUS   The conjunction and the other difficult and challenging aspects such as the square and opposition give the same Uranian qualities of intuition, originality, mechanical aptitude, and independence, as do the more fortunate sextile and trine aspects.

The problem is, that unless there are stabilizing factors elsewhere in the chart, the control and persistence necessary for eventual achievement are often lacking because of willfulness, lack of discipline, and a restless eagerness for new excitement and experiences. With the conjunction, the temperament can be emotionally volatile along with a very bright and ingenuous mentality. The square increases the temper and insistence of independence to the point of rebellion against social mores and restrictions. With the trine the mind can be particularly inventive with mechanical aptitude. There can be a daring courage allied to the vision and drive of a pioneer in some field. The opposition often gives an eccentric, willful temperament leading to conflict and loss in relationships.

MARS-NEPTUNE Humanity as a whole is not yet tuned to the higher spiritual vibrations of Neptune. Confusion, illusion, dis-illusion, and deception are often found accompanying Neptune's House position and aspects. The conjunction, square, and opposition with Mars can indicate obscure and difficult-to-diagnose conditions that find their way to the psychiatrist such as nervous disorders, sex illusions, and perversions, drugs, and alcoholism. Neptune always figures in alcoholism and drugs. There can be danger from food or water poisoning. If the 8th House is involved there can be mystery surrounding the death.[2] However, the conjunction is the most powerful magnetic aspect in any horoscope; the energies of Mars are given an intuitive, almost magical delivery. The difficulty with all Neptunian aspects is that fantasy can replace reality. Even with the magnetism and vision of the Mars-Neptune conjunction the energies of Mars can be directed down some very weird paths or—some very spiritual ones. The square gives a combination of forceful energy and spiritual insight, but in a weak chart self-delusion is possible. The trine and sextile give personal magnetism, spiritual and/or mental power. Often there is talent in some aesthetic, artistic, or musical field. The opposition denotes deception and illusion in some form.[3]

MARS-PLUTO Major aspects between these two represent perhaps the most intense expression of concentrated power to be found in any chart. There is a boundless potential for constructive or destructive action. Often the methods of achieving goals are secretive, devious, or extreme. The conjunction emphasizes the concentrated drive toward dominance and power. Persons with the square often have the added difficulty of very violent tempers. With the sextile and trine there is the same drive toward power but with less inner tension; the individual seems better able to accept the need for control of his tendency to ruthlessness and fanaticism. The danger is that once arriving at the stage of seeing the need for reform, he tends to turn that same demanding ruthlessness upon himself that he once forced upon others with the result that repression and self-anger only lead to frustration, guilt, and increased tension. The only antidote is to develop understanding and forgiveness of oneself as well as of others and to realize that the process of self-reformation takes time. And always remember—we have eternity to accomplish anything and everything we set as a goal. The opposition adds brusqueness of manner and more ill-temper so that relationships suffer. There may be a battle between the personal will, directed toward personal aims versus the use of personal energy for the growth and transformation of the collective whole.

The condition of Mars in the horoscope always indicates the use or misuse of that driving energy in past lives and what form it took in general.[4] For example, a difficult aspect between Mars and Moon could show that Martian energy was used to dominate or bully females, or tyrannize within the family unit. Or it could mean that in the past, other circumstances and other people were so crushing that an oversensitivity about asserting yourself was brought over into this incarnation. If, from your horoscope, you can see that you must meet a certain amount of difficult karma because of your Martian aggressions in the past, then, instead of reacting instinctively to aggression from others, you must seek to understand, responding with cooperation and love instead of anger. The failure to assert yourself carries a karma of weakness and *that* also must be met with self-understanding and with an effort made to develop the needed strength and courage in order to stand up for what is right.

Mars Retrograde

The expression of Martian energies and self-assertion for material, physical, and emotional fulfillment is a vital factor in the evolution of the Soul. When Mars is retrograde at birth, or goes retrograde (by progression) during the life, it means that there is a recapitulation of certain Martian experiences. These are lessons to be more thoroughly learned and qualities to be more firmly built into the character. The House in which Mars is found, and the Houses ruled by Aries and Scorpio indicate the particular areas of that needed experience. With retrogradation, there is a certain inhibition of the normal outpouring, resulting in a more subtle, inward-flowing of the planetary energies.

NOTES

[1]Pluto should also be considered, being part-ruler of Scorpio; but in this case Pluto makes no aspect to Venus.

[2]The horoscope of a young nephew of a friend of mine showed Mars and Sun in the 8th House in opposition to Neptune. While traveling through a mountainous region in the Far East he disappeared. In spite of a large

reward offered for information, numerous search parties and a great deal of money and effort expended, no trace of him or what might have happened to him was ever found.

[3]It is difficult to judge from a Neptune aspect whether the individual is liable to deceive others, or be deceived by them, or just deceive himself. C. E. O. Carter once discussed that interesting point, *see* his *Astrological Aspects* (Romford, Essex, England: L. N. Fowler & Co., 1977). His feeling was that it was a case of opposite sides of the same coin; other people being really our other selves; they cannot deceive us unless we have first deceived them at some point in time. They cannot deceive us even in the present unless we have deceived ourselves first via some fantasy, illogic or wishful thinking.

[4]It is possible to get greater details of past lives through meditation, regression or focussing upon the horoscope. *See* Chapter XIV.

X

JUPITER: FORTUNE OR EXCESS

In the symbol of Jupiter the crescent and the cross are combined: the reflection of the spirit overshadowing the cross of material manifestation. Manly P. Hall, in *Astrological Keywords*,[1] describes Jupiter's symbol as a "conventionalization of an eagle with outstretched wings and the first letter of the Greek name Zeus." In the Greek and Roman pantheon of the gods, Zeus or Jove was the father of the attendant gods. Our word "jovial" springs from the name Jove and describes one of the personality traits attributed to that planet.

Jupiter symbolizes benevolence, enthusiasm, optimism, expansiveness, honor, knowledge, and opportunity. He is called the "Greater Fortune" whereas Venus is called the "Lesser Fortune". His influence brings an emphasis upon the abstract mind, higher education and learning, religion, philosophy, and law. Jupiter gives the key to understanding the ability to prosper, the ability to grasp opportunities, and the person's general ability to grow in physical, mental, and moral ways by his placement in a Sign, a House, and the strength of aspects. He could also be called the "Preserver", for his influence often seems to preserve a person from harm if only by "the skin of his teeth". I recall two serious automobile accidents in which the cars were demolished. In one of the accidents five people were killed,[2] yet neither of the people with Jupiter aspects suffered even a scratch!

However, Jupiter does not always bring the cornucopia of riches that people expect from his favorable aspects. While abundance may be his keyword, it can mean too much of a good thing if he is weak or afflicted. Where Saturn's "afflictions" are characterized by a *lack* of something in the character, in the physical constitution, or in one's circumstances, with Jupiter it is an excess of something. For example, Jupiter in the 1st House often gives a good opinion of the self and a larger than average body. But it can also mean conceit and obesity in certain Signs and/or with difficult aspects.

Jupiter is the agency by which spiritual forces are made manifest to the lower consciousness. Jupiter's vibrations are not transcendent as are those of Uranus, Neptune, and Pluto; but Jupiter provides an exoteric (outer) channel for esoteric (inner) truths which are too subtle for comprehension by the average person. Jupiter shows our capacity to give—wisely, sincerely, and abundantly. If one has a birth chart Jupiter whose condition indicates problems in character and life, these conditions can be mitigated or changed by a conscious effort to express benevolence and generosity in thought, word, and deed. George S. Arundale once stated, that to progress spiritually, one must always be generous, never mean or petty. Of course, that applies not only to money but to attitudes, judgments, actions, etc.

Jupiter shows his power most effectively when the person gives, as an expression of gratitude, to another person or to God. This creates a condition of openness in the psyche to which the karmic response[3] is so healing, profound, and far-reaching that its effects are sometimes called the "Grace of God". No aspiring person should let a day of his life pass without feeling or expressing gratitude sincerely and deeply in some way.

One of the best illustrations I have found of Jupiter's influence is in the horoscope of Joy Mills—teacher, lecturer, writer, past president of the American Section of The Theosophical Society, and international vice-president of The Theosophical Society. In her chart, Sagittarius is on the Ascendant with its ruler, Jupiter, in the 9th House. This marked her from birth as one destined for some field in religion or higher education with extended travel of mind and person. She lost her mother early in life (Moon, ruler of the 8th House, conjunct Saturn and square Mars), and spent her childhood moving from relative to relative (Aries on the 4th House with Mars square the Moon, semi-square Mercury and Venus, and square Saturn). This loss and the ensuing difficulties in her formative years profoundly affected her values, giving her a deep sympathy for humanity. Later, she was able to translate this fine quality of understanding into teaching and practical service for the Society (Capricorn on the 2nd

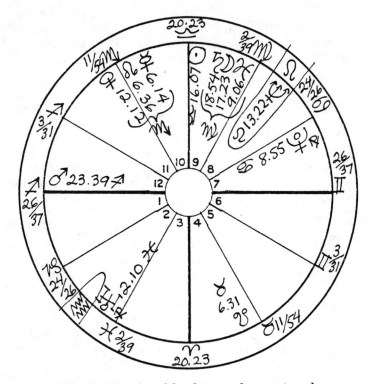

Joy Mills—Theosophical leader, teacher, writer, lecturer.

House cusp with its ruler Saturn conjunct Moon and Jupiter in Virgo, 9th House). She joined the staff of the American Section at age 21 and, except for several years teaching in public schools, has continued in one position or another for the Society all these years.

Jupiter in the 9th House denotes the *field* of that planet's expression. Virgo is not the happiest Sign for Jupiter's placement, for that planet's natural expressiveness is limited by Virgo's passion for detail and analysis. However, the very care and caution and dedication to service that Virgo induces eventually gains the support of others in service or financial backing.

Jupiter's sextile to Mercury gives expansion in intelligence and communication; the sextile to Venus in the House of friends and group associations gives many affectionate relationships with both individuals and groups. The major emphasis in Joy's life—on religion, teaching, and travel—is shown by the conjunction with Saturn and the Moon. Her travels in the service of the Society have taken her all over the world, and the opposition to Uranus gives her independence, as well as intuition, and attraction to the occult.

The almost exact sextile to Pluto in Cancer (7th House) shows the strong link with the public in some psychological or spiritual type of service. A sextile or trine between Pluto and one of the "personal" planets indicates that the person has an innate understanding of the processes of growth and transformation; taking for granted that life is always demanding, one must discard the old and open up to the new. The square and the opposition generally mean the person does not recognize that process and so they will fight it. This does not mean that the sextile and trine obviate the disturbance and pain of Plutonian changes, it is just that those persons intuitively feel that any pain experienced is a necessary part of growth.

Pluto in Cancer shows that the difficulties and sorrows in her childhood and youth were probably necessary to free her from attachment to the restricted nest of personal home and family so that she could give a greater service to a wider family. Both the Lights—Saturn and Jupiter—in the 9th House make it the most important section of the chart by far. The Sun close to the Midheaven often gives executive position, and Mars conjunct the Ascendant gives the energy and drive necessary for success though with times of inner and outer struggle.

Signs and Houses Ruled by Jupiter

Jupiter is the ruler of Sagittarius and, through that Sign, ruler of the 9th House. Also some consider it a part-ruler of Pisces and, through that Sign, ruler of the 12th House. His greatest influence is on the House in which he is placed.

There is always a plus quality to Jupiter's vibrations. Jupiter's placement in a Sign is likely to bring out the best qualities of that Sign; the opposite of Saturn's effect which can be relied upon to produce some sort of difficulty, taking on the style of the Sign in which it is placed. Jupiter will give opportunities though we do not always recognize them as such. Through Sagittarius Jupiter brings emphasis upon the higher mind, religion, philosophy, law, publishing, and extended travel of the mind (such as higher education, development of the abstract mind) and body, such as long journeys, and residence in foreign countries and places far from the place of birth. His vibration expresses most purely in Sagittarius and the 9th House. Jupiter indicates our basic attitudes toward religion and spiritual aspiration. If he is unaspected, the 9th House empty of planets and the ruler of that House unimportant in the horoscope, then that person is usually not attuned to an inner understanding of life. The person with a strong Jupiter and 9th House has the urge to keep seeking until he finds the religious concept, teaching, or teacher which most satisfies his needs. When he does find it he is likely to recognize it almost immediately.

Jupiter sometimes shows in the horoscope as a symbol of the father, the actual parent, and indeed he can be taken as one of the archetypes of the father along with the Sun and Saturn. Psychologists who use Astrology in their work state that "invariably if Saturn, Jupiter or the Sun is in the 7th House, we project our father onto the partner, or in the case of Jupiter, some aspect of the father. This projection comes from men as well as women."[4] That "aspect of the father" could be the masculine version of the feminine nurturing urge.[5] Certainly Jupiter nurtures the spiritual urges and he is the symbol of the teacher or spiritual father expressed often in human form as priest, minister, guru, or school teacher. Any teacher is a spiritual parent, for his work is to guide the younger or unevolved person to mental or spiritual unfoldment. Jupiter's position and aspects in the horoscope show how and by what means, if any, we feel the urge to teach. He shows how we, as individuals, need to discipline and train ourselves to be moral exemplars or teachers in some manner giving guidance to others.

Jupiter, Pisces and the 12th House

As the co-ruler of Pisces, Jupiter brings the highest levels of expansive, lofty awareness. If Sagittarius and the 9th House symbolize the priest and teacher, Pisces symbolizes the mystic and hermit. His urge toward something greater than the little self (which is expressed in the 9th House through religion, philosophy and higher education) is, in the 12th House and Pisces, often expressed in formless, mystical at-one-ment with the universe or God attained within the secrecy of that "inner cave of the heart", or by physical withdrawal from the outer world's busy-ness. The

12th House rules monasteries, convents, and all places of confinement and retreat.

Jupiter also expresses through Pisces, not as teacher or priest but as savior and healer, giving himself to all who are suffering or in need—teaching by the example of his life rather than in laying down religious laws and systems.

It may be difficult to associate the exuberant, expansive Jupiter with the 12th House—the most difficult House to interpret—which rules hidden things, the unconscious, serious illnesses, and places of confinement such as hospitals, prisons, asylums, monasteries and convents (see Chapter IV, page 43). It is also the 12th House that rules the *expansion of the self into universal consciousness*, which is very Jupiterian. The 12th House is most clearly involved with the heaviest past karma. This would seem, on the surface, to be more like Saturn than Jupiter, but the two planets work as a pair, mediating between the personal factors and the transpersonal factors. Saturn symbolizes the *process* of the Law of Karma; Jupiter symbolizes reincarnation in the sense of expanded opportunity, new life, a second chance. Together, Saturn and Jupiter establish law and order. Meeting the trials that reside in the 12th House is meeting yourself and giving yourself the opportunity to clear away something which is impeding your growth.

Some astrologers believe that enclosure in a monastic order appears in the horoscope as a misfortune, indicated by the more difficult and unfortunate aspects or planetary placements. I disagree and offer as an example the horoscope of a woman who had been a nun for over two decades before leaving the convent. Like Joy Mills, she had Jupiter in Sagittarius but hers was retrograde, indicating that his influence was more inward-turned, and that there was to be a recapitulation of religious experience in this life.

Clare had Neptune and the North Node in the 12th House and she had Pisces on the cusp of her 8th House. When she first entered the convent as a novice, her progressed Sun exactly squared Saturn. [Saturn, Pisces, and the 12th House are the astrological factors most related to nuns and nunneries.] This showed the self-denial and discipline of a nun's life but a square, conjunction or opposition between Sun and Saturn nearly always marks an important step in the career.[6] At the same time, her retrograde Venus made an exact trine to Mars in Pisces (7th House), showing that her relationships with others were ex-

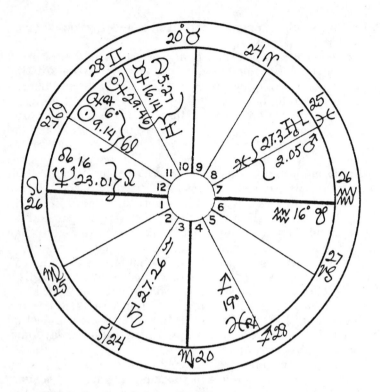

Clare—Jupiter and the 12th House: the life of a nun.

tremely balanced and harmonious. In other words, Clare was not entering the convent because she was at odds with the world. Her transitting Saturn was moving through the 10th House indicating a time of climax in her career. The interpretation of the North Node in Leo is "Learn to open up your heart, to take personal responsibility." The South Node in Aquarius showed that in her past life, or lives, she had operated well on the group level; the three planets in the 11th House, well-aspected, underline that fact, though not on the personal level. It seems possible that she was inwardly directed to become a nun because for her that was the best way to achieve the opening of her heart and to take such responsibility.

Jupiter at birth was strongly placed in Sagittarius, 4th House, in trine with Neptune in the 12th House (Leo), again emphasizing the heart and showing that her religious aspirations were true and wise.

Pisces on the cusp of the 8th House showed the connection with regeneration and rebirth—the dying to the old self—that entering the convent would demand. At the time she took her final vows, her Venus (in Cancer), which was retrograde at birth, turned direct and repeated the trine to Mars in the 7th—she was "married" to Christ by those vows. Venus, changing direction, showed that her capacity for love and affection had "changed direction" and expressed differently by flowing outward to other people as well as to her Divine Spouse (7th House).

The dynamic energies of Mars were pulled forth with the all-encompassing compassion of Pisces. When she eventually left the convent, her Sun had progressed to an exact conjunction with Neptune, and her Venus was exactly conjunct her Natal Sun. Leo, her Ascendant, stretched back over most of the 12th House so that there would always be an intimate relation between the 1st and 12th Houses in her life.

Clare did not tell me her reasons for leaving the convent, but from her horoscope and the above-mentioned aspects I might hazard the guess that some inner vision illuminated her decision to take that step. Her Jupiter in the 4th House (the latter part of life) trine to Neptune will continue to inspire religious expression in her life.

♃ Rulership

Some of the people, vocations, and things ruled by Jupiter are:
1. Ministers, priests, lawyers, senators, physicians, bankers, clothiers, merchants, philanthropists, publishers, gamblers.
2. Ceremonial things, the feet, toes, thighs, hips, liver, pancreas, diabetes, sciatic nerves, rheumatism, coxaglia, gout, obesity and tumors.

Jupiter in the Modes, Elements and Signs

Modes: Jupiter varies in expression according to the Mode, Element, and Sign in which he is placed. In **Cardinal Signs** he expands in activity and leadership, self-promotion, and self-confidence. In **Fixed Signs** he organizes and accumulates, expanding the scope of his profession or financial assets in order to buttress his security. In **Mutable Signs** he expands into so many channels of expression that there is a danger that his interests will be spread too superficially over too many things.

Elements: In **Fire,** Jupiter is more often than not lucky, his enthusiasm and optimism carrying the person over most obstacles, though there is a tendency to over-expand or take risks. Jupiter in a Fire Sign afflicted, and without balancing factors in the chart, can make the compulsive gambler. In **Earth,** Jupiter expresses his qualities in the here-and-now reality of the material world with innate caution controlling his expansiveness. The importance of the physical senses to the Earth Signs can, with Jupiter, lead to over-eating, over-drinking, and other excesses. In **Air,** Jupiter expresses his qualities in the world of large ideas, grandiose and visionary concepts of future social, business and city planning schemes. The Air Signs are the most social of all the Signs, for they are able to objectively appreciate (unlike the emotional reactions of Water or the suspicions of Earth), another person's thoughts regardless of whether they agree with them. In **Water,** the emotions and sensitivity expand, the natural urges of Jupiter toward faith in a benevolent Providence and self-improvement combine happily with the soul yearnings so characteristic of Water Signs.

Jupiter's expression in a particular Sign in which he is placed at birth varies considerably depending on his aspects and other factors in the horoscope. His positive expression is an innate faith—in a higher power, or universal plan, and in self-confidence. There is an optimism and benevolence with an insistent urge toward self-improvement. Negatively expressed, it can be laziness, over-confidence, false pride, arrogance, religious pretensions, irresponsibility, and exaggeration.

Jupiter in Aries increases the desire to enlarge the scope of personal expression; challenges are seen in terms of personal ability and personal success.

Jupiter in Taurus seeks opportunity and rewards in accumulation of money or property. There is frequently a love of the beautiful, and of sensual comforts.

Jupiter in Gemini—his Sign of Detriment—gives diversity, changeability, quick mental facilities, and often indicates travel. This position does tend to superficiality with the interests being spread over too many things and changing often. The spirit of inquiry and adventure is keen.

Jupiter in Cancer—his Sign of Exaltation—expresses most fully his best qualities in benevolent emotions, kindness, sympathy, and protectiveness, the spiritual, nurturing father.

Jupiter in Leo shines gorgeously but when afflicted, self-justification and conceit are strong. There is a dramatic, even theatrical touch along with loyalty, generosity and exuberance.

Jupiter in Virgo circumscribes his natural expansiveness because that Sign so often is analytical, detailed, fussy and fault-finding—the opposite of big, generous Jupiter. However, the critical faculties are not always a drawback because they can serve to direct Jupiter's expansiveness into constructive, if more modest, channels.

Jupiter in Libra indicates social expansiveness that can present opportunities from many directions. There is a natural desire to be companionable and well-loved. A favorable influence for a happy marriage, fortunate partnerships, and professions that call for diplomacy or arbitration.

Jupiter in Scorpio intensifies that planet's spiritual dimensions. There is an expansion of the self through deep feelings and wide sympathies. In some horoscopes it can mean religious fanaticism, the powerful drive for improvement turned upon the world or the self.

Jupiter in Sagittarius, his own Sign, usually means ideals and enthusiasm can reach lofty heights. Wisdom and understanding are prized. It gives a love of liberty and free movement, sports and the outdoors.

Jupiter in Capricorn, his Sign of Fall needs to learn how to give without consideration always of what he will get back in return. The religious urge, mixed with Saturn's vibration, tends to dogmatism. With positive attitudes, scope for expression can be found through careful preparation and planning. Any favorable Jupiter-Saturn connection is good for business.

Jupiter in Aquarius seeks to establish and maintain many friendships and group activities. He can be humanitarian, unconventional, and scientific. He is happiest in discussion of large scale humanitarian schemes.

Jupiter in Pisces, the rulership of which he shares with Neptune, expresses in a strong, intuitive imagination, overflowing with kindness and the desire to help others. Helpful for the arts and psychic work. If afflicted, the imagination can run to exaggeration and confusion.

Jupiter in the Houses

Keywords for Jupiter are expansiveness, opportunity, ethics, and personal growth. Jupiter amplifies whatever he touches, for better or worse. Depending on his aspects the affairs of the House in which he is placed are marked by abundance. For example, Jupiter in the 2nd House well-aspected brings financial abundance. At the least, he preserves the person from serious loss or need. But if Jupiter is afflicted, it gives extravagance or financial loss, usually owing to over-optimism and lack of careful planning or investigation before investment. Jupiter in the 6th House, unafflicted, is a preserver of health; afflicted, it can mean illness or accident to the parts of the body ruled by Jupiter. Such illnesses are usually of the type caused by overindulgence or too much of something in the system. Wherever placed, Jupiter's benefits seem to flow more generously if the person makes an effort to improve himself or the conditions ruled by that House. For example, in the 5th House difficult aspects may give troubles with children, usually due to lack of discrimination, overindulgence, or over-protection. If the person makes consistent efforts to develop a more detached, impersonal attitude, improving his understanding and judgment along with giving love, Jupiter will reward him by expanding his life with amplitude through relationships with the children. Remember, Jupiter is the planet of abundance and self-improvement. To call forth his rewards you must feel and express gratitude, give generously, and work on self-improvement.[7]

Jupiter's Aspects

Jupiter as the principle of abundance and self-improvement amplifies the qualities of the planet aspected for better or worse. An unaspected Jupiter indicates that the time has come to begin giving, as in Chapter VIII the man with the unaspected Venus was told it was time he started learning to love.

JUPITER-SATURN   The joining of the principles of limitation and expansion makes contradictions. This usually causes alternating periods of optimism and depression. Self-understanding is the key to achievement; learning to work hard in expansive periods and remaining of good cheer in constrictive periods. With the square and opposition, success may be achieved but only at the cost of hard work or personal hardship and long delays. It will be difficult during those times to see the potentials of self-improvement because conventional attitudes limit the vision. The sextile and trine often give controlled expansion, sure and steady success, patience and progress.

JUPITER-URANUS   The conjunction of these two planets can give sudden and unusual luck, success in large enterprises and humanitarian awareness. It can also, depending on the rest of the chart, make one excessively willful, independent in unconventional ways, and give a tendency to go to extremes in religious or philosophical matters. The square and opposition give the same originality or eccentricity, willfulness, and love of freedom as the conjunction but with less control. There is increased tactlessness and bluntness that offends others, breaking up personal relationships and often making the person highly egocentric. The sextile and trine give unexpected good luck, often from unusual sources. The personality is forceful, magnetic and frequently the trine indicates genius.

JUPITER-NEPTUNE   The conjunction of these two makes one expansive and idealistic. There is often a great attraction to the sea, but most marked are the qualities of kindness and philanthropy—the Good Samaritan. This conjunction often gives talent, or even genius, in the arts. All intuitions and sensitivities are increased, with psychic abilities common. If the rest of the chart is not strong or if it is afflicted, there can be much daydreaming, fantasy, and deceit of the self and others. The square and opposition give vision in religion, philosophy and a mystical approach to life which can in certain charts depart from reality. The challenging aspects always give more energy, a compulsion toward achievement, than the "soft" aspects but also more difficulty. Jupiter can exaggerate the sensitivity of Neptune leading to psychic disturbance, escapism, involvement in weird cults, danger from alcoholism, drugs, gas, poisons, and anaesthetics. The most common negative expression is a lack of just plain commonsense! The sextile and trine give an easy flow of benefits typical of the conjunction. Benefit comes often from hidden sources or comes in subtle ways. There is often spiritual insight and personal magnetism with lucky "hunches".

JUPITER-PLUTO   Aspects involving Pluto are among the most difficult to evaluate. It seems to make little difference whether the aspect is fortunate or unfortunate: the so-called stressful or difficult aspects are often found in the horoscopes of the most spiritually aware and creative individuals. The conjunction, square, and opposition often indicate a confrontation with religious or educational taboos in which some sort of breakthrough is necessary in order to grow. The square and opposition produce a resistance or rebellion against the purgative processes of change that Pluto brings. The sextile and trine show an acceptance of the need for change and growth, and an openness to the new—new people, ideas, and attitudes—with an easy flow of inner power.

Jupiter Retrograde

Retrogradation is the principle of recapitulation wherein the thoroughness of the evolutionary process is insured. With Jupiter, it might mean that certain aspects of religion, education, ethics, self-improvement, etc., must be re-experienced and the lessons of giving and gratitude more thoroughly learned.

NOTES

[1]Manly P. Hall, *Astrological Keywords* (Totowa, N.J.: Littlefield, Adams & Co., 1975. A well-organized and comprehensive compendium of everything related to the Signs, Houses, Fixed Stars, and other astrological subjects.

[2]These two cases bring up the perennial question of free will versus fate, the first accident in particular. Forewarned of the danger of accidents around a certain date, the woman and her husband took extraordinary precautions and care with their car and travel. Yet "on impulse" she accepted an invitation to drive 100 miles in a fellow worker's car to a neighboring city. The friend was driving and, rounding a mountain curve, they came upon a parked truck. Swerving to avoid collision, they smashed into an oncoming car killing every occupant in it.

[3]Everything that happens is karmic—the result of some cause in present or past lives. C. W. Leadbeater gives a good analogy to help understand the workings of *karma* in his *Inner Life* (Wheaton: Theosophical Publishing House, 1978), page 359: "There is another aspect of *karma* the consideration of which I have found helpful in the effort to understand its working; but it belongs to a plane so high that it is unfortunately impossible to put it clearly into words. Imagine that we see each man as though he were absolutely alone in the universe, the center of an incredibly vast series of concentric spheres. Every thought, or word, or action of his sends out a stream of force which rushes toward the surfaces of the spheres. This force strikes the interior surface of one of the spheres, and, being at right angles to it, is necessarily reflected back

unerringly to the point from which it came. "From which sphere it is reflected seems to depend upon the character of the force, and this also naturally regulates the time of its return."

[4]Luella Sibbald, "How I Use Astrology As A Psychotherapist", in *American Theosophist*, Special Issue, Fall, 1978.

[5]The crescent part of Jupiter's symbol conveys the essence of Moon's function of nurture.

[6]To emphasize that difficult Saturn aspects are far from negative, it should be remembered that Sun-Saturn aspects crystallize the ambition and direction of the personality: 27% of all U.S. Presidents through Nixon were born with Sun conjunct, square, or opposition Saturn. Another 25% had the moon conjunct, square, or in opposition to Saturn.

[7]While writing this chapter, I received letters from two friends, one inveighing against God, fate, faithless or unappreciative lovers, friends, and employers. He had given all and received nothing but grinding poverty and loneliness. The other friend had just lost her job but was busy cheerfully working out ways of earning money at home while looking for another job. Her past life had been far from easy but she considered herself blessed in the things that counted. Somehow things always seemed to work out for her. Both friends were talented, hard-working people with afflicted Jupiters in their Natal charts. The second friend was some years older than the first but neither was young. I felt that the difference lay in their relative "openness" to Jupiter through gratitude and giving. The first friend considered life a swindle, being grateful for nothing but the second friend gave her "widow's mite" with both hands, constantly grateful for whatever came her way.

XI

ħ

SATURN: MOST MISUNDERSTOOD PLANET

In the symbol of Saturn, the cross of matter takes precedence over the reflection of the spirit—the crescent. Saturn is the symbol of the physical plane, of matter personified through which emotion, mind, and spirit must manifest for evolutionary purposes.[1]

An eminent astrologer was once asked to list the planets in order of importance and his reply was "Saturn, Saturn, and Saturn!" An exaggeration, perhaps, but Saturn is indeed of prime importance in the analysis of any natal horoscope. Just from the position and aspects of that planet, an astrologer can glean many of the essential factors in the character and life. Some of Saturn's most important principles are that of self-preservation, contraction, crystallization, form, structure, stability, and time.[2] Saturn has always had a "bad press". Most astrologers give him negative meanings because his vibrations so often result in obstruction, disappointment, poverty, frustration, and the like. I hope to show that Saturn has a very positive side without which no material or spiritual progress could be made.

Saturn represents concentrated experience and learning which come to the soul only through incarnation in a physical body on the physical plane. On the higher planes, our soul—higher Self, or whatever one wishes to call that individual spark of the Divine—is splendidly free and powerful. It is only through the limitations of bodily form and the challenges of material life that we have the opportunity for developing the qualities of patience, endurance, resourcefulness, hard work, and organization. Saturn also shows us what we lack and need to develop by the lessons he teaches us through daily experience. Saturn tests us every step of the way and shows up the folly of self-deception, escapism, or rationalization so typical of most of us. He does not allow us to pass on to a higher stage until his demands have been fulfilled. Saturn's position in the horoscope shows the point of greatest responsibility, the area of unfulfillment in past lives (duties ignored, lessons evaded, weaknesses and faults uncorrected), and, therefore, the area needing the greatest effort in *this* life.

Anne's horoscope is an example of what most astrologers would term a most unfortunate chart with two dominating "T" crosses and a few "good" aspects. A "T" or a Grand Cross in Fixed Signs[3] is one of the most difficult configurations to cope with. In Anne's chart Saturn is conjunct the Midheaven and Neptune in Leo on one arm, with the Ascendant, Sun, and Mercury conjunct in Scorpio on another arm, and last, Uranus in Aquarius opposing the Leo group and squaring the Scorpio group. The natal aspects can usually be expected to manifest no matter what happy sextiles and trines the planets make as they progress. A square between two planets in the Natal chart will manifest as a square when, by progression, the planets form a sextile or trine—*unless* there is a radical change of character and much effort is made toward self-understanding. The "T" and Grand Crosses give difficulties but they also give much energy and strength. A spiritual orientation enables one to turn that energy and strength into constructive channels.

Saturn conjunct the stationary Neptune[4] in the 9th House shows a conflict or contradiction in religious matters. Neptune represents the urge to escape from the limitation of the material plane into union with the All, and Saturn represents the orthodox, structured, or materialistic religion, or even a complete lack of religion. In Anne's case, her family was materialistic and agnostic so there was almost a complete denial of religion in her youth. In its place she put romantic books, fairy tales, and an extraordinary amount of daydreaming—very typical of Neptune. In later life she leaned to the mystical, but she always tried to put whatever mystical inspiration that came to her into some *practical* form that would be of use in the world. Saturn in a Fixed Sign is almost always indicative of strong willfulness and rigid habit patterns that block the flow of love and the energy of life (Leo and the Sun). Saturn's square to the Ascendant-Sun-

Mercury reinforced that, but the opposition to the revolutionary Uranus exactly on the Nadir—the very foundation of any chart—guaranteed that the structure would be shaken again and again until that energy and love could be released.

When Anne was 12 years old, the progressed Saturn became stationary and stayed in the same degree for the next 7 years. Her father suffered financial reverses and shot himself on her 14th birthday. The progressed Midheaven was conjunct Mars in the 10th House, which rules the father; progressed Mercury was trine Saturn, but since the two were square at birth it was the square that manifested. After that, for several years, the family moved about, the mother in an unhinged emotional state, shown in the chart by Uranus in the 4th House (mother) opposition Saturn. When Anne turned 16 her progressed Saturn turned retrograde and she left school to try to earn a living in the depths of the Depression. The following years saw unemployment, family troubles, poverty, disastrous romances, and attempted suicide. Life was so terrible that she began a desperate search for some meaning to life and, at 19, stumbled upon Astrology and Theosophy. (Progressed Sun trine Neptune, opposition Jupiter; Mercury sextile Uranus; Jupiter sextile Neptune; and the progressed Moon was moving through the 8th House, the House of rebirth.) Despite a complete lack of spiritual training or religion in her youth, she immediately recognized these ancient wisdoms as truth, providing a purpose to life. Circumstances did not instantly become easier but her feelings of despair and injustice were gone. She began to study and change herself. (At 20, Saturn began to retrograde from the degree where he had been stationary for 7 years.) When her progressed Sun exactly opposed the natal Jupiter, instead of further financial misfortune she obtained a good job and worked with determination instead of with her former arrogance. Within two years she rose to a much more responsible position. Three years later the progressed Sun trined Saturn, an aspect which might have brought all the difficulties of the natal square. Instead, Anne became active in The Theosophical Society and entered upon three happy years of concentrated study and self discipline, all very characteristic of Saturn and the 9th House. At 28 she married but her husband opposed her theosophical activities (progressed Venus opposition Neptune, Jupiter square Mars) and so the marriage broke up. When Saturn had retrograded back to his natal position and Sun sextiled Uranus, Anne went to Adyar, the international center of The Theosophical Society for a year of study.

After a divorce she married again and had several children. There were major changes in residence over the years and eventually that marriage broke up when Venus conjunct Uranus and Sun opposed Pluto. Pluto's vibrations can produce drastic changes: after 14 years a housewife Anne found herself at middle age forced to go back to work with three young children to support. The whole structure of her life changed again but the progressed Midheaven trine Jupiter brought an influential connection leading to a good position. She prospered and after two years went into business on her own. Anne had always kept up her studies in Theosophy and Astrology and eventually when the Midheaven trined Uranus (exact opposition at birth) and the transitting Saturn passed over his natal place, she was given the opportunity to combine the two in lecturing, writing, and counseling.

Anne's horoscope and life are proof that you *can* change your fate as mapped in the birth chart. The birth chart pattern shows *potentialities*, not unchangeable destiny, and an afflicted Saturn need not mean unending misfortune. The difficult aspects are the most energizing, challenging, and inducive to real accomplishment if they are understood and used constructively. Any planet touched by Saturn, through the difficulty or challenge offered, is shown in practical as well as psychological terms to be an opportunity of revealing a deeper, richer, and more purposeful expression of its meaning. Thus, those with a badly afflicted Saturn have a great propensity for discovering meaning and purpose in their lives. Those with a Grand or "T" Cross involving Saturn have the possibility of becoming strong, well-integrated persons.

Signs and Houses Ruled by Saturn

Saturn is the ruler of Capricorn and, through that Sign, ruler of the 10th House. Saturn can also be considered the part-ruler of Aquarius and, through that Sign, part-ruler of the 11th House. Saturn's vibrations aid in the consolidation of the self, helping us to establish a firm base of operations and in no Sign more than Capricorn is Saturn's urge to defend the self's safety and security through tangible achievement more in evidence.

In the natural order of the Signs, Capricorn rules the 10th House. The essential meaning of the 10th House is the expression of the self in the outer world, especially regarding one's attainment in a career.[5] So, Saturn and Capricorn, wherever they may be placed in the individual chart, along with the 10th House, show the ambition of the individual, the degree of seriousness or the lack of it, and the particular direction of his drive toward self-perfection and achievement in the world. Ambition can be a destructive thing, but it is absolutely necessary in the earlier stages of evolution, for without it no progress would be made. It is only when the individual evolves to the point where he wishes to hasten his progress spiritually that he is instructed, in *Light On The Path,*

> Kill out ambition. Ambition is the first curse: the great tempter of the man who is rising above his fellows. . . . Yet it is a necessary teacher. Its results turn to dust and ashes in the mouth: like death and estrangement, it shows the man at last that to work for self is to work for disappointment. Work, as those work who are ambitious.

Few of us have reached the stage of not needing some personal ambition to prod us on to effort and achievement, but we can *begin* to practice discrimination, detachment, and selflessness in our ambition. We may miss feeling the hot joy of personal triumphs but we shall also be able to endure the inevitable career frustrations with equanimity and patience.

The traditional rulership of cautious, stable Saturn over Aquarius seems completely at variance with its other ruler, the independent, unconventional Uranus. (See Chapter IX, page 105, regarding joint rulership.) But taking a closer look, who is more set in his ideas than the typical revolutionary? It is obvious that the 11th House and Aquarius, wherever placed, will have something of Saturn's gravity. But as both this Sign and House are concerned with larger objectives, they will not express it primarily in a self-seeking way or in such a practical form as in Capricorn. Saturn's principles will be expressed in more widespread channels; objectives for humanity, group work, and studies that are out of the ordinary—frequently of the very old or very new such as archeology or electronics. In Aquarius the Saturnian tendency to self-enclosure means that fellowship in clubs, societies and other groups will be more congenial than in a one-to-one relationship.

♄   Rulership

Some of the people, vocations, and things which are ruled by Saturn are:

1. The father, farmers, elderly people, state officials, financiers, miners, all conservative lines of business, real estate dealers, jailers, undertakers, bricklayers, time.
2. The skin, teeth, gall bladder, ligaments, the skeleton, knees, auditory organs, chronic diseases, rheumatism, gout, paralysis, deafness, skin diseases, atrophy, hardening of the arteries, impeded circulation, consumption, some cancers.

Saturn in the Modes, Elements and Signs

In the **Cardinal Mode,** Saturn is at his most positive and most negative. Capricorn is his home Sign, where he expresses his qualities most naturally. Libra is his Sign of Exaltation and Aries is his Sign of Fall. Saturn's natural reserve, caution, and aptitude for careful planning are at its best in Libra but those same qualities clash with Aries' fire and combativeness. Cancer is the Sign of Saturn's Detriment and in that Sign the planet's urge to build a self-protective shell is increased, sometimes to the extent that the tendency to brood and take offense forms a difficult barrier to normal relationships.

In the **Fixed Mode** there is consolidation, the slow steady work of attaining security. There is often a strong willfulness and fixed habit patterns that block the flow of energy.

In the **Mutable Mode,** Saturn's tendency to crystallization is balanced by the flexibility of the Mode but there is a need to restructure the thinking patterns, eliminating the compulsion to worry and be overly opinionated.

The Element wherein Saturn is posited indicates a particular problem represented by that Element, especially with stressful aspects. There is always a special *need* to express the energy of that Element and yet a fear or inhibition in doing so. Saturn's position shows where one needs to develop faith in a greater power than the little self, making the effort to transcend selfish considerations. For example, **Saturn in Air** indicates the need to develop understanding and powers of communication.

Saturn in Fire shows a need to stabilize the identity in new forms of creative self-expression instead of being confined to old, sterile self-images.

Saturn in Earth needs to express precision and reliability in work, proving his efficiency and thereby building self-confidence.

With **Saturn in Water** there is often fear of the emotions, either fear of outward emotional expression disclosing vulnerability to other people's attitudes or criticism, or inwardly repressive of emotion for a variety of reasons. Obviously, before Saturn's best qualities and those of the Element through which he is functioning can be expressed—the fears, inhibitions, and sometimes just blindness must be overcome. Saturn's position in Element and House marks the area that needs attention.

In **Aries** there is a struggle between the intrepid, forcefulness of that Sign and Saturn's concept of goals to be reached along careful, structured lines. There is often a self-defensiveness about expressing the ambitions.

In **Taurus,** Saturn's conservative temperament blends perfectly with that Sign's practical acquisitiveness and security goals. The danger lies in too much materialism, too stolid an immersion in the practical with a neglect of important intangibles.

In **Gemini** the intellect may be somber, its expression persuasive and clever with words. The perception is keen and the ambition often finds expression along more than one line.

In **Cancer,** its Sign of Detriment, the early home life can be so lacking in supportiveness that self-confidence suffers. There are likely to be problems with the mother or other women due to rejection or a "mother complex".

Saturn in Leo needs to learn to express affection spontaneously, to help others generously. Willfulness and rigid habit patterns inhibit the flow of love and elan. A flare for the dramatic leads Saturn in Leo people to dramatize their lives, usually in the form of a tragedy.

Saturn in Virgo is the original worrier. Hard working, critical, orderly to a fault, and often seeming to go out of his way to assume responsibilities and burdens. If you want to irritate a person with Saturn in Virgo, just tell him that there is nothing to worry about—he knows better!

Saturn in Libra, its Sign of Exaltation, finds balance in the social awareness of the Sign. Loneliness is a characteristic of Saturn stemming from fears, inhibitions, timidity, or too rigid a protective shell of self-enclosure. The vibrations of Libra ease that blockage and his positive qualities find fruitful expression in esthetic and social enjoyment, diplomacy, and philosophy.

In **Scorpio** there is a fixed intensity to the emotions and ambition. Saturn's natural reserve deepens to secrecy and sometimes deviousness and intrigue. The memory is long for injuries and injustice, real or fancied. In times of trouble sex may be sought as giving renewal and self-affirmation.

With **Saturn in Sagittarius** a lift is given to ambition, the innate coldness is warmed and powers of organization expanded in administrative work. There may be a philosophical or religious attitude to life, international travel and larger ethical concepts.

Saturn in Capricorn (the Sign of Rulership) expresses his qualities easily. Ambition plans the goals carefully and hard work is welcomed. If there are difficult aspects, there may be a selfish arrogance that considers any means justified to attain one's ends. Materialism and the desire for recognition are important motives.

In **Aquarius** (Sign or Rulership shared with Uranus) Saturn's ambition seeks outlet in group activities, humanitarian objectives and his powers of organization and aptitude for careful, hard work are utilized for social planning and schemes. The Saturnian "heaviness" is lightened by innovation and intellectual liveliness.

In **Pisces,** Saturn's austerity and self-enclosure is softened. The usual drive of his ambition with its motives and rewards is questioned with the result that there may be confusion or more than one change of profession. There can be sorrows early in life that later lead to periods of moodiness, depression, and doubt.

Saturn in the Houses

There are as many "keywords" for Saturn as there are astrologers: limitation, cold, ambition, lack, the heavy hand of karma, etc. I hope that I have been able to show that the positive qualities of the planet are vital to progress and achievement. To the negative keywords should be added discipline, concentration, power of organization, responsibility and perseverance. We only suffer the negative qualities because in the past or present we have avoided our just responsibilities and lessons.

The House in which Saturn is placed at birth shows the area of character and life where you are too attached, too rigidly self-centered, too defensive so that you can be tied up in a knot of negativity. Therefore, it is the area where you must strive to overcome this limitation through experience and by serious, thorough effort. It shows where and how we will meet the particular karmic obligations that serve to discipline our desires and ambitions. We may instinctively intuit this karmic pattern and, therefore, dread it, for there are a few of us who happily embrace such difficulty and effort. Avoidance only puts off the day, because Saturn will not let us pass until we have fulfilled the demands of our karma.

In the **1st House** Saturn nearly always gives a feeling of personal insecurity and inadequacy, especially in the early years. There is a strong sense of perfectionism which can make the person over-meticulous and add to his sense of "not measuring up to standard" and so suffer periods of depression. In a strong character this sense of limitation may act as a spur to achievement; in a weak character, timidity and inhibitions may block the person from any forceful expression in life.

In the **2nd House** the person is responsible and careful with financial affairs. Depending on the aspects it can run to a slow accumulation of money and property, miserliness, or failure and poverty. Whatever is accumulated may come after much hard work and delay.

In the **3rd House** there can be loss or responsibility connected with brothers or sisters. I once read the chart of a friend with Saturn in 3rd House so I asked her if her sister was dead. She replied that the sister was very much alive but, although they lived in the same house, they had not spoken to each other for eight years! The "coldness" of Saturn need not be that of death. Often this position implies a lack of education or difficulties in learning especially in elementary school. Depending on other factors in the chart, it can give a depth and seriousness to the mind with caution and commonsense exercised in all matters of correspondence, communication, education, or literary work.

In the **4th House** there can be much discipline, coldness, or difficult conditions in the home or early childhood. This position can indicate depression caused through lack of a proper home or loss of a parent or, later in life the responsibility for the home or the parents.

In the **5th House** there can be disappointment or delay in an area of life that should bring joy and relaxation. Children can be denied or become the cause of anxiety and extended responsibility. Saturn in this House is unfortunate for risk-taking or gambling.[6] As the 5th is the House of "love given", Saturn's position here can sometimes mean that the person has much difficulty in feeling or expressing love for others.

In the **6th House** there can be health problems, usually according to the Sign on the Cusp. Depending on the aspects, Saturn here may give periods of unemployment, troubles with fellow workers and employees, or problems arising from service given to others. The 6th and the 12th Houses are the least *free* areas in the horoscope and Saturn here usually brings rather heavy karmic obligations or burdens. I have had a number of charts where the person undertook long-term service to another (such as the care of a bedridden relative or friend) when there was no legal or moral necessity, because they felt it was somehow their duty. Looking into their past lives I always found that they had, indeed, incurred a debt of care for the unfortunate one.

Saturn in the 7th House can deny or delay marriage or give marriage (or a business partnership) to an older, more serious person. According to the aspects or other planets in 7th House, there can be frustration and loss from others in close partnership such as marriage or business, or they may bring much responsibility. The 7th House rules other people in general so Saturn here can mean difficulty or inadequacy in forming happy relationships. With good aspects it can mean a very stable, long-lasting partnership bringing permanent benefit.

In the **8th House** there can be loss or responsibility through the finances of others, difficulties through death and inheritance. A seriousness over sexual matters, interest in psychic matters, death and the after-life.

In the **9th House,** frustration or denial of travel, difficulties in foreign countries, with foreigners or while traveling on business or duty. Depending on other factors, the religion or philosophy is likely to be orthodox or materialistic but it can denote profundity in questions of faith and beliefs. As with all Saturn placements, long-term results can be good if one's duty is fulfilled and sustained effort put forth.

In the **10th House,** there is a serious application to the career. This position of Saturn is supposed to give assured success in the career after delays and much hard work with disappointments along the climb. If the rest of the chart is weak, the person may avoid responsibility, blaming everyone else or unkind fate for the resultant setbacks and failures.

In the **11th House** there may be lack of real friendship or many friends. It is the House of "love received" and the affectionate response from friends may be small. It can mean few friends but those few will be serious, long-lasting friendships. Elderly friends prove to be the most satisfying companions or there could be loss and disappointment through friends or group affiliations. One's hopes, dreams, long-term goals are serious and carefully planned.

In the **12th House,** Saturn can mean sorrows borne in secret which, frequently, may be of one's own making. This placement can indicate loss of the father through death or separation. As it is the House of the subconscious, Saturn's presence here may indicate a deep seated neurosis, a "hang up", or some fear amounting to a phobia. Well-aspected, it can mean a serious commitment to those who suffer or are in need or imprisoned.

Saturn Aspects

The aspects to and from any planet have much to do with whether the positive or negative qualities of that planet will find ready expression. With the dynamic planets—Mars, Sun, Jupiter, and Uranus—there may be more difficulty along with positive results. For example, Saturn with Mars shows as clash or harmony between impulse and delay; with the Sun, there may be wisdom or arrogance; with Jupiter, we find good business judgment or financial frustrations; and with Uranus, you have a clash between conservatism and unconventionality. With the more negative planets—Moon, Mercury, Neptune, and possibly Pluto—Saturn's negative qualities of fear, inhibition, and limitation seem stronger. The whole chart, as well as other Saturnian aspects, must be taken into consideration. So remember, *no single factor can ever be considered alone.*[7]

SATURN-URANUS In a strong chart, the conjunction can give an aptitude for practical planning and a determined independence which works to produce unusual results. Or, it may produce a nervous tension and confusion because limitation and freedom do not mix easily. Danger from accidents such as falling or being in a plane or car crash can be attributed to this configuration. The square and the opposition give much the same but the contradiction of the two planets is emphasized. Nerves can suffer and the individual is awkward in relationships and there are often radical changes in the life of one who has one of these difficult aspects. (Anne's horoscope, p. 129.) The planned goals, dictated by ambition, are often upset by impulse and independence. With the sextile and trine, the ambitions can express along unique, unusual, or revolutionary lines. Uranus often gives brilliance of mind and originality, even genius. Or, if the rest of the chart agrees, eccentricity plus an arbitrary, brusque manner that drives people away and frustrates really worthwhile projects.

SATURN-NEPTUNE The conjunction between these two can give a peculiar magnetism attracting other people; intuition aids the ambition and there is often a very vague sense of time. Except in a conjunction or opposition with Neptune, people with Saturn strong in their charts usually have a very keen sense of time though it can amount to an obsession, the person going to extraordinary lengths rather than be five minutes late to an appointment.

The sextile and trine give good sense of timing, that person being always at the right place at the right time with the right qualifications and equipment to succeed in a venture. Neptune also enhances the imagination and vision. With the sextile and trine aspects, these qualities can be channeled into practical, well-planned expression.

With the square and opposition, the same qualities are present but its practical expression may be frustrated because the planning was confused and impractical. With Neptune's emphasis on the boundless and timeless, there would be conflict with the exactitude of Saturn. Sometimes the conjunction square, or opposition can show death or separation from the father, often under peculiar circumstances. I had a friend, Marion, whose Saturn was conjunct Neptune in the 12th House. This configuration gave her musical talent which she expressed in a practical way by teaching music. She had been an only child, living happily with her parents in a small town when one day a foreign woman presented herself at the door claiming the father as her husband. He admitted to the fact, packed his things and left with her. Neither Marion nor her mother ever heard from him again.

SATURN-PLUTO Aspects with Pluto are even more unpredictable than those involving Uranus. Pluto rules death, regeneration, rebirth, and transformation. The conjunction, square, and opposition may be more stressful than the sextile and trine but only because the latter seem to give the person an innate acceptance of the necessity for change and growth. There often seems to be something compulsive about any of the aspects involving Pluto but in the long run the effects are purgative; old relationships, habit patterns, obsessions, etc., are wiped out so that the next stage can be entered. In some way the perspective is deepened and widened. There is often a drive—with the stronger aspects—to rebellion or reformation. With certain horoscopes, the ambition is ruthless in manipulating or dominating others to further one's ends.

To sum up, the primary lesson of Saturn is responsibility and facing up to reality. The adult soul takes responsibility for all his actions. Putting the blame onto parents, spouse, circumstances, or fate for one's weaknesses, failures, and mistakes is childish. The person who expresses the positive qualities of Saturn is a mature person. Saturn rules time and time brings many sorrows derived from the Saturn principle such as those of illness, bereavement, and the enfeeblement of age. But no person who has met Saturn's demands positively needs to fear old age.

Saturn Retrograde

With Saturn it implies a recapitulation of responsibilities avoided or lessons only partially learned in the past.

NOTES

[1] I have always felt that the Church erred in stressing the crucifixion of Jesus Christ as a historical happening with all the accompanying physical suffering, "guilt" of the Jews, and vicarious atonement all of which have caused so much trouble and confusion in the ensuing centuries. It

obscured the deeper meaning of the cross symbol, which is the crucifixion of the spirit, i.e., every soul is "crucified" in matter for evolutionary purposes and is his own savior, not just one man in one point in time.

[2]For a most comprehensive analysis of Saturn in line with modern psychological, spiritual and occult thought read Stephen Arroyo, *Astrology, Karma and Transformation: The Inner Dimensions of the Birthchart* (Vancouver, Washington: CRCS Publications, 1978); and Liz Greene, *Saturn, A New Look At An Old Devil* (N.Y.: Samuel Weiser, 1976).

[3]A Grand Cross is a planetary configuration where four or more planets form a cross, usually in the same Mode. A "T" Cross differs in that one arm of the cross is unoccupied. In Anne's horoscope, the Fixed Signs—Leo, Scorpio and Aquarius—are occupied with Taurus empty. The empty arm of the "T" always exerts a powerful attraction, the person seems to feel a lack in that area and often marries or engages in some interest related to the empty Sign. Both Anne's husbands had their Suns in Taurus, the empty arm of her "T" Cross.

[4]A planet is considered very powerful when "stationary" or "direct". The effect has been compared to the heat of a candle or light bulb. Moving over one's hand, the heat is only mild warmth, but held in one position, the heat becomes extremely perceptible! A planet is stationary when it remains in the same degree of longitude just before or after changing its motion to either retrograde or direct (after being retrograde). This is marked in the ephemeris by the letter "D" or "R" on the day the motion changes.

[5]Every person has a "career" and a 10th House to interpret, even a woman who is a homemaker and does not hold down a paying job outside.

[6]I have a friend with Saturn in the 5th House who is the epitome of Saturnian responsibility. Her favorite relaxation is a holiday gambling in Las Vegas using only a pre-determined sum of money. Though never spectacularly lucky, she has hit upon a wonderful safety valve to mitigate the strictures of Saturn in her character and life!

[7]To avoid repetition, the aspects between Saturn and the faster planets can be found in the chapters covering those planets.

XII

URANUS, NEPTUNE AND PLUTO:
AMBASSADORS FROM THE GALAXY

After many lives in which the qualities of the more material planets are expressed, the soul's basic drive shifts from the personal to the spiritual level. The higher octave planets—Uranus, Neptune and Pluto—challenge the individual to become more than human. It may cover a period of several lifetimes for the person to become consciously aware of this change in motivation, but that does not negate the power of this evolutionary drive. That drive, always growing stronger, continues to attract outer events and situations into the life which reflect the inner needs and which provide the stepping stones for spiritual growth.

Uranus represents mental understanding of the higher planes of consciousness.

Neptune represents a mystical and emotional yearning for at-one-ment with the Higher—be it the soul, personal God, or the nameless, boundless One.

Pluto represents the total commitment to self-transformation which, in the process, involves the purging of all desires, attachments and motives that stand in the way of that transformation.

Uranus, Neptune, and Pluto symbolize the forces that constantly prompt change and growth in our consciousness. Dane Rudhyar called them "Ambassadors of the galaxy" explaining that they do not completely belong to our solar system: they are the great transformative agents that act as intermediaries linking our small system with the larger system of the galaxy. This may be an explanation, in part, of the statements in the Secret Doctrine that there are only seven planets in our solar system and Neptune is particularly mentioned as not belonging to it.[1]

Elman Bacher puts it that Neptune parallels, on a vast transcendent scale, the functions of our Moon. The Moon, working locally between the Earth and Sun, is the mother in a personal sense with reference to relationship, home, and nation. Neptune, functioning as a transmitter of galactic energies working between the Galaxy and our system, is Mother in a universal sense, all-embracing, all-forgiving, all-redeeming.[2]

All of the planets are concerned with our spiritual and material evolution but the Sun, Moon, Mercury, Venus, Mars, Jupiter, and Saturn manifest more noticeably in our everyday lives. The effects of the higher octave planets depend upon whether we have truly learned the lessons of Saturn, fulfilling his "demands". If we have learned those lessons then we will not be lacking in the self-discipline and moral sense needed to deal with the vibrations of Uranus, Neptune, or Pluto in the Natal chart or when, by progression or transit, those planets contact sensitive points in the horoscope.[3] Otherwise, a strong contact can have a very overbalancing effect.

Those who have contributed to pioneering in the frontiers of human knowledge and achievement were born at a time when Uranus, Neptune, and Pluto were in mutual aspect or in close aspect to Sun, Moon, or Ascendant.[4] To give but a few examples: Galileo was born with his Sun in a "T"-Cross with Uranus and Neptune and in conjunction with Pluto almost exactly on the Ascendant. Although this pioneer in Astronomy was born long before the discovery of the higher octave planets, their vibrations clearly affected him. Sir Isaac Newton had Neptune and Pluto in opposition and Sun in sextile to Uranus. Thomas Edison had the Sun conjunct Neptune, sextile Pluto and Moon, in square to Uranus. Marconi, inventor of the wireless, had Sun square Uranus, Moon trine Neptune. Charles Lindbergh's Moon was rising in conjunction with Uranus and in opposition to both

Neptune and Pluto. Perhaps the most extraordinary scientific discovery of the century was the discovery of atomic energy. The first chain reaction was set off when the Sun was in close trine to Pluto. At the completion of the experiment the Moon was conjunct Neptune and trine Uranus. The Sun was conjunct Pluto when the first atom bomb was dropped on Hiroshima. Harry Truman, who ordered the bomb dropped on Japan, was born with his Sun conjunct Neptune and trine Uranus, with Pluto also in trine to Uranus. Astrologer Dane Rudhyar has Pluto and Neptune on the descendant and his Moon in square to Uranus. Marc Edmund Jones has the Sun in trine to a Pluto-Neptune conjunction and Moon in sextile to Uranus. Astrologers are usually associated with the planet Uranus but the true astrologer seems to be strongly influenced by Neptune and Pluto as well.

In the world of art, long before the discovery of the outer planets, Michelangelo responded to the vibrations of Neptune and Uranus bracketing the Midheaven and Pluto sextile Neptune, his Moon on the Ascendant in a fan formation with Neptune and Pluto, his Sun in trine to Neptune and in opposition to Pluto. Neptune is on the Midheaven of Picasso's horoscope, trine to Uranus. Salvador Dali, the surrealist, has Uranus in opposition to Neptune with his Moon in square to both. These artists, in their different ways, have attempted to add an extra dimension to their paintings by distortion (which is an example of one kind of Uranus-Neptune influence). Of the prominent teachers, leaders, and gurus in spiritual fields, G. I. Gurdjieff, the controversial Russian with his methods of teaching through humiliation, had his Sun close to the Nadir, conjunct Jupiter and Mercury, and all of them squaring the Ascendant as well as Mars in the 7th House, making, in effect, a Grand Cross with the Midheaven. Uranus in Leo is a singleton by quadrant and virtually by hemisphere, the signature of a loner. It is also square Pluto in the 8th, indicative of his drastic and original methods of spiritual training, but his Moon in close conjunction with Neptune pictures the mystical side of him known only to genuine seekers.

Swami Vivekananda, probably the most influential of all the earlier apostles to the West of the theory and practice of Indian philosophy and religion, had his Moon, Part of Fortune, and Saturn all conjunct in the 9th House opposed by Neptune. His Pluto was in opposition to the Midheaven. The name

"Vivekananda" means "spiritual discrimination", a very appropriate name for a mystic with Virgo on the cusp of the 9th House and Neptune in the 3rd House in close sextile to Mercury in Aquarius (1st House).

Vivekananda's great teacher, Sri Ramakrishna, had his Sun conjunct the Ascendant, Uranus, and Mercury. Neptune was in close square to Saturn in the 9th House and, incidentally, was exactly conjunct the Vivekananda's Mercury. Ramakrishna's teachings, with their Neptunian call for renunciation, found worldwide expression through the speaking, writing, and travel (all ruled by Mercury) of his disciple, Vivekananda. Uranus conjunct the Sun and Mercury in the 1st House gave Ramakrishna's methods of teaching his disciples such an originality that some people considered him mad.[5]

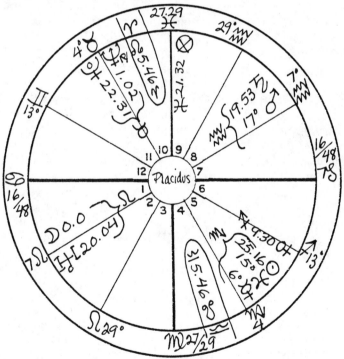

The Theosophical Society—Nov. 17, 1875   8:00 PM.
New York City, N.Y.   Lat. 41 N. Long. 74 W.

The Theosophical Society has also been most influential in bringing the spiritual and occult wisdom of the East, the Ancient Wisdom behind all religions to the world. In the Society's chart and in the charts of all those prominent in the first fifty years, Uranus stands out. The horoscope contains a Grand Cross in Fixed Signs with Uranus in Leo opposing Mars and Saturn conjunct in Aquarius, squaring Pluto in Taurus and squaring Sun and Jupiter in Scorpio. The Moon in Leo, Neptune in Taurus and Mercury in Scorpio form a "T" Cross in Fixed Signs. There is a Grand Trine between Moon, Sun, and the Midheaven. Moon is in 0 degrees Leo, still within orb of trine to the Pisces Midheaven and Scorpio Sun, which is of some help in balancing the many difficult aspects. In spite of many trials and tribulations through the one hundred years of its life, The Theosophical Society is proof that an entity with such an abundance of "challenging" configurations can be successful. One of the founders, H. S. Olcott, had his Sun trine Pluto and opposition Uranus. The other founder, H. P. Blavatsky, had Neptune on the western horizon (she was perhaps one of the world's most extraordinary mystics with great psychic powers), with Sun opposition Uranus and Moon opposition Pluto. Her methods of teaching varied with the pupil and could be anything but gentle! Annie Besant had Uranus rising in opposition to the Sun with Pluto sextile to Neptune. Krishnamurti whose promotion by the Society and subsequent departure caused such upheaval in the 1920s has his Sun opposing Uranus forming a "T" Cross with his Aquarian Ascendant. He was born while the Pluto-Neptune conjunction was some three degrees apart but as these two planets were not otherwise significant in the chart, his contribution appears to be very largely Uranian—preparing people for the coming Aquarian Age by looking to their own selves for illumination rather than to a master or other font of authority.

♅　Uranus

The symbology of the higher octave planets is not as clear as that of the personal planets. The symbol for Uranus is said by some to be the "H" of its discoverer Herschel; but others say the two half-moons represent the reflection of the Spirit bracketing the Cross of Matter. The tiny circle below might be the Soul.[6] The discovery of Uranus in 1781 coincided within a few years of the

American and French Revolutions, the beginning of radical changes in all phases of human life. Uranus is the disintegrator of forms, the enemy of crystallization, the opener of doors. He symbolizes the alchemist, the magician, the occultist, the astrologer, the creative artist, and the political, religious, and social revolutionary. His vibration brings progress after the fulfillment of Saturn's obligations and responsibilities. His influence is felt at those points in evolution when the individual automatically begins to function on progressively more impersonal phases of experience. There is nothing superficial or comfortable about the influences and effects of Uranus; his sorrows are agonies, his punishments catastrophic, his loves have nothing to do with social respectability. In the horoscope, Uranus shows the urge to freedom; his position marks the area in which the person must have freedom to grow and express himself. Uranus gives the power to create, to intuit, to invent, and to achieve independence and inner freedom. Uranus symbolizes the divine purpose of liberation which must, and inevitably will, release the consciousness of man from ignorance and slavery to outworn concepts. Sometimes the ruin of material or emotional foundations is the fastest way in which the individual can become aware of a greater purpose in life.

Uranian vibrations manifest in sudden changes of the life pattern—a major progressed aspect or heavy transit can have an effect like the closing of one volume and the opening of another with new scenery, characters and plot. A dominating Uranus in a horoscope can mean the liberator, awakener, illuminator, inventor, genius or, the rebel without a cause, the constant troublemaker, the dictator.

The Sign and House Ruled by Uranus

Uranus is the ruler of Aquarius and of the 11th House. He shares that rulership with Saturn[7] and no matter where Uranus is placed in the chart there is a relationship to matters of the 11th House and the House on which Aquarius is placed. For example, one of my clients had Aquarius on the cusp of the 9th House with Uranus posited in her 4th House. She has made of her home a gathering place for friends of her spiritual persuasion. In some ways it is like an ashram without a guru-in-residence, where friends congregate for spiritual discussion or to live for varying lengths of time, sharing the work. Another friend has Aquarius on the 2nd House with Uranus in the 5th. She has what might be called an unconventional love life with unconventional friends who often become her lovers with resultant financial entanglements.

Rulership

Some of the people, vocations, and things ruled by Uranus are:

1. Lecturers, inventors, astrologers, scientists, psychologists, aviators, radio operators, electricians, revolutionaries, occultists, antiquarians; sudden and unexpected things, photographers, radiologists, television, telepathy, aeronautics, cooperative societies and clubs.
2. Shin and ankle, circulatory system, pituitary gland, higher nervous system, spasmodic disorders, acute nervous conditions, cramps, ruptures.

Uranus in the Modes, Elements and Signs

The Mode and the Sign in which Uranus is placed is of less importance than the House in which the planet is posited. Like Neptune and Pluto, Uranus is many years in one Sign so obviously almost everyone in a generation will have their Uranus in the same Sign. Therefore, the Sign position will be more indicative of a generational attitude. Those individuals born between 1968 and 1974 will show, in their adult lives, the radical changes in attitudes toward marriage and partnership which were started when Uranus moved through Libra. Those born between 1974 and late 1981 when Uranus moves through Scorpio will show in their lives the radical changes in attitude toward death and sex that we have seen begun in the last few years.

While in outer, more obvious ways the effects of the Sign in which Uranus is placed may be shared with millions, it would be a mistake to overlook its importance for those seeking illumination. For that individual the Sign would color his attunement to truth and experimentation with the forces or change within and without.

In **Aries,** the urge to independent action, self-assertion, and new experience could lead to spiritual leadership.

Taurus is the Sign of Fall for Uranus: the lightning flash of

Uranian intuition is impeded by the materialism of the Sign. Still, within the field of *values* the aspirant may make great changes and find a true awakening.

In **Gemini,** Uranus expresses easily with quick inventiveness, independence of thought and speech. But versatility and even brilliance over many areas can lead to superficiality. There can arise a contempt for those more slow-witted and inarticulate and the aspirant must learn true appreciation for other qualities than those of the intellect.

In **Cancer** there can be a struggle between the claims of home, family and tradition conflicting with the urge for freedom leading to a deeper insight into this age old problem.

Leo is the Sign of Detriment for Uranus under which the leadership qualities of the "royal" Sign can color Uranian expression with arrogance and even dictatorship if the heart is not listened to.

With Uranus in **Virgo,** the lessons of spiritual discrimination, the first step on the Path, can be learned. It is the first step, but one that must be practiced every step of the way until one transcends the human kingdom. It is also the Sign of Service and the intuition of Uranus can guide the aspirant to his particular Work in the universal Plan.

In **Libra,** unusual conditions in marriage or partnership often bring deeper insight into the problem of attaining a balance between the bonds of marriage and the need for freedom.

Scorpio is the Sign of Exaltation wherein the intuition of Uranus allied to the persistence and depth of Scorpio can lead to a profound grasp of the basic mysteries of life, death and regeneration.

Sagittarius can be the Sign of the spiritual pioneer if the individual can control intense restlessness and direct the zeal for change and exploration into constructive, selfless channels.

In **Aquarius,** the Sign he rules, Uranus is strong and the urge for freedom can be directed into humanitarian efforts. There is a deeper meaning to Aquarius: that true freedom can only be found with self-knowledge—"know yourself and you will be freed."

In **Pisces,** the dynamic forces and intuition of Uranus can be used by the aspirant to pierce the emotionalism of the Sign, to realize inspiration, healing compassion, and self-renunciation.

Each Sign has hidden depths, an esoteric side hidden from the unquestioning mass of humanity. Most, if they believe in Astrology, are happy with the popular prediction books, astrological magazines, and newspaper "forecasts". There is nothing evil about that, though when one thinks of the complexity and depth of every horoscope the few lines or paragraphs pretend to analyze, predict, and guide an evolving soul!

Uranus is usually the first of the three higher octave planets to break through the *maya* of material life, awakening the person to growth and unfoldment. As long as we are immersed in material desires and self-seeking, we are enslaved. Our true goals lie elsewhere and Uranus aids us to self-knowledge and liberation.

Uranus in the Houses

The affairs of the House occupied by Uranus will show the sphere in which the individual will feel change and disruption, either initiated by himself or by external causes. But more than that Uranus is the creative power of the universal mind, so evident in the extraordinarily intuitive perceptions that result from a Uranian attunement. Like a flash of lightning on a dark night, the whole landscape of one's life can be illuminated and seen with an entirely new perspective. The House position of Uranus shows us where we can potentially experience and use this awakening power.

In the **1st House** the personality will be out of the ordinary, independent and unconventional. If there are difficult aspects, there can be willfulness, eccentricity, impulsive changes of direction.

In **2nd House** there may be periods when material security is shattered, or there are sudden and unexpected gains, both of which may seem to appear through accident or luck. These sudden losses and gains in the area of finances and resources carry the lesson, teaching the need to break free of identification with matter, to reshape one's values.

In the **3rd House,** odd and interesting happenings can be expected on short journeys. Brothers and sisters may be unusual in character or circumstances with separation from them likely. The mind may be original and inventive, or arbitrary and eccentric. The attitudes can change radically several times in the life.

In the **4th House** are frequent changes in the home, or separation from it and the family, or unusual conditions in the home.

One of the parents may be an unusual person. The 4th House, and particularly the Cusp (the Nadir), shows how the individual regards himself, which lays the very foundation of his being. Uranus here indicates that at some time in the life there may be a dynamic breakthrough into spiritual realization. (Realization is one thing which, though it may change the life, usually requires the total commitment of Pluto to accomplish full transformation. Much depends on the entire horoscope of course.)

With **Uranus in the 5th House** there is little regard for convention in love affairs which can start suddenly and end in the same manner. Unusual children often indicated by this position and just as often, separation from them. Uranus always speeds up the rhythm of a person's nature and in this area it presses one to a restless, new excitement-seeking in love affairs, hobbies, gambling or speculations, sports, and ways of finding enjoyment. Whether aspects are favorable or difficult, it can give brilliance in creative ability.

In the **6th House** Uranus can bring changes and new ideas concerning diet and health. Clever and inventive in work, often with a scientific bent. There are usually sudden changes in employment and upsets in health according to the Sign on the cusp. For the person aspiring to the spiritual life, it can mean intuitive guidance toward a selfless, humanitarian, or occult type of service.

Uranus in the 7th House gives unusual conditions in marriage or partnership. It is not the happiest augury for a lasting marriage, for the urge to independence often brings divorce which is frequently precipitated by meeting someone else who appears to promise a new, exciting relationship. All too often, that one also ends in divorce or separation. If, with Uranus in this position, the marriage *does* last, it will be because both partners are very unusual people with circumstances and attitudes quite different from the normal marriage. It can also mean that the partner, whether in marriage or in business, is a foreigner, eccentric, or somehow out of the ordinary.

In the **8th House,** money from others may come in unusual ways such as unexpected inheritances and the like. An 8th House Uranus may give odd and unconventional ideas about life, sex, and death. One's death can be sudden and unexpected, possibly in an automobile or plane accident.[8] To the spiritually-minded person, this position of Uranus can mean a breakthrough in the mysteries of death, contact with the other side, recollection of past lives, and other so-called occult matters.

Uranus in the **9th House** often means an unorthodox philosophy or approach to religion, or it may indicate a change from one's early beliefs, and possibly study and interest in the occult. Changes when far from home, exciting new experiences while traveling are also a mark of a 9th House Uranus. If afflicted, there can be sudden accidents or difficulties while on long journeys.

In the **10th House,** Uranus can point up a person who could be an outstanding, charismatic leader in world affairs or any field he chooses, using his vision and originality to change old ways. Or it can mean one who is brilliant and original but so arbitrary, changeable, or resistant to routine business that he invites opposition, antagonism, and failure. The vocation most suitable for this position of Uranus would be one that calls for originality and change, such as the fashion industry. There are sure to be changes in the career which could range from government work to electronics to design. Combining the New Age Uranian influences with the 10th House rulerships you can get a glimpse of the wide range of professional possibilities in this position.

In the **11th House,** unusual objectives in life. Friends who are unconventional, much older, younger, or in some way very different from the person himself. Attraction to humanitarian or altruistic societies or groups. Sudden and unexpected separation from friends or group affiliations.

In the **12th House,** Uranus attracts one to unusual and secret interests. Occultism can be positive and forceful. Arbitrary and impulsive attitudes and actions rising from unresolved conflicts in the unconscious. It can mean insight and intuitive perception of cosmic truths.

Uranus Aspects

Uranus acts electrically, speeding up the individual's tempo so that under a progressed or transiting aspect Uranian he becomes excitable, restless, "turned-on", and with an urgent desire for change and freedom. If, at birth, there is an aspect between Uranus and another planet, or with the Midheaven or Ascendant, the effect will be very strong.

Uranus does not afflict any planet in the chart unless there is a karmic tendency toward crystallization to be counteracted. Uranus does not shake us up unless we need to be freed from our inclination to cling to some outworn structure in our lives whether it be a relationship, concept, "security blanket", or whatever. The aspects involving Uranus show where we have to open up, experiment with new ideas and relationships and become more receptive to truth. Having said that, it must be stressed that the actual expression of Uranian aspects is unpredictable, there is always an element of the unexpected, unusual, the sudden. And even the creative manifestations are usually accompanied by some of the less desirable Uranian characteristics. From a spiritual standpoint, Uranus serves the purposes of the higher Self by radically repolarizing an individual's position in a particular area of life and cutting away all remnants of past life patterns that have been blocking growth.

It must be stressed again that the aspects formed between the higher octave planets are sometimes in orb for many years. That is because of the frequent retrograde and direct motion of these three planets. For example, Uranus and Neptune were in square aspect on and off from 1951 to 1958. Obviously, therefore, many people born during those years would have that square in their charts. It would serve to color their characters and attitudes but the degree of expression would depend upon the individual chart and stage of evolution.

URANUS–NEPTUNE   With all the aspects, the intuitions and psychic impressionability are increased. In a strong chart of an evolved individual this can make for tremendous vision and sensitivity to the higher planes. In a weak chart it may have little effect or lead to fantasy, deceit of self and others. In any chart there is a likelihood of conflict between the Uranian drive for individualistic freedom and the Neptunian urge to renounce individual freedom for union with the boundless All or some cult (or drug) that promises escape from the problems of individual freedom. The square and opposition increase the conflict and nervous tension but also can increase the efforts to attain the ideals in unusual ways.[9]

URANUS–PLUTO   If the action of Uranus is unpredictable, the action of Pluto is even more so. The reason for this is, I believe, because all of the higher octave planets are functioning from a range of values or principles beyond our human comprehension. The effects of their vibrations depend often upon the individual's stage of evolution or sensitivity. Therefore, it is impossible and misleading to give an exact description of Uranus to Pluto aspects. In certain strong individuals, the will power can manifest as an arbitrary willfulness or a ruthless domination and manipulation of others for selfish ends. The sextile and trine can mean that the energies of the two planets may be expressed in a creative way but this is not invariably the case.[10]

Uranus Retrograde

The individual with a natal retrograde Uranus tends to be a rebel against all that binds him. The expression of this in the life varies with each horoscope. He has learned *how* to be independent in former incarnations and now must discover the purpose of independence.

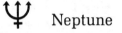

The exoteric symbol of Neptune is the trident or forked spear held by the Greek and Roman god of the ocean. Esoterically, the symbol represents the upturned crescent (Chapter VII, page 79) or sacred cup open to receive the inflow of Buddhic intuition, understanding, and compassionate, boundless love. Neptune is also the planet of creative inspiration; all great artists have Neptune strong in their charts. Michelangelo, Picasso, and Dali have already been mentioned. Omar Khayyam was born with a Uranus-Neptune opposition, Pluto in trine to Uranus and sextile Neptune. Edgar Allan Poe had Moon conjunct Pluto in square to Neptune and trine to Uranus. Uranus was conjunct his ascendant. His strange genius for macabre stories and his addiction to alcoholism and drugs demonstrates one kind of Neptunian (allied with the influence of Moon, Uranus, and Pluto) manifestation. The horoscope generally attributed to William Shakespeare shows his Midheaven bracketed by Venus and Neptune with Pluto squared by Uranus. The Moon is sextile Pluto and the Part of Fortune is square Uranus and opposition Pluto. Many of his plays are allegorical representations of eternal truths, which is one reason they have survived. In the horoscopes of nearly all of the great composers Uranus, Neptune, and Pluto are prominent. Neptune is strongly connected with the arts because it is related to imaginative inspiration.[11]

Neptune in the Natal chart shows where it is easiest to surrender to a greater whole. It is inspiration, imagination, sacrifice, sublimation, and the highest idealism. Neptune is also the planet of camouflage; things are never what they seem to be where Neptune is placed or in a Neptune progression or transit. Neptune rules the love that unites all as well as the never-sleeping forces of decay and dissolution.

Never count on anything *material* promised by Neptune, particularly his aspects. So often what appears to be an ominous storm on the horizon of life will produce only a light shower, an imminent bonanza will deliver 10% of its rosy promise. It is wisest to look to Neptune only for non-material gains such as idealism, inspiration, imagination, and creativity. Neptune can be the planet of deception or chaos until one has learned the lessons of Saturn relating to self-discipline, commonsense, and an honest appraisal of oneself. With so many people, Neptune's manifestation can be that of self-aggrandizement, self-dramatization, and fantasy; a lot of talk but no real effort. Sometimes all recognition of one's actual abilities and importance are dispensed with. Saturn sets boundaries, Neptune dissolves them, so great discrimination must be practiced to avoid illusion. The infinite expansion of some ideal can be noted in the examples of Napoleon, the Kaiser in W.W. I, Philip of Spain, and Hitler. They had not learned the lessons of Saturn and so their karma brought inevitable disaster. There are no limits to *spiritual* expansion for those who truly seek the way within but outward expansion of an ideal (especially when it involves the use of force) is another matter.

Neptune sensitizes individuals to become their own teachers by attuning them to the reality of the unseen, the immaterial forces of life. There is an element of renunciation related to Neptune, a renunciation of personal requirements for the sake of the greater whole. Neptune rules alcoholism, drugs, hallucination, and escapism; those things which singly or in combination have been used to attempt a short cut to Nirvana. Any such attempts to achieve heavenly bliss without effort can only bring disaster.

The Sign and House Ruled by Neptune

Neptune is the ruler of Pisces and the 12th House, sharing that rulership with Jupiter.[12] Wherever Neptune is placed in the chart there will be a relationship between the things ruled by that House and the matters ruled by the 12th House and the House upon which Pisces is placed. A friend of mine had Neptune in the 9th House, very close to the Midheaven, with Pisces on the Cusp of the 6th House. She is a mystic and very psychic. When she was a young woman, a friend sent her some wooden carvings from Africa. As she opened the box, a cloud of fine dust flew up into her face from the packing. Shortly afterwards a strong infection started spreading across her face under the skin, eating away flesh and bone. Doctors were mystified and it was not until there had been considerable disfigurement (she had been an extraordinarily beautiful woman) that it was discovered to be a fungus growth known only in Africa. She believes that it was the karmic result of a past life in Africa as a witch-doctor who misused his powers. Neptune rules certain types of fungus, placed in the 9th House (foreign countries, religion and religious practices), Pisces is on the 6th House of health, and the 12th House (Neptune's natural rulership) rules hospitalization, past karma and "self-undoing". The Moon (also a ruler of fungus growths) was part of a Cardinal "T" Cross in exact square to Jupiter (co-ruler of Pisces, 12th and 9th Houses, whose aspects often show religious karma from the past). Jupiter is posited in the 1st House in opposition to Mars in Cancer, 4th House. She also had two serious operations for cancer in later life. Along with the negative expression of Neptune, the lady has great Neptunian spiritual and psychic qualities, spending much of her life helping others.

Another case, which demonstrates the positive manifestations of Neptune's vibrations, is that of a man with his Sun in the 7th House exactly trine Neptune in the 3rd House, with Pisces on the Cusps of the 8th and 9th Houses. Music was his great love but when he found it could not provide him with an adequate livelihood he went to work for a large corporation (12th House) involved with travel and credit cards (9th and 8th House matters). He rose to executive level and is now in the auditing department (8th House) where his duties entail foreign travel (9th House). In his spare time he studies Astrology (Neptune, 3rd, and 9th Houses), and does volunter hospital work (12th House).

Rulership

Some of the people, vocations, and things ruled by Neptune are:

1. Artistic and literary people, philosophers, mystics, black magicians, ascetics, occupations connected with the sea, oil, chemicals, television and films (all such occupations in which illusion is involved), anaesthetics, spiritualism, the sea, plastics, mind-altering drugs, alcohol, sleep, dreams, fish, psychism in all branches, idealism, hypnosis, the intangible.
2. The Pineal gland, spinal cords, nerve fiber, the feet, lymphatic system, allergies, obscure diseases such as comas, catalepsy, hypochondria, poisoning, toxic conditions, drug addiction, alcoholism.

Neptune in the Modes, Elements and Signs

These factors are of less importance than the House in which the planet is placed. As remarked previously, the higher octave planets stay so many years in one Sign that many millions will have their Neptune in the same Sign, thus sharing generational attitudes and conditions in those things ruled by the planet.

Neptune first entered Sagittarius in 1970 but did not settle there until 1971. It will take approximately fourteen years to traverse that Sign. The most outstanding material change wrought so far has been the oil crisis of 1973-74 which has had such a worldwide effect. Oil, energy, inflation (a Neptune-Jupiter expression), and politics have been interlaced ever since.

But Neptune is also connected with death, and passing through Sagittarius there will be many new ideas and discoveries in that field, perhaps producing new evidence on survival after death.

For those individuals endeavoring to grow spiritually, the Sign in which Neptune is placed at birth would color his attunement to creative or spiritual inspiration.

In **Aries,** the imagination will be strongly expressed, the often brash assertiveness of the Sign softened. The will to dominate can, in some charts, show a person who will resort to subversive means to attain his ideals, rationalizing that the ends justify the means.

In **Taurus,** imagination and psychic sensitivity can be ex-

pressed in a practical way or in sensual fantasies with careless-
ness over resources. Taurus is related to values and, to the
aspirant, this means expressing his ideals in practical, honest
ways even in money and business matters where dishonesty in
all shades is common practice.

In **Gemini** Neptune passed through that Sign between 1887-
1901; the many modes of communication—speaking, writing,
traveling, advertising, etc.—must measure up to the highest
ideals, which means that one's thoughts as well as speech and
writing must be free of distortion, exaggeration and deceit in
order to be "true of sound". Like a coin whose sound, when
struck or dropped, proclaims its falsity or verity, we are each one
sounding our note in the world through our emotions, speech
and thoughts. In **Gemini,** Neptune can make one more mentally
intuitive or too susceptible and changeable, allowing the per-
suasions of others to deflect us from our ideals.

Cancer (traversed between 1901-1913) is supposed to be one
of the best Signs for Neptune, being of compatible nature. The
characteristics of Cancer include the urge to nurture and protect,
fluidity and sensitivity. These can be very helpful qualities to
one seeking to forget the self in service of others, but as both
Cancer and Neptune vibrations are strongly emotional, care
must be taken to avoid excess sentimentality and muddled emotionalism. It is good to feel compassion but a waste of energy and
spiritual purpose to lavish it on every stray animal and human
that appears on the horizon. One can only do so much and there
must be sensible priorities.

Neptune in Leo (1915-1929) has sometimes been called "religion on fire" and indeed when Neptune is in this Sign of its
exaltation and the person finds a religion or philosophy, he
tends to dramatize it and himself with enthusiasm! This can
become a form of fantasy (making oneself the star of a drama) or a
bid for recognition. Pride may produce self-aggrandizement.

In **Virgo** (1929-1943) Neptune is in its Detriment, its qualities
finding difficulty to express, perhaps because the critical, analytical qualities of the Sign inhibit Neptune's compassion. Virgo
likes to measure, to set tidy limits and Neptune seeks the infinite. I have known quite a number of women with Neptune in
Virgo who, though very intelligent, attractive, and eager for
marriage had never found the man who could measure up to
their ideals. If they married, it did not last. Discrimination is

absolutely necessary with all Neptune's influences and ruler-ships for no planet can be more illusionary and misleading. Especially with Virgo, the discrimination, the ability to analyze critically, must be applied carefully to the right subjects. There is often an attraction toward chastity and asceticism, vegetarian or special diet, or healing through the laying on of hands. Virgo ideals often find expression through service of the sick.

Neptune in Libra (1943-1956) increases the aesthetic and ar-tistic qualities. The ideals seek a balanced expression, though the desire for harmony may lead to weakness and vacillation. The marriage ideals go through subtle changes, illusion and disillusion, eventually putting those ideals on a sounder, more spiritual basis.

Neptune in Scorpio (1956-1970) can make one highly sensi-tive and inspired either in the arts or psychically. The aspirant must guard against being oversensitive to slights, imagining injury or lack of appreciation where none is intended. There is much intuitive understanding when in love. Occult studies can spiritualize the expression of this Sign and matters of the House it rules in the chart.

Neptune in Sagittarius (1970-1984) is the planet of vision and during its passage through the Sign far-ranging explorations of the world, mind and spirit, many boundaries will be dissolved. It will be a time of confusion and mysticism in religions, with many new prophets and cults rising. Neptune seeks to bring people closer together, dissolving separations, so that many who are born in this period will gravitate to living in a religious or idealistic community. Boundaries will be dissolved between far parts of the world through the speed and availability of travel and communication. Sagittarius is the Sign of the law and medi-cal professions and there will surely be a change in attitude and administration of these professions. All these things and much more will bear fruit more fully when the children born with Neptune in Sagittarius come to adulthood. Their point of view will be very different from ours, their ideals much more open, free, and forthright, as is the nature of Sagittarius but since Neptune is the planet of mystery there will still be mysteries into which only the pure and totally committed may safely probe.

Neptune in Capricorn (1984-1997) will bring new political concepts, the dissolution of old ambitions, and the emergence of new ambitions that would be strange to our hearing now.

And beyond that, when Neptune moves through **Aquarius** from 1998 and then into **Pisces,** its own Sign, we can only guess and reason from our knowledge of planet and Sign. The *forms* of our yearning for union with others and a greater Being may change radically but the principles that govern the universe remain unchanging.

Neptune in the Houses

By House position in the Natal chart, Neptune indicates the potentials for tuning in on transcendental influences, either constructively or destructively. All three of the higher octave planets do that, but each is different and no one of them alone can be called *the* planet of spiritual intuition or psychic power. The House position indicates the sphere in which the imagination can be used most fruitfully and easily, in which one can most easily surrender to a greater whole. At this stage of evolution (for all but the most selfless and evolved) there is always a degree of illusion—things are not what they seem to be about the affairs of the House in which Neptune is placed.

Neptune in the **1st House** increases the sensitivity enormously. It can be a physical sensitivity leading to allergies and ailments that are mysterious, resisting ordinary medical treatment. Psychologically there is a tendency to daydreaming, escapism of various kinds, and the person can easily lose himself in a world of the imagination. With Neptune in the 1st House, drugs should never be taken, even antibiotics may produce severe side effects and narcotics can lead to addiction. This position often gives psychic or creative ability.

In the **2nd House** imagination and psychism can be brought into money-making purposes or there can be vagueness about financial matters leading to loss or deceit. Depending on the aspects there can be danger of fraud or, if well-aspected, idealism about possessions.

In the **3rd House** the mentality can be imaginative and intuitive, or vague and unstable, depending on the aspects. It can indicate occult or artistic studies—the example of this follows.

In the **4th House** there may be peculiar conditions to do with the home, often a substitute home and parents, such as foster parents or adoption. Idealism about home, parents, and ancestry is another mark of this position. Sometimes there car be peculiar complications in the home or misunderstandings within the family. I have often found it to indicate some mystery about the person's parentage, such as illegitimacy or uncertainty about their identity. The 4th House shows the individual's self-regard (which so often is conditioned by his parents' attitudes and early childhood) and Neptune here can indicate very negative, inferiority feelings or self-exaltation based on illusion.

In the **5th House** there can be unrealistic expectations of children or love affairs. Peculiar happenings in regard to children and deceit in romances. Investments in things of the sea, oil, or art—but the profit or loss depends upon the aspects. A tendency to take risks without using commonsense or careful forethought. Romances can be very secretive and involved.

In the **6th House** much depends on the aspects; a well-aspected Saturn can do much to balance Neptune here. Health may suffer through hidden, peculiar causes such as toxic or food poisoning, drugs, escaping gas. Work conditions may be difficult because of intrigues, double-dealing, and gossip. The person may be over-sensitive to the attitudes and emotions of those with whom he works and allow it to poison his satisfaction with his job.

In the **7th House** there can be peculiar conditions in marriage or partnership. Here are examples from cases. In one marriage the couple had not had sexual relations for twenty-five years; it was really a marriage in name only although to all outer appearances it was a very successful, happy marriage. In another marriage, Neptune in 7th indicated a subtle disintegration. And in yet another, Neptune's position meant that the lady always idealized her partner so much that no mere human could possibly measure up and when they proved fallible she never recognized it was her own illusions to be at fault, the men had "deceived" her. The partner is likely to be spiritual or artistic but unless well-aspected, difficulties arise and disillusion sets in.

In the **8th House** Neptune gives an easy understanding of spiritual matters with the ability to attain heights. The person may be mystic or mediumistic, dreams or visions may be precognitive. There may be deception or mismanagement in financial matters, inheritances or other people's money. Difficult aspects may give deception through illusionary ideas regarding persons or conditions on the other side of death. Neptune in the 8th can indicate disillusion in sexual matters. Whatever the aspects, death is likely to come while asleep or under anaesthetic.

In the **9th House** there can be significant dreams, visions, or intuitions that aid religious/spiritual comprehension and studies. These can be used to advantage in publication. Romantic adventures or confusion on long journeys. With difficult aspects, higher studies become confused because ideas or goals are not thought through. The person's approach to all religious, higher educational, or serious studies tends to be very idealistic or mystical.

Neptune in the 10th House can be excellent if the life work lies in artistic, psychic, or inspirational fields. Even with favorable aspects, a strong Saturn or other stabilizing factors are necessary to avoid the fantasizing about one's place on the world stage that seems to accompany this position rather often. For example, one woman I know with this position, always dramatized herself in the lead role until she became so overbearing that she lost her job. In later years, to make up for her lack of achievement, she adopted the achievements, travels and adventures of others as her own. In other cases success is imagined but not worked for, secret or psychological reasons being the cause. Usually there is strong idealism as to the personal prestige in life.

Neptune in the 11th House gives strange and peculiar, sometimes deceptive friendships with dishonesty or misrepresentation at their hands. Wherever Neptune's position in the chart, it often indicates one's "blind spot". The 11th House is the area where one has a responsibility to a larger group of which he is a part. He has to learn selflessness by being at the mercy of others (his friends or group), if his eyes are closed to his real motivation. The lesson to be learned is, that one is never deceived unless one deceives oneself first. Long-term goals may be very idealistic or vague and on the level of fantasy. Ideas and ideologies should be carefully scrutinized before being taken up.

The **12th House** is the natural House ruled by Pisces and Neptune. The intuition and psychic power can be at work in hidden ways expressing through mediumship, art, dancing, music, and other aesthetic interests. Neptunian expression can be peculiar, even distorted and perverse, but it is never coarse or crude. There is always a refinement, a delicacy, a subtlety about Neptune's activities. If Neptune has difficult aspects, there can be neurosis stemming from repression of things in the subconscious. There is an example in the case of the woman whose bigamous father was claimed by another wife (Chapter XI, page 139) when she was a small child. At birth, Saturn and Neptune were within one degree of conjunction in the 12th House. When Marion reached age 28, her progressed Neptune made an exact conjunction with Saturn. She was about to graduate from college with honors, no worries and everything to look forward to, but for no reasons that any doctor or counsellor could discover, she lost all interest in life and for a year went through a completely incapacitating depression. Transitting Saturn was also completing his cycle of the twelve Signs, returning to his Natal position in the .2th House.

Neptune Aspects

It should be noted that the difficult, more stressful aspects involving Neptune are more indicative of artistic creativity and spiritual progress than the harmonious aspects. The "divine discontent" which presses most of those seeking creative or spiritual goals is frequently the manifestation of Neptune's difficult vibrations. In the charts of all persons actively pursuing some kind of spiritual path as their main vocation, Neptune was in conjunction, square or opposition with the personal planets, Ascendant, or Midheaven at birth.

Every aspirant must always remember that Neptune is the most subtle planet in its mode of operation, so there is often misunderstanding and misapplication of spiritual ideals. One need only remember the devout men of the Inquisition who tortured, burned, and imprisoned thousands, sincerely believing themselves to be carrying out the will of the God of love. After lives of illusion and disillusion we realize that no true realization of the spirit can be achieved through goals that are sought in the world outside ourselves. Such goals are achieved only when we accept the responsibility for making our characters and lives ideal. Difficult aspects of Neptune can give self-delusion about one's high level of spiritual development leading to spiritual pride. Humility and discrimination are the only safe-guards against the illusions of Neptune.

NEPTUNE-PLUTO Any planet touched by Pluto shows ways of action governed by past attitudes, where the need for elimination and renewal is necessary. Neptune reveals the visionary and imaginative capacity which too often manifests as illusion. Pluto forces us to see our illusions and ideals for what they *really* are. There will be larger forces working for social change to which one must respond, and also periods of subtle psychological change.

The opposition aspect often takes the form of disappearances of persons, circumstances, or possessions important to the individual.

Neptune Retrograde

In any line of endeavor or expression of organic life whether involuntary, voluntary, or evolutionary, there are always periods of review or recapitulation. It is no different with the spiritual life with which the higher octave planets are so closely related.

A retrograde Neptune indicates a period in this incarnation when the individual is living through the karma of learning what is real and what is unreal in his ideals. There develops a deep inner need to view all material matters in terms of their significance to the Soul, forcing him to live in this world but not be identified with it.

♇ Pluto

There are two symbols for Pluto in common usage. One is shaped like a combination of the first two letters, "P" and "L". The other, more to my liking, is the upturned crescent over the Cross of matter, symbolizing the sacred cup uplifted to receive the powers of wisdom, foresight, and spiritual will. Within the cup is the sphere symbolizing the Spirit. Appropriately named for the Roman god of the underworld and the dead, Pluto rules the 8th House and the Sign Scorpio. His keywords are elimination, renewal, regeneration, endings and new beginnings. He seems an enemy because he brings us in touch with death of one kind or another. But, like Uranus and Neptune, his vibrations are always seeking to make the individual aware of the unreality and impermanence of the mundane world against the reality and eternity of the soul. His work is to bring freedom from bondage to forms no longer useful to the Spirit. Old conditions, complexes, patterns of thought and behavior are highlighted or flushed to the surface. These factors so often have a compulsive or obsessive quality about them that it *forces* us to deal with them. Above all, Pluto is the planet of transformation, urging us toward that final goal of all those many incarnations, to transcend the human kingdom and become more than human, a being "whose growth and splendour have no limit." Uranus and Neptune awaken and inspire us, then Pluto gives us the indomitable will, the total commitment to cleanse ourselves of all impediments in character and our past so that we can achieve that final transformation.

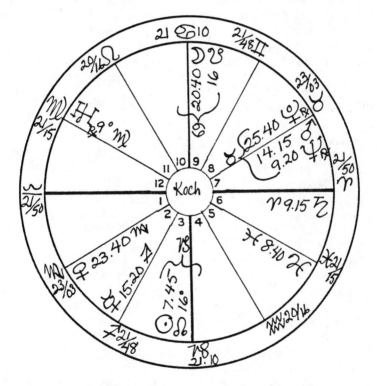

Sri Ramana Maharshi—South Indian saint
Born Dec. 30, 1879   1:00 A.M. Thiruthuzi,
India Lat. 7N55 Long. 78E10

Astrologers have noticed that those who have contributed most to the psychological and spiritual integration of their fellows have a strong accent on Pluto in their charts. Such a one was Sri Ramana Maharshi, the sage of Arunachala. Born in 1879, the life of this South Indian saint illustrates Pluto's influence in his total commitment to self-transformation from early youth accompanied by drastic austerities taken to eliminate any element that stood between himself and God. The Moon is conjunct the Midheaven, square the Ascendant, trine Venus in the 2nd House and sextile Pluto in the 8th House, Pluto making a close opposition to Venus, the ruler of his ascending Sign, Libra. The two are also in Mutual Reception; Pluto in Taurus and Venus in Scorpio. With Pluto in the House of death and regeneration, Maharshi accomplished the death of the personal self. The essence of his teaching is embodied in the Self-Inquiry: the Vichara. This is a meditation in which the individual asks, "Who am I?", continually confronting and eliminating the unreal and the impermanent not-selfs until the consciousness reaches the realm of the unchangeable Spirit-Self.

When Maharshi was a boy he had an extraordinary experience. While alone in his room one day, a terrible fear and realization of death overcame him. Though in perfect health and without any suffering he felt his last hour had come. He quietly lay down on the floor, saying to himself: "Death is coming to me, but death of what? My body is already lying without movement, it is becoming cold and stiff, but I, my consciousness, is not affected at all. I am therefore independent of this dying form. I am not this body." After some time life came back into the corpse-like body but the young boy was changed. His experience brought to him the conviction of the independence of his real Self from the temporary form falsely called I. Shortly after that he left his family for years of extremely ascetic life, keeping complete silence in the caves of the sacred mountain of Arunachala. But even sitting in isolated silence, his spiritual presence was so powerful that pilgrims and devotees came from all over India and the world to sit at his feet. Eventually he was persuaded to leave his solitary existence and take up residence in an ashram at Tiruvannamalai.[14]

Maharshi's horoscope shows strong influence of the other higher octave planets. He has a Grand Trine in Earth Signs with Uranus in almost exact trine to Neptune, and both trining the

Sun. Uranus is also in exact opposition to Jupiter and both are in square to Mercury, making a "T" Cross in Mutable Signs. Jupiter aspects both the Sun and Neptune within a one-degree orb of an exact sextile to each.

Sign and House Ruled by Pluto

The planets visible to the naked eye were named for Roman gods long ago by astrologer-astronomers and the practice was continued when Uranus was discovered in 1781, Neptune in 1846 and Pluto in 1930. It is a curious thing that the qualities, powers, and rulership attributed to those particular gods so perfectly fit the qualities, powers and rulership of the planets astrologically. Out of all the considerable pantheon of Roman and Greek gods it is remarkable that the names of those *particular* gods were chosen.[15]

Pluto was the god of death, ruling over the underworld—that which is submerged. Most astrologers now give Pluto rulership over Scorpio and the 8th House, sharing the rulership with Mars.[16] The 8th House is the House in which, symbolically speaking, the soul undergoes the trials that eventually free him from identification with the exclusive personal self of the first seven Houses to the all-inclusive Self identified with the last five Houses. I have noticed that every time the progressed Moon moved through the 8th House, it coincided with a time of loss and disillusionment. When the Moon moved on into the 9th House, ideals, hope, and a better perspective were regained and established on a more sound foundation. Thus we pass through many little deaths and rebirths in one incarnation and in the larger span of many incarnations. We don't often have progressions or major transits of Pluto in effect, but the Moon is always making aspects, stirring up each House and planet as she progresses.

Wherever Pluto is placed in the chart there will be a relationship between the things ruled by that House and the matters ruled by the 8th House and the House upon which Scorpio is placed. For example, one can take the horoscope of Annie Besant who played so many different roles in her remarkable life. Scorpio was on the 8th House and Pluto posited in the 1st House, in Aries. With typical Aries zeal plus Pluto's urge for reform, she was a social reformer, working to aid downtrodden working women, one of the pioneers in birth control (a most appropriate field for Scorpio-Pluto), a leader and reformer in education, independence for India, religion, and not least of her accomplishments was the transformation of herself. Wherever Pluto is placed, there is the area where we meet our old unredeemed self but also where one is in immediate contact with a deep reservoir of concentrated power. In Mrs. Besant's chart, Pluto in the first House, along with Uranus and Mars, gave her the total commitment and the power to reform herself as well as others. In another case, one of the most spiritual women I knew had Pluto in the 12th House with Scorpio on the cusp of the 5th House. In her case there was the death (8th House) of her child (5th House) causing long-lasting suffering (12th House). Then again, in later life, she and two people close to her were seemingly "obsessed." She was only freed from the dark forces (a negative expression of Pluto—the psychic underworld, the 12th House), that were destroying her life by the help of a saintly man who providentially entered the scene at that point.

Rulership

Some of the people, vocations and things ruled by Pluto are:
1. Atomic scientists, insurance agents and companies, tax collectors and taxation, sanitary inspectors, sewage disposal, surgeons, undertakers, nuclear power, atomic energy, underground activity, organized crime, purgatory, life after death, birth, death, cataclysms, sorcery, kidnapping, psychotherapy, possession, fanatics, plutonium, beginnings and endings, elimination.
2. Generative organs, genital disorders, venereal disease, hemorrhoids, elimination of body wastes, cancer.

Pluto in the Modes, Elements and Signs

These factors are of less importance than the House in which Pluto is placed. Pluto was discovered in Cancer in 1930, the year the worldwide Depression began during which, for the first time, programs such as the NRA, the WPA, Social Security, etc., organized the economy and life in the United States. Other countries also instituted their national programs. There were banking and tax reforms. When World War II broke out, Pluto had just entered Leo, royal dynasties crumbled, war became total war, totalitarian states and dictators proliferated. After peace was declared, the United Nations was established with international programs, nations set about instituting cradle-to-grave welfare plans or at least putting into effect far-reaching health and welfare programs. In 1958 Pluto entered Virgo, health and employment received increasing attention, food and drugs were increasingly regulated. In 1972 Pluto entered Libra. It is yet early to grasp all the changes Pluto will bring in Libra matters but we are already seeing changes in marriage and divorce. Pluto's principles of elimination of the old and outworn, total commitment to get to the root of things, transformation, and rebirth express on a national and international scale as well as on the personal.

For those individuals endeavoring to grow spiritually, the Sign in which Pluto is placed at birth would color his need to let go of the old and begin anew. With the very evolved person it would influence his total commitment to transformation.

Pluto in Gemini (1884-1914) would emphasize communication as a means to elimination of the past and outworn habit patterns. Through thinking, reading, studying, traveling—communicating in the fullest sense of the word—the aspirant should work toward dispelling prejudice and ignorance, one of the greatest blocks to spiritual growth.

In **Cancer (1914-1939),** an exaggerated adherence to family, tradition and the home can delay evolution. The family matrix is like a protective shell from which the eaglet must break out if he is to try his wings and soar to the heavens.

In **Leo (1939-1957),** arrogance must be supplanted by the power of love. It will be remembered that at that time the Nazi ideology emerged, manifesting a negative expression of Pluto, the importance of the individual was submerged for the glory of the totalitarian state. Not that every one with Pluto in Leo is a "little Hitler" but pride, arrogance, and disregard for another's rights to a minor or major degree can be stumbling blocks for the aspirant.

Pluto in Virgo (1957-1972) brings danger of too much attention to practical, material things. Concern over health, employment, working conditions looms large, distorting the spiritual perspective. The critical mind sees details but not the whole. The aspirant must learn to let go of those welfare worries and think of himself only as a server.

In **Libra (1972-1984)** relationship with others particularly in business or marriage partnerships is important. By reforming his attitudes to others, he reforms himself. The greatest conflict will come when Pluto demands that the aspirant probe to the core of his motivations and attitudes regarding his relationships no matter how ugly they may turn out to be. To ignore a subconscious ugliness is only to have it rise again and again with increasing compulsiveness.

When Pluto crosses into **Scorpio (1984-1996)** those children born then will experience the full power of Pluto in his own Sign in their lives. For the aspirant, it will come as a great time of testing. The mysteries of sex, birth, death, and regeneration will press upon him and he will experience them according to his commitment and his evolutionary status. Through the turmoil and pain these words of *Light On The Path* apply:

> Stand thou aside in the coming battle, and though thou fightest be not thou the warrior. Look for the Warrior and let him fight in thee. Take his orders for battle and obey them. (The "Warrior" is the Soul, the higher Self, which the personality must realize is his *real* self.) When once he has entered thee and become thy Warrior, he will never utterly desert thee, and at the day of great peace he will become one with thee.

Pluto in the Houses

Pluto's House position shows where one is living out an old pattern of behavior which, often, is compulsive and pain-creating. It is the area in which we are most intensely meeting that which needs elimination in our characters. We meet our old self, our past desires, our past karma.[17] The "letting go" and elimination is especially difficult for people with Pluto in the 8th House or the Sign Scorpio prominent. They subconsciously fear that they will become vulnerable and thus give into the hands of others the power they want to keep for themselves. However, the position of Pluto is also the area of greatest potential for regeneration and transformation.

Pluto in the 1st House   This is the House of the personality and the identity, so Pluto's presence therein suggests that in this incarnation the individual's sense of identity must be changed.[18] There is often great reserve and insecurity which inhibits him from cooperation with others at a deep personal level. His defensiveness makes all relationships difficult, preventing openness so that he is frequently very lonely, even alienated from family and friends. Although persons with Pluto in the 1st House often have Pluto's powers of wisdom, foresight, and spirituality, their insecurity and reserve prevents them from expressing it effectively unless they are sufficiently evolved. Pluto's methods of elimination apply to both physical and psychological organisms and his influence acts to flush hidden conditions to the surface so that spiritual energy can be released creatively.

An afflicted Pluto indicates difficulty of elimination which psychologically means suppression of unpleasant feelings with the resultant risk of obsessive and neurotic conditions.[19] Complexes are associations of ideas; usually rooted in past lives or the early childhood of this life, which are beyond conscious control. These old patterns of thought and behavior hold us in bondage and prevent us from acting with psychological freedom. Pluto transits stir up these karmic patterns and push them to the surface for destruction. If there are good aspects to Pluto then regeneration is not so difficult and can follow along with transits or progressions.[20] Persons with Pluto in the 1st House tend to be very bottled up and defensive which makes it difficult for them to face themselves. Once they can do that, they can draw upon the tremendous Plutonian energy showing powerful concentration and depth of insight into life's deeper meanings.

Pluto in the 2nd House This position indicates the necessity for a regeneration of one's sense of values, especially concerning possession of or control of material resources. The 2nd House is the House of *physical* values; the 8th House, Pluto's natural House, is the House of *emotional* values. There is always a close connection and interaction between opposing Houses. In the effort to achieve security there is often a great covetousness and desire for possessions but that attitude, instead of bringing peace of mind, only becomes a source of turmoil and anxiety. Sometimes there can be compulsive spending that leads to trouble.

There can be extremes of behavior such as a total surrender of material concerns to the point of asceticism, or the individual may stoop to the lowest level in order to make financial gains. Pluto is often found in the 2nd House of millionaires and is a good position for tax matters, banking, collective funds, corporations, monopolies, etc. There is often considerable resourcefulness in attaining material security. With the evolved person there can be an intuitive comprehension of the deeper energies which money represents.

Pluto in the 3rd House   This position of Pluto often produces compulsions in the field of communication. The person may go to extraordinary lengths to put himself or his ideas across to others. His speech and writing are forceful and reiterative to the point of irritation. There is great mental energy expended in pursuance of a goal and there is nothing lukewarm about the intellectual interests. The 3rd House is supposed to rule the sense of humor (it is surprising how few astrologers ever consider the importance of a sense of humor to the point of doing research) and Pluto would tend to give a bite to the wit producing an able satirist or critic. This is a good position for scientists, orators, writers, researchers, and healers. The intellectual powers are usually good, though elementary schooling may be found dull and frustratingly superficial (this placement is often found with school dropouts). At some point in the life, the individual will be forced to take notice of his failures in communication and his ways of thinking.

Pluto in the 4th House   This placement can indicate the early loss of a parent or a difficult youth due to other circumstances. It could also mean some mystery or scandal in the family background. It can indicate a home life which is subject to all kinds of turbulence due to the person's compulsive need for control and domination within the home. This stems from a desire for a home as a place of rest, security, and retreat from the worldly battles. Unfortunately, such willful demands on other members of the household provoke rebellion rather than the desired peace. It can also mean contention with a Pluto-type dictator in the home. Pluto's presence here indicates that a complete reorientation is needed in the individual's deepest feelings about himself and his sense of security and inner peace. When these depths are plumbed and attitudes truly regenerated, the security and contentment attained within will be reflected in the home conditions. The influence of this house lies like a great moving river beneath the surface of the personality. It represents the very base of the individual himself in terms of the family, roots, childhood, and home that he has come from and symbolically in terms of his inner sense of security and safety. Any planet, but especially Pluto, points to something in the psyche which must be first discovered and brought to the light before it can be dealt with constructively. Not until then will the person be free from compulsive attitudes concerning home and family and be able to penetrate into the unconscious mind, using that insight to discover "the kingdom of heaven within." Pluto in this House can give that power as well as great insight into the needs of others.

Pluto in the 5th House   There can be a compulsive desire to be somebody important, to express one's individuality regardless of circumstances. This can lead to a ruthless risk-taking without concern for consequences such as in speculation, pleasure, love affairs, sports, life-or-death type adventures. Often these attempts to be best or be recognized are thwarted, leading to a reevaluation of *why* there is such a need to be important. The key to this position of Pluto is learning to express oneself through creativity, producing something unique instead of trying to *appear* unique. Close emotional relations with lovers or children can help the person to appraise himself and his true needs realistically, although the compulsive elements in such relations should be eliminated.

Pluto in the 6th House   Often a person with Pluto in this House has a compulsive desire to serve others but in that desire is a strong element of the reformer and not all people are appreciative of his efforts to improve them! There can be a deep interest in the healing of mind and body perhaps through research work. This placement of Pluto has much to do with collective bargaining in the labor field with the individual working for the betterment of work conditions. This position can lead to drugs and alcohol, weakness in the intestinal or elimination areas. Difficult aspects can lead to trouble with employees and fellow workers, poor work habits, resentment over real or fancied lack of appreciation for one's work. Matters concerning personal health or even one serious illness or accident can lead to great changes of attitude, perhaps directing the individual to serve in a more humble spirit, expending his energies on reforming himself rather than others. In some cases it may show an ability in the healing arts.

Pluto in the 7th House   With Pluto in this House, the person will find marriage and other close partnerships the best field in which to find his own regeneration. Similar to Pluto's position in the 1st House, relationships with others are very difficult and, therefore, are the very areas in which deep-seated attitudes and habits must be brought to the surface and faced. The individual may be compelled by an unconscious urge to seek the ideal mate or some unconventional union. Many marital adjustments are called for, with periods of intense loneliness due to lack of understanding with the partner. There is a high likelihood of divorce or of some great difficulty or crisis within marriage when everything that the person is attached to seems to be torn from him. Pluto can be agonizing in his effect because every shred of what we consider stable can be destroyed. Often there are compulsive and painful emotional problems in close relationships. The individual may want desperately to be loved, yet he is unable to establish a rapport with those who are a power in his life. Marriage requires deep-seated personal changes if it is to last. With Pluto in the 7th House, public exposure comes naturally with an intuitive sense of what the public wants or needs. Whether the relationship with the public benefits or harms depends on the rest of the chart and Pluto's aspects. This placement often means success in legal affairs and an enigmatic charisma.

Pluto in the 8th House When Pluto is placed in this House the person seeks to destroy within himself that which is negative, in order to rebuild the self on a higher level. Remember, it is the House of emotional values and often everything to which one is emotionally attached is destroyed or removed. Often there are difficult sexual experiences. It is a position that tends to evince a compulsive desire to influence others through the use of power of some nature—financial, authoritative, psychological, sexual, or occult. There may be a tendency to manipulate others and insist that others change themselves to conform to the individual's particular values. In fact, the often unconscious (and unreasonable) demands made by the person upon others is the fruitful source of much of his emotional frustration and trouble. Pluto is often found in the 8th House of mediums and occultists, research and laboratory workers, economists, and those who work for the reform of large groups or even a nation. Like those with Pluto in the 6th House, persons with Pluto in the 8th have a reforming zeal that is not always appreciated by those whom they have selected for reform. They would do better to let others be themselves and concentrate instead on self-reform. It often indicates a long life, success in legacies, and attracting the money of others. Death and the afterlife can fascinate and often through intuition, research, or actual experience the person will be able to transcend the limitations of the physical world, overcoming all fear of death in realization of the continuity of life. There is a need to totally adjust the use of all power in relationships.

Pluto in the 9th House   With this position there is a religious ardor that could shade into fanaticism. It can mean much spiritual expansion and involvement along philosophical, religious, and mystical lines. There is a certain adventuresome quality, a desire to explore new intellectual and religious fields. Expressed negatively, Pluto in the 9th can take the form of dogmatism and self-righteousness. Again, there is the necessity to attend to one's own reform and allow others to find their way of mental or religious expansion. There may be much travel to and involvement with foreign lands. There is an insatiable urge for learning and a need to communicate ideas and beliefs to a large scale audience rather than to a small group of friends. In the 9th, Pluto usually gives deep spiritual experiences in the latter part of life which can serve to transform the attitudes concerning religion and God.

Pluto in the 10th House   This position of Pluto strengthens the authority and energy of the individual resulting in head-on collisions with others who also have convictions of their own authority. One of the parents was probably too dominating, so in adult life there is a resentment of all those in authority and a compulsion to establish independence and power for oneself, plus a drive for worldly recognition. This can be the placement of an innovator, planner, government leader, or a dictator. There is usually a tenacious drive to attain the top and the person can often attain his goals but at a cost. There can be notoriety and many changes of career. The person is either loved or hated but never ignored. This position often gives leadership ability, magnetic attraction to and from the public, and speaking ability. The need is for total transformation of the person's attitudes and values concerning worldly success, authority, and status before the true creative power of Pluto in the 10th House can be expressed.

Pluto in the 11th House   Friends are very important to one with Pluto in the 11th House, so they may influence him too strongly. Often Pluto manifests here as an overpowering friend or the wrong kind of friends who pull him down. There is a compulsion to be accepted and loved by other people and, with certain aspects, there can be a ruthless behavior with friends that spoils the give-and-take of good friendships. With a positive expression of Pluto in 11th, the individual can be a joy and support to friends and humanity, active in altruistic group endeavors. (Many priests and doctors have their Plutos in 11th House.) Ideas about long-term goals are not consciously very clear and the present can be neglected because the interest is so fixed on the future. The real need for a person with Pluto in this position is to learn self-reliance, and they also need to learn that their ultimate desires can only be achieved through daily attention to the task of personal transformation.

Pluto in the 12th House   In this position, the "secret enemies" lie within the personal subconscious in a very real way. It can be called a karmic position—though everything is really karmic—pointing to a past life in which the individual avoided learning certain lessons or using a special talent. Pluto in the 12th House brings one face to face with temptations and previous failings. The person must transform the quality of his emotional life by adherence to some belief or transcendental truth in order to overcome the confusing miasma of emotions, feelings of guilt, and self-persecution which lurk within and destroy the soul's effective expression in the life. Often the re-orientation needed to effect that transformation will require long periods of solitude, for intercourse with others serves to stir up the old chaotic emotions and thought patterns that the individual is attempting to transcend. Once the person has established firm spiritual attitudes, uncovered and understood his frustrations and fears, he can experience the unity of all life without losing his balance. He may achieve this alone or with others.

The integral transformation of man was and is the goal of many esoteric systems; it goes under names such as initiation, individuation, and the "Great Work". Whether they consciously realize it or not, it is the goal of every man and woman who is striving to be a better person, live a more rewarding life, and be of some unselfish use to their fellows. Pluto's action brings into the consciousness the accumulation of psychological rubbish impeding progress toward that transformation. He marks our past which eventually has to be faced. In any House, the dynamic, regenerative power of Pluto can be drawn upon to provide the will power and impersonal consciousness necessary for transformation. Pluto's power only expresses in a negative form when we struggle to cling to outworn forms.

Aspects of Pluto

These have already been covered but a few observations might be helpful. The aspects involving Pluto are among the most difficult factors in the horoscope to understand because the astrologer never knows on what level they are going to manifest. It is a common misapprehension to think that the most important manifestations are on the objective, physical plane. Another common misapprehension is that the difficult aspects are "bad" and the so-called fortunate, easy aspects "good". Even from a materialistic point of view this is not invariably true. With the higher octave planets there is an even greater blurring of what is really fortunate or unfortunate. From the higher standpoint, of course, *all* things happen for the best to achieve our ultimate liberation from bondage to forms into the limitless power and love of the Spirit. It is Pluto who brings us to the point of total commitment to spiritual growth after flushing to the surface aspects of our old, unredeemed self. Pluto is the outermost planet, yet its action is within our most personal, secret depths.

Pluto Retrograde

Since Pluto is retrograde nearly half of the time, a very high percentage of the world's population has this configuration in their Natal horoscopes. These individuals will ultimately become more concerned with transforming themselves than trying to reform the people and world around them. The individual with a retrograde Pluto lives through a karma of experiencing mass consciousness within himself. There are few in this century of graphic television and instant news who do not feel, to some extent, the sufferings of the millions torn by war, oppression, concentration camps, and refugee status as a part of their own personal suffering. In time, and depending on the stage of spiritual evolution, a person with a retrograde Pluto feels the ills of society as a personal reason to transform himself to be of a greater help to suffering humanity.

NOTES

[1]H. P. Blavatsky, The Secret Doctrine, Vol. V (Adyar, India: Theosophical Publishing House, 1938), p. 222.

[2]Elman Bacher, Studies in Astrology, Vol. II (Oceanside, CA: Rosicrucian Fellowship, 1973), p. 57.

[3]The transits of Uranus, Neptune, and Pluto over sensitive points in the Natal chart are the most penetrating, far-reaching, and long-lasting (ultimate) effects of any transits.

[4]For one of the best explorations of this theme, using the charts of pioneering scientists, musicians, politicians, saints, etc., see R. C. Davidson, "The Disciples of Uranus, Neptune and Pluto", a two-part article in British quarterly, Astrology, Vol. 51, Fall and Winter, 1977 issues.

[5]Christopher Isherwood, Ramakrishna and His Disciples (N.Y.: Simon & Schuster, 1965).

[6]The shape of the Uranus symbol is often reproduced in the roof antennae of that very Uranian invention, the television set!

[7]For analysis of this joint rulership, see Chapter IX, pp. 105–6 and Chapter XI, p. 132.

[8]No astrologer can be certain in predicting the time of death. Many a person has survived the most ominous of configurations to confound the prognostigator! Even if one could be sure, most people do not welcome death and would brood about such a prediction so (unless the person and the circumstances are very unusual) I will never give more than a carefully worded warning to guard against ill-health or accident.

[9]This conjunction indicating a union of positive intuition and receptive mediumship was frequently found in the charts of those who were adult when the spiritualistic movement began after 1846. The last conjunction occurred about the time they were born around 1820. The next conjunction of the two planets will occur in 1991. Elman Bacher states that trines involving Uranus, regardless of the evolutionary status of the person, indicate he is in advance of his time, place and background.

[10]Uranus squared Pluto 1930-1935, and was conjunct Pluto 1965. The opposition between the two at the beginning of the 20th century characterized the generation born then. Uranus was in Sagittarius and Pluto in Gemini.

[11]Composer Cyril Scott in his book, The Occult Influence of Music Down the Ages, develops the theme that music—the power of organized sound—has been used by the Inner Government of the world to work on the emotional bodies of people in order to bring about desired changes and offset the less desirable features of the period in which they lived.

[12]See Chapter IX, pp. 105–6 and Chapter XI, p. 132.

[13]Annie Besant and C. W. Leadbeater, Talks on the Path of Occultism, Vol. III (Adyar, India: Theosophical Publishing House, 1965), p. 402.

[14]*See* Mouni Sadhu, *In Days of Great Peace* (London: George Allen & Unwin, 1957). The author gives a moving account of his experiences living in the ashram of Sri Ramana Maharshi as well as insight into the teachings and life of the saint.

[15]Pluto was named from the suggestion made by a small English girl, the first suggestion to be received and accepted.

[16]*See* Chapter IX, pages 105–6.

[17]Saturn is labelled the planet of *karma*. It does present karmic tests resulting from past evasion of responsibilities and self-discipline. Pluto in the individual chart reveals the habit patterns we carry over from the past which have to be eliminated at deeper levels of our being.

[18]Although Pluto has been "on the scene" for almost fifty years, it has taken time, experience and research for astrologers to comprehend that planet's effects and still longer to get their observations into print. To my thinking, there has been very little that is useful available to the student outside of a few articles in magazines and Stephen Arroyo's books so I am treating "Pluto in the Houses" at greater length.

[19]I remember the noted clairvoyant, Dora Kunz, describing the human aura in a lecture. She said that complexes, "hang-ups" and phobias show in the aura as congested blocks of matter, like warts on the etheric, emotional and lower mental bodies. The circulating flow of atoms through those bodies with its vitalizing, cleansing effect cannot penetrate those blockages but must circle around them. If the blockage is severe enough there can be a mental or physical breakdown.

[20]Pluto moves so slowly that he does not make many progressed aspects in a life time but the faster moving planets can make progressed aspects to Pluto.

XIII

ASCENDANT, MIDHEAVEN AND NODES

It is an extraordinary fact that very few astrological books give any information (or at least, very little that is useful), concerning those vital points in the horoscope—the Ascendant, the Midheaven and the Moon's Nodes.[1] The Ascendant is of primary importance to the way the entire personality is integrated and expressed. The Midheaven shows highest projection of the personality in the outer world and answers the question, "What am I going to do in this life; what is my destiny?"

The Ascendant, or Rising Sign,[2] constitutes the "window" through which the individual views life, as well as the "persona" or mask that the soul is wearing for this incarnation, the image which is seen by others. That image may not be an accurate portrayal of the real Self, but it is the one which comes across most vividly to other people. It shows the way in which the person is most sensitive and aware, the way in which he must express himself to feel spontaneous, whole, and *alive*.

The Ascendant is intimately related to the physical body, which is why progressions and transits to the Ascendant have such a marked effect upon the general health, vitality, and appearance. The body, from birth to death, constitutes the individual's most immediate physical environment, through which all impressions from the outer world are filtered. The Ascendant reveals the way in which a person feels himself to be a unique "I".

To understand the full importance of the Ascendant in any horoscope, it is necessary to consider more than just the degree and Sign on the horizon at birth, along with the 1st House. Of first importance is any planet within 6 degrees preceding or following the Ascendant degree, especially the 6 degrees above the Ascendant (in the 12th House). Next in importance are any other planets in the 1st House, the planet ruling the Ascending Sign, the House, and Sign in which it is placed, and aspects to the Ascendant degree from planets elsewhere in the chart. All of these factors modify or accentuate the qualities of the Ascendant.

Planets near the Ascendant

Any planet in conjunction with the Ascendant degree brings to unusual prominence that planet's particular qualities in the personality and life of the person. The **Sun** conjunct the Ascendant often brings an arrogance and self-centeredness, but also a vitality and the ability for leadership. **Moon** conjunct the Ascendant makes one motherly, sensitive, and often changeable. With **Mercury** there, you usually find a strong emphasis on learning and intellectual abilities, worry (fussing over every little problem), a quick wit, and ease in communication. **Venus** nearly always gives charm and an attractive appearance unless there are contradictory factors elsewhere.[3] **Mars** conjunct the Ascendant marks the natural leader with an unusual degree of courage. (Joy Mills has Mars 3 degrees above her Ascendant). It can, of course, make for a very hot-tempered, impulsive, aggressive individual!

Jupiter conjunct the Ascendant gives a generosity of mind and emotion. Individuals with this placement always have a good opinion of themselves, but if Jupiter is afflicted there can be false pride, arrogance, and pretension. **Saturn** can give wisdom, practicality, and a capacity for good timing. In my experience I have nearly always found that this position tends to much shyness and feelings of loneliness and inferiority especially in youth. Certainly, the person is always more serious than the average person and can have periods of emotional depression.

Uranus on the Ascendant gives a restlessness, an eagerness to try the unorthodox, the unconventional, the new, and different. A prominent Uranus makes for willfulness; such people are often a law unto themselves, rebelling against authority or what seems to them outmoded. **Neptune** gives charisma—a real magnetism, often beauty of person, refinement (or perversity), and sensitivity. There can be too much sensitivity, both physically and emotionally, so that things which constitute mere petty irritation to most people, can make someone with Neptune on the Ascendant really ill. With **Pluto** on the Ascendant, the personality expression would resemble that of Scorpio rising—moody, reflective, and intense.[4]

Any planet on the Ascendant, either in the Natal chart, or by transit or progression shows that the individual is becoming intensely aware of that planet's particular principle as it manifests under universal law. A planet in the 1st House (or in the 6 degrees above the Ascendant) is a much more concentrated focus of energy than is a Sign and it can overshadow the influence of the Ascending Sign. For example, Jupiter near the Ascendant can give the impression that Sagittarius is the Sign rising. If it is Sagittarius rising, then a double emphasis is given to Jupiter/Sagittarius qualities. Sometimes the planet will be close to the Ascendant degree but in a different Sign. This is conducive to a more complex personality and approach to life. Every planet in the 1st House, whether conjunct the Ascendant or not, adds another dimension to the personality. Many planets in the 1st House can make for a very strong and complex personality, or a very confused one, if the planets are expressing contradictory qualities and/or if the rest of the chart is weak.

Ruler of the Ascendant

The planet ruling the Sign on the Ascendant, and its House and Sign position are extremely important factors in any horoscope. Aspects to that planet are also very important, being on a par with aspects involving the Sun, Moon, or Ascendant. An example of the modification the ruling planet of the Ascendant can make: a client had Aries rising with Sun in the 1st House. One would therefore look for a very dynamic, aggressive person. But her Mars (ruler of Aries) was placed in Pisces, considerably softening her personality and approach to life.

Aspects

Aspects to the Ascendant show how one characteristically expresses oneself in the outer world.

Sextiles and **trines** show avenues of easy, spontaneous expression in the things of the House (or Houses) ruled by the aspecting planet and also the things of the House in which that planet is placed; the energies of that planet express harmoniously in concert with the qualities of the Ascendant.

The **squares** and **oppositions** express with tension, stress, inhibition, or difficulty those things ruled by the aspecting planet and the House in which it is placed or ruled by Sign. However, difficult aspects can provide ambition or a drive which the softer aspects rarely give. Most of us are not inclined to strive very hard unless we are urged on by difficult circumstances or an inner discontent! .

The **square** to the Ascendant often manifests as some kind of oppression or inhibition in the early environment, especially when the aspecting planet is in the 4th House. There may be an unusually strong pressure toward achieving recognition or success in a career if the aspecting planet is placed in the 10th House. The 4th House type of square often shows emotional patterns that hold one back from expressing the qualities of the Ascendant, while the 10th House square pulls one toward some kind of achievement.

An **opposition** to the Ascendant often means an inner division or tension because the individual is torn between two modes of conduct or two equally desirable objectives. Sometimes the person will alternate for years between the two types of expression or objectives emphasizing first one and then the other.

The Midheaven

This significant point in the horoscope is usually called the M.C. (Medium Coeli) and is the zenith or meridian which is immediately overhead at the moment of birth. The M.C. degree and Sign, the ruler of that Sign and any planets in the 10th House and in the last 6 degrees of the 9th House before the M.C.: all these factors constitute a magnet toward which the individual grows as he gets older. It is the magnet of capabilities, qualities, and levels of achievement that the person admires and works hard to develop and attain. For example, Taurus on the M.C. may show that he admires reliability, patience, trustworthiness, and he works to exhibit these characteristics to the world. He also values security and seeks a career that will bring him solid and steady advancement. The planet ruling the Midheaven Sign often shows, by its House position, where the person's true vocation lies. The word "vocation" means literally "that toward which one is called". All the 10th House factors are closely related to your "calling" in life, the meaningful work, ambitions, and attainments of this incarnation.

Planets Near the M.C.

The planets in the 10th House, and especially those conjunct the M.C. in either the 10th or 9th Houses, show the qualities, activities, and achievements that are extremely important to the individual and which that individual desires to express in such a way that his reputation will be enhanced. This is why the M.C. and related factors are so often connected with honor, fame, reputation, or the opposite, if there are very difficult configurations. For example, in Anne's chart (Chapter XI) Saturn is conjunct the M.C. though still in the 9th House. One of her strongest ideals was to be like a rock of support and stability to those about her, a typically Saturnian quality.

Both Robert K. (Chapter IX) and Joy Mills (Chapter X) have the **Sun** conjunct the Midheaven. Robert's Sun is in the 10th House and he always wanted to be the "boss". Joy's Sun is in the 9th House, four degrees from the M.C. and her ideal is to be a person who can give spiritual leadership. Both of them are expressing Sun qualities in their careers in different ways. The Sun in the 10th nearly always brings that person to a position of some kind of authority or into dealings with government, heads of state, leaders, etc. The affairs of the House which has Leo on its cusp will be brought into connection with the business, profession, or whatever constitutes the person's life or career in the outer world.

The **Moon** in the 10th House or conjunct the M.C. often gives a life lived very much in the public eye. This can mean fame or notoriety, for whatever the person does will receive the limelight. There is great sensitivity to the opinions of others.

If **Mercury** is in the 10th or conjunct the M.C. the career is often in one of the communication fields. Virgo on the M.C. or Mercury therein also attracts men as well as women into secretarial and clerical work. Education is important and knowledge respected.

With **Venus** in the 10th, beauty, charm, artistic and esthetic expression are important and the person is attracted to a career in which those things are an integral part (such as cosmetics, fashion, art, etc.) or in which the surroundings are harmonious and attractive.

Mars in the 10th nearly always brings achievement—it is called "the planet of success," most likely because of the work and energy earns achievement of material goals. There is always a degree of struggle and strife in the career.

Jupiter in the 10th is an excellent indication for success in the affairs of the world, in business, professions, politics, or society. The person admires the qualities of benevolence, openhandedness. If afflicted, there can be financial difficulties through over-expansion, over-optimism and lack of careful forethought and planning.

Saturn in the 10th is frequently an indication of success in the career though success often comes late after much hard work and disappointment. There is a serious application to the business of getting ahead and often shouldering of heavy responsibilities.

Uranus in the 10th gives the urge to be independent or at least be independent-minded. It often denotes a career in government. I have two friends with Uranus in the 10th with very different careers. One has been in the fashion business most of her life, for many years the head of a firm. The other is a high government official. This emphasizes the fact that the planet or Sign in the 10th House or M.C. can indicate the kind of vocation or it can indicate the qualities that enabled that person to achieve success or attracted him into that particular vocation. Certainly, in the cases mentioned, Uranus gave an independence and intuitive sense of what will "sell," qualities needed in fashion as well as government life.

Neptune in 10th can give a charisma that attracts people so that it can bring a position of inspirational or artistic leadership. Idealism concerning career is strong but often there is much illusion concerning one's importance. I have had a number of horoscopes where the people with Neptune in 10th grew increasingly divorced from reality; just plain nutty, in fact! Much depends on the rest of the chart.

If **Pluto** is in the 10th House, it is important to the person to be powerful and wield authority and influence. This can be either good or bad depending on the use made of the power once it is achieved. Each planet in the 10th House (or near the M.C. in the 9th House) will be connected to the Sign and House it rules, wherever they are placed in the chart. For example, if Neptune is posited in the 10th House and Pisces is on the Cusp of the 5th House, then the affairs of the 5th House will be brought into connection with the career.

Aspects to M.C.

The aspects made to planets in the 10th House or to the M.C. influence the person's public expression, vocational goals and recognition from the outer world. The precise type of aspect, whether harmonious or difficult seems to be less important than the qualities and urges of the planet making the aspect. Conjunctions and aspects involving the Midheaven are extremely important for they are intimately connected with the *purpose* of the individual's incarnation. We take on physical, emotional and mental bodies life after life in order to grow personally in character and evolve spiritually but also in order to contribute our bit to society, and to that universal entity "in which we live and move and have our being".

☊　Nodes　☋

Astronomically, the Moon's Nodes[5] are the two points at which the Moon's orbit intersects the plane of the ecliptic (the Sun's apparent orbit or path around the Earth) as it goes from North to South latitude, and vice versa. The North Node is the one given in the Ephemeris, called the "Dragon's Head" and is traditionally given a nature similar to that of Jupiter. The South Node or "Dragon's Tail" is exactly opposite and is considered of a nature similar to Saturn. The Nodal axis (the line from Node to Node across the horoscope) shows the direction of one's destiny.
THE NORTH NODE indicates a new learning; where you are going; what you are going to develop and carry on with you.
THE SOUTH NODE shows what is instinctive and well-known because it is rooted in past life patterns.

The thing to remember is that *both* Nodes are valuable. Like two ends of a bridge, both are necessary to the traveler crossing it. The South Node shows what we have brought with us into this incarnation, the instinctive habit patterns which must be understood; to be changed if negative, or utilized to the full if positive. The North Node is our destination, pulling us forward into new patterns of learning and growth.

In interpretation of the Nodes, four factors are considered: the Signs and Houses in which the Nodes are posited, aspects to the Nodes (especially the conjunctions), the planets ruling the Nodal Signs, and their aspects, especially their relationship with each other. For example, if the North Node is in Aries and South Node in Libra, the aspect between Mars and Venus should be considered.[6]

☊ ♈ **North Node in Aries or 1st House** Learning to stand on one's own two feet, must become more assertive. Life will seem to force one constantly into situations where the person must rely on his own judgment and act on his own initiative.

☋ ♎ **South Node in Libra or 7th House** Brought over from the past diplomatic talents and appreciation of the arts. Partnerships and unions tend to become too involved and overwhelming so that the individuality may be eclipsed. There is overidealization of the marriage partner so that dissatisfaction eventually results.

North Node in Libra or 7th House Learning to experience the "We" consciousness, cooperation. Must overcome the tendency to work by one's self, develop the ability for close personal relationships with others. Once the balance is achieved, the person can become an able diplomat or arbitrator; needs to develop an appreciation of the arts.

☋ ♈ **South Node in Aries or 1st House** Egotistical habit patterns which can give a strong pioneering spirit but with a "me first" attitude. The problems in life are much concerned with the personal self. Look to the rulers of Aries and Libra, if Mars and Venus are in harmonious relationship, the individual will be able to get along with others. If the planets are in difficult aspect; inharmony and lack of cooperation.

☊ ♉ **North Node in Taurus or 2nd House** Things in Fixed Signs always seem to be more of a crisis. Learning to accept life and beauty, looking upon things of Earth as a cornucopia. This position gives the problem of earning and managing resources for oneself rather than depending upon others. There is a need to develop practicality, physical endurance and perseverance. There will be changes in values, money and possessions.

☋ ♏ **South Node in Scorpio or 8th House** Habit patterns of past turbulence, revolution. Difficulty in accepting love and life and perhaps in accepting money from others. Instinctive fear that things are not going to go as planned. A natural talent for the occult arts, a desire for knowledge of the hereafter. There is usually no fear of death and death seems to play an important part as a regenerative force in the life. Often a preoccupation with sexual knowledge and prowess.

☊ ♏ **North Node in Scorpio or 8th House** Fundamental, dynamic changes are to be made in this life. At some point the individual will be forced to learn to accept help from others, even the humility of accepting financial aid. There is a need to learn the rightful and beautiful purpose of sex.

☋ ♉ **South Node in Taurus or 2nd House** Brought over from the past a tendency not to listen. Determination is a keynote with this position. Dissatisfaction with money earned or working conditions which may give many changes in jobs or holding down more than one job at the same time. The drive for financial security can lead to financial difficulties, success in that area is usually delayed. A need to learn balance and control of the sensual appetites. Look to the Sign rulers, Venus and Pluto (ruling the opposite end of the nodal axis) for a stressful aspect can mean a battle over possessions.

☊ ♊ **North Node in Gemini or 3rd House** This is a position of one who is naturally attracted to and finds more fulfillment in city living in spite of, or because of, the previous life in a country environment. Learning to communicate effectively—it is difficult for this individual to express his deepest feelings, but he can only find true fulfillment when he learns to participate freely in a give-and-take relationship with others.

☋ ♐ **South Node in Sagittarius or 9th House** Habit patterns from the past of freedom loving, the "wide open spaces" of mental and physical living. This is the Nodal position of one who was in the past a "country person". There is much instinctive knowledge and a wanting to know "why". Religious karma from the past, which will be shown by the aspects of the Sign rulers, Jupiter and Mercury (ruler of the opposite end of the axis).

☊ ♐ **North Node in Sagittarius or 9th House** The goal in this life is to see what is true. Higher education and beneficial travel aid in this search. Religious karma surfacing in this life forces the person to develop a greater regard for religion and ethics. Learning to become more objective in one's thinking and studying in order to expand mentally and spiritually.

☋ ♊ **South Node in Gemini or 3rd House** Habit patterns from the past of great curiosity and emphasis on the development of conscious mind. There is a strong psychic tie to brothers and sisters and could mean the loss of one of them through death or separation. There is a strong urge to share knowledge with others. Difficulty in elementary education, much impatience, and difficulty with neighbors.

♌ ♋ **North Node in Cancer or 4th House** Learning through emotional experiences, opening up oneself in order to break up old emotional patterns. The home and domestic relationships are very important to spiritual growth. There may be a problem with a parent either through greater love for one than the other, or losing one parent at an early age.

☋ ♑ **South Node in Capricorn or 10th House** Rigid emotional patterns from the past often making the person in this life "a law unto himself". These people seem old even as children. They do not take time to relate on a personal basis because of a need for public recognition. It can bring many changes, disappointment and dissatisfaction in regard to the vocation. For the aspirant the great lesson in this life will be the control of selfish desire and use of ambition and power.

♌ ♑ **North Node in Capricorn or 10th House** Learning to grow up, to face life as a mature person, work with the public in some way. Sometimes home and domestic life is sacrificed in order to follow a career. The Sign on the 10th, (if the North Node is in the 10th House but in another Sign than Capricorn) the rulers of the Nodal Signs and aspects to those planets and to the North Node will show the area of sacrifice as well as indicating the type of career.

☋ ♋ **South Node in Cancer or 4th House** Emotional family patterns from the past. Fear of failure or fear of failing to get to the top generally due to a stress pattern between career and family expectations. Many changes in residence with a deep desire for a secluded, subjective life.

♌ ♌ **North Node in Leo or 5th House** Learning to open up one's heart, to take personal responsibility. There is a need to learn to love intensely on a one-to-one basis. A deficiency or delay regarding children in the life (the children can be physical or creative offspring). Leo and the 5th House are the areas that show the ability to give love and with the North Node here, the person must learn how to love.

☋ ♒ **South Node in Aquarius or 11th House** Eccentric habit patterns brought over from the past, the person can operate well on a group level but not on a personal level. It is a position of unattached love—too detached. Friendships, group relationships, altruistic movements and utopian concepts for humanity are prominent in the life of a person with South Node here. But he needs a truly intense love affair to fulfill the need for a better balance in the love nature.

♌ ♒ **North Node in Aquarius or 11th House**   Learning to use the mind in a scientific, mental way. Learning to develop group identification in order to act less like "King Leo" looking upon others as his subjects. The type of friends chosen is of great importance. Someone with North Node in the 11th House will be helped greatly by another with their South Node in the 11th. There is a need to learn the art of friendship and people who have the same nodal axis bridging the 5th and 11th by House and/or Sign, seem to understand each other and therefore can be of mutual help.

☋ ♌ **South Node in Leo or 5th House**   A person with this nodal position is used to operating from the heart level, everything is very personal. He is used to having his work or his way taken without question. There is an almost constant interest in love and its pleasures, and loves that are always changing with the result that a permanent love relationship is often delayed. There is an immaturity about this constant searching for romance and pleasure and the person will not know real love until he is able to give it selflessly.

♌ ♍ **North Node in Virgo or the 6th House**   Learning to make manifest one's dreams, learning to be more practical. The individual must learn to work for others, be of service to them without self-interest. He must develop discrimination and care in details. Health matters should receive adequate attention.

☋ ♓ **South Node in Pisces or the 12th House**   Habit patterns brought over that make the person feel as if he had come out of nowhere and that everything was going to evaporate, nothing is solid and dependable. There is a tendency toward escapism in some form. For example, if the ruler of Pisces, Neptune, is placed in Virgo, work may become the escape. There is often such a sensitivity to pain that he may not be able to deal with it. Psychic ability or some unusual talent.

♌ ♓ **North Node in Pisces or 12th House**   Learning to open up and become more of a listener, more sympathetic. Developing faith instead of reacting to everything with doubt and analysis. Learning to trust the intuition. This position of North Node takes self-sacrifice. It means helping those less fortunate in a quiet, unassuming way, learning to accept others just as they are. This is a position of karma which seems to call for payment, which may explain the many doctors and nurses who have the North Node here (as well as those with S. Node in Pisces) and have instinctively chosen work with the sick and suffering as a means of meeting that karma.

☊ ♍ **South Node in Virgo or 6th House**   In the past the individual criticized those who were ill and in trouble, telling them analytically why they suffered. In part this is because the person has an instinctive knowledge on health matters and a drive to learn more concerning the subject. There can be mysterious illnesses, which are difficult to diagnose or treat. Sometimes the person can become a hypochondriac. Many doctors and nurses have South Node in the 6th House. There is a strong tendency to take everything apart, to doubt and criticize.

Nodal Aspects

A planet conjunct or in aspect to the South Node will stimulate the past habit patterns with its characteristic planetary energies. With the North Node the qualities we most admire and strive to develop will be stimulated. And of course the things ruled by the particular House and Sign in which the Node and planet are posited. For example, if Mercury squares or conjuncts the South Node, it ends to stimulate excessive criticism and lack of tact but it can also act as a challenge, spurring the person on to greater mental achievement. The Moon conjunct the North Node can give a physical beauty and a sensitive personality which meets favor with women and the public. When a planet is in conjunction with the South Node, a lot of energy goes to that area unless the North Node is also conjunct a planet. In which case the energy is equally distributed so that neither planet nor House is the sole focus. A man carrying a heavy load divided on either side would find the weight bearable but if he tried to carry it all on one side, he would hardly be able to stagger a few steps! In Anne's chart (Chapter XI) Pluto is conjunct South Node in opposition to Venus conjunct the North Node. There have been great difficulties at times with financial resources, the affections, sex, death, and self-reform, but nothing that she felt unable to handle.

North Node conjunct the Ascendant usually gives a tall, attractive appearance and charm. It is supposed to be especially favorable for a man's good looks. Conjunct the Midheaven, there can be delays in finding the vocation until after the age of thirty.

South Node conjunct the Ascendant often causes uncertainty as to identity, who you are and what sort of personality you are. My feeling about the reason for this is that the identification with the past life is still so strong that the person feels confused wearing a new personality in this life. Sometimes there is something unusual about the appearance, the person may be very short or very tall.

Life development often starts off on a path connected with the South Node position and later develops and fulfills itself through the North Node position. Under stress we may revert to the South Node habit patterns. An example could be given of Janis Joplin, the singer who apparently died of an overdose of drugs. When she couldn't cope with her North Node in Leo (learning to take personal responsibility, learning how to love on a one-to-one basis) she reverted to her South Node in Aquarius saying in effect, "I'm just one of the group".

NOTES

[1]See Stephen Arroyo, *Astrology, Karma and Transformation: The Inner Dimensions of the Birthchart* (Vancouver, Washington: CRCS Publications, 1978), Chapter 10.

[2]The Ascendant in astrological parlance can mean the Sign on the cusp of the 1st House, the whole 1st House with all the planets if any within it, or the exact degree on the horizon at birth.

[3]John Coats, international president of The Theosophical Society, has Venus exactly conjunct his Ascendant degree and has both extraordinary charm and good looks.

[4]Read the chapters on the planets and Signs to obtain a full understanding of their qualities and then apply them to the personality.

[5]I am indebted to Mr. David Railey of Atlanta for first demonstrating to me in his excellent American Federation of Astrologers lecture, how important and usable the Moon's Nodes were in horoscope interpretation.

[6]This is not the book to go into great detail on the Nodes. For that, see Bernice Prill Grebner, *Lunar Nodes* (Tempe, Ariz.: American Federation of Astrologers, 1976), and Isobel Hickey, *Astrology: A Cosmic Science* (Bridgeport, Conn.: Altieri Press, 1970). Marc Edmund Jones and Dane Rudhyar have also written on the Nodes.

XIV

DOORS TO THE SOUL: THE USE OF INTUITION

Each Sign, House, planet, and aspect contains many meanings. The combinations, with their myriad subtleties of application in each horoscope, can be very confusing to the student. On top of that, it is very difficult to know the level of evolution on which the owner of a particular horoscope stands. A man of genius and a primitive savage may share the same time of birth: it is the consciousness and level of evolution that makes the difference. The interpretation that would be helpful to one would be meaningless to the other.

Every astrologer, sooner or later, has to work out some kind of solution to these problems according to his background, abilities and psychological predisposition.[1] There are astrologers who base all their interpretations on the traditional Astrology handed down through the centuries and on the results of research now being done all over the world. Then there are some who have a knowledge of Astrology but use the horoscope more as a point of focus, like a crystal ball. Their Astrology, therefore, is only as good as their psychic powers. Most astrologers of any stature, I believe, use tradition, study, research, and experience *plus* their intuition (or ESP) to pull the many, and sometimes contradictory, factors in a chart into a meaningful whole.

It is only after a careful study of all the factors in a chart, drawing on her sound astrological background, that British astrologer Rose Elliott tries to contact the "ego or spirit" behind the chart.[2] She first describes herself as beginning to think and feel in the manner of the person whose chart she is doing. The identification—the empathy—is so close that in doing one chart she relates she felt a great fear of death; in another, she felt a great urge to get into the country and among trees.

She related how, by getting into a chart in this way, one instinctively knows or feels how a certain planetary aspect will become externalized. In a particular case, a Moon conjunction with Neptune in Virgo had brought out irrational fears during childhood which no one understood and had called silly. The child had felt hurt and puzzlement and Rose Elliott was able to relive these emotions through her contact with the chart.

Mrs. Elliott tells of concentrating on the center of the chart, as one would with a mandala. The center becomes a golden orb and she begins to feel as if she is *inside* the chart, standing in that center, with all the planetary forces playing around her like the rays of the sun. These rays are brilliantly hued, of many colors, which blend and interweave—the color of a planetary ray blending with or tinted by the Sign through which it is working. Centered in this way, she sees the twelve sections of the chart around her as different colors; for instance, Aries is red, Cancer a greyish-blue, and Leo is gold.

As she reaches a certain point of transcendence the central golden orb where she stands seems to open out and she finds herself in a corridor. This corridor represents time. The point at which she stands represents the present in the life of the subject. From this "present" point she can look back down the corridor into the past, and forward into the future. She can also see rooms which open off the corridor and light up, allowing her to see within them. She relates that as she peers into these lighted rooms she sees pictures, like a cinema portraying incidents in the past—perhaps in this life, perhaps in a past life—and certain incidents in the future. These always have a bearing on the chart and, she feels, are shown her only if it will help her client to understand more about himself and the reasons for certain karma in this life.

Of the several interesting cases Mrs. Elliot related (see Chapter VII, p. 80) one involved the chart of a man who had practically no Saturnian influence in his chart except for one very difficult aspect. He was, from a worldly point of view, a failure; could stick to nothing, with no will power to make anything of his considerable mental gifts. This did not worry him for he was quite happy drifting through life. It was not he but his mother who consulted Mrs. Elliot. She was a strongly Capricornian woman, with some Aries, determined, ambitious, and desperately disappointed that her son was such a failure.

"I was shown a picture of a brother and sister ruling in Egypt; she completely dominated him, making him do what she wanted. Then another picture of a rich woman in Rome forcing her son, who was connected with the legal profession, to carry out her wishes almost like a puppet. It seemed that because she had dominated him in at least two previous lives, in this life she had produced a weak man, with no will power and has to suffer agonies to her pride and ambition because he is no credit to her and not like the sons of her friends."

Another friend, who is both a psychic and astrologer, says that she often sees the line from the Midheaven to the Nadir as an electric blue line which runs through the person's aura, with the degree and Sign of the Midheaven on top. A gift that many astrologers wish they had when it comes to rectifying uncertain birth times! It also suggests that our horoscopes may be literally as well as symbolically a part of our being. She also sees the symbol of the dominant planet over a person's head.

My own method of "going through the horoscope" to make contact with the Soul may differ from that of Mrs. Elliot. I see the birth chart as a mandala expressing symbolically the character of the Soul's will to incarnate, the kind of personality, environment, experiences, and crises which that spiritual entity needs in order to become a mature, integrated, and creative being on earth as well as on the higher planes.

The birth chart only shows what kind of a human being the person *can* become, it does not tell whether this person will fulfill the potentialities. So I ask myself, "What is the Soul trying to accomplish in this incarnation?" The present is always rooted in the past (while it is being drawn to the future) so, after carefully studying the whole chart I meditate upon those factors I feel tell most about the past—the 12th House Sign and planets and the major configurations in the chart. Usually, by that time I have developed a close identification with the person whose chart I am doing.

No matter how dull or superficial or unlovable I may have thought him to be at the beginning, at this point I can only think of him as an endlessly fascinating and infinitely lovable being. I *will* myself to enter the horoscope and open up to whatever the Soul within and behind this personality can communicate to me. Perhaps it is only my own Soul or Higher Self that I hear, or perhaps it is our Souls speaking to one another, it hardly matters. All separation is only an illusion, separation between entities whatever their level and separation between past, present, and future. I could not enter into a horoscope to any depth until I

could get past the illusion that there was a wall between individuals and between past, present, and future that only rare and
spasmodic intuitions or psychic experiences could pierce. What
happens next is usually a vivid unrolling of certain past scenes,
personalities, and relationships. Like Rose Elliot, I feel I am only
shown those fragments of the past that have relation to the
present life and knowledge which will be of help to the person
whose chart I am reading.

A natural question would be, "How do you know this is not
just your imagination spinning romantic pictures?" The answer
is that I do *not* know, for verification is usually impossible.
Being an artist, my powers of visualization are perhaps more
developed than the average person's[3] and my imagination more
trained by my daily work. There is a convincing reality about
these insights which, incidentally, are rarely very exciting. Usually just the ordinary stuff that makes up most lives.[4] Nevertheless, I keep my Astrology "straight" and am always careful to tell
my clients to accept my impression of past lives only if it "rings a
bell inwardly" with them and if it proves helpful in explaining
present life relationships and difficulties.[5]

Having been a commercial artist for most of my working life, it
is natural for me to use art in interpretation. Meditating over a
chart I will take paper and some easy medium like colored pens
and watercolors and put down the symbols and scenes that come
before my inner eye. To give an example, I did the chart of a
friend with a Grand Trine in Water Signs: Pluto in Cancer conjunct the 4th House Cusp, Mercury and Venus in Scorpio and all
of them in close trine to the cusp of the 12th House. Meditating
over this configuration, I saw a semi-circle of white Grecian
pillars around a pool of water. It was night and the water reflected the stars so perfectly that the night sky and stars seemed
to be in the water below as well as above. I sent the sketch to her,
not knowing what if anything it would mean to her. She wrote
me that it was a scene she saw in her dreams repeatedly, and
went on to tell me that in her youth she had been nearly blind but
not until her eleventh year was notice taken of her handicap. The
night of the first day when she acquired glasses, her family
found her lying on her back in the garden just staring at the stars.

"To this day I have never lost the wonder and thrill I felt that
night. Most of my life I have been accused of walking around
with my head in the stars and your picture reminds me that the

stars and all they stand for not only circle my head but also are mirrored in my soul".

Another example of what someone termed my "visual horoscopes" involved the chart of a friend who had the Sun conjunct the Moon in Leo in the 4th House. This brought to me a picture of a woman in blue robes nursing a babe with hundreds of little hands reaching up to her. Beside her stood a Roman warrior sword in hand, all in fiery gold, bearing a round shield with tiny flames carved in circles on its surface. Behind and between the two figures was an arch through which the Sign Aquarius could be seen. My feeling was that her task in this life was to harmonize the masculine and feminine polarities within herself during this life in order to form the right base for her next life's work.

Quite different was the picture gained from the chart of a middle-aged, unmarried principal of a large school, a very brisk, no-nonsense sort of woman. The 12th House contained the South Node, Mercury, Saturn, and Venus intercepted in the Sign Taurus with Aries on the cusp.[6] Meditating upon these factors, I found myself thinking about the Earth and all its beauties. No artists have captured this better than the Chinese and Japanese and I found myself painting a picture in the Japanese style with craggy mountains, clouds and water. One mountain was particularly prominent with a cave high up on its face. Before the cave sat a hermit in meditation. Near his feet a waterfall broke out and fell in a silvery-white ribbon to the land at the foot of the mountain. My feeling was that from the hermit came the water of spiritual nourishment. The masses of brilliant flowers that grew below the mountain, watered by the waterfall, symbolized beauty and its appreciation which this lady needed. I mailed off the picture with the horoscope reading, thinking I would surely get a snorting reply taking me to task for associating her with such an incongruous symbology. However, to my surprise, she replied that she had been told (and felt it to be true) that her Master was a Japanese. She loved all things Japanese and was at that moment taking a class in Japanese flower arrangement.

One picture that came to me was definitely rejected by a friend who said it didn't make sense at all. The ruler of her 12th House was Scorpio. Pluto (ruler of the 12th House) was conjunct Mercury in Cancer in close trine to Uranus in Pisces, sextile Saturn in Virgo. Uranus was posited in the 3rd House, in exact opposition to Saturn in the 9th House. Her Ascendant's ruler, Jupiter, was conjunct Neptune in the 8th House squared by Moon in the 4th. This lady was young, very beautiful, and happily married to a prosperous husband. The picture I got was in the form of a warning: a Central American-type pyramid with a small temple on top submerged under the water. Water always means emotion to me and the strong emphasis in Water Signs, her ruler conjunct that watery planet Neptune in the House of death and Uranus in Pisces exactly opposed to Saturn, in the two Houses ruling the mind suggested to me that without mental control and discrimination, her emotions and illusions might sweep her to disaster. Within two years she was divorced and went to live with a cult that seemed to be a combination of pseudo-occultism and old-time revivalist emotion. She became ill but was given no medical attention because the leaders of the commune told her her sickness was caused by a curse put on her by an enemy which could only be removed by prayer. She died in a short time of a massive cerebral hemorrhage.

Making objective the whisperings of the subconscious or super-conscious is used quite often by mental patients and children in drawings and paintings. Actually *all* art is just that: the expression of the inner Self in some form. When it comes to Astrology there is such a wide range of expression to any planetary symbolism that it becomes a challenge to the creative imagination and the creative imagination is the magic key that can transform the horoscope interpretation.

What is our highest good? It is quite probable that it is different from the material things that most of us picture as good. The Cosmos may function within a different scale of values and with different priorities than are common to humanity. The average person's relationship to the Cosmos and to his own evolution is largely passive, involving a slow and uncertain course. But we can, by changing our attitudes and efforts, raise the relationship to another level where cooperation with both is the rule.

It has been said that originally each soul came forth from "the bosom of the Father" through one of the twelve Signs of the Zodiac. Sparks of the One Flame sent forth to attain perfection on all the seven planes, returning in the fullness of time to the Door from which they first issued. I do not think this necessarily means the particular Ascendant or Sun Sign under which we were born in this life, for surely we must experience the qualities of all twelve Signs to become whole human beings. And there are new factors aiding spiritual evolution.

Uranus, Neptune, and Pluto, the higher octave planets, were always in the heavens though unknown, their transforming energies absorbed and put to use by only a few. Their discovery during the last 200 years is very significant. I believe it means that all humanity, not just a few rare leaders, is able for the first time to make *conscious* use of those planetary energies in its psychological and spiritual life. More individuals will have the capacity to absorb, assimilate, and then release the vital zodiacal energies particularly emphasized at their birth.

The Natal horoscope holds the blueprint for this incarnation. We can use it to try to get what we want emotionally and materially, or we can go deeper into it by seeking to fulfill the spiritual potentialities sketched in the chart. By consciously aligning our will with those cosmic energies pouring through the Signs and planets, it is possible to raise our level of being. The change automatically reflects in outer circumstances—the people and events that are drawn to us. The energies known by the names of the planets and Signs create disharmony only when harmonious expression is denied them so if we work *with* those energies, expressing as far as possible their spiritual qualities, then our whole life and character can only be transformed, our true destiny fulfilled.

We may not be free to choose all of our circumstances, for this is where karma operates in the form of environmental conditions and unconscious inner pressures. But we are free to give positive or negative *meaning* to our experiences. Unless we understand our path and the tasks that are appropriate to our essential nature, we may waste our lives pursuing inferior goals. If we are earnest students, no lesson ever comes to us in vain and no lesson ever leaves us where it finds us. This is the purpose of transpersonal Astrology, which should expand our awareness and assist us towards psychological maturity and spiritual transformation. Surely, these are the goals most worthy of attainment!

What is our horoscope trying to tell us of things left undone or badly done in the past which now must be rectified? Or what does show about the good qualities, talents, and other skills which can be built upon in order to make us even more useful to others and ourselves? Can we find what it tells us of the relationships that need refinement, understanding, or strength so that we may shed old, debilitating emotions and walk freely in loving companionship in future lives? We should not only interpret the stars, we should interpret the events that come to us. Sometimes it may take a lapse of months or years to evaluate the dimensions of an experience, but as we identify increasingly with our higher Self, our Soul, our vision will be closer to truth, thus accelerating our progress toward that glorious day when we will become more than human.

NOTES

[1]Before a psychologist can practice his profession, he must go through personal analysis by a qualified analyst. One reason for this requirement is so that he will be aware of the areas in his character that would lead to over-reaction or bias involving some of his patients. Likewise, an astrologer should recognize the elements in his chart that could give rise to antagonism or lack of understanding with certain clients. Some astrologers have a prejudice against certain Signs. For example, an astrologer whose chart was strong in Fire might have little patience with a client with a flock of planets in Pisces.

[2]From an article, "Astrology and the Psychic Faculty", in *Astrological Journal,* Autumn, 1974. In a letter to me, Rose Elliot emphasized an important reservation she had concerning her visions, "Although I am quite often shown pictures apparently relating to the past, I think it would be wrong to suppose that these are *always* of previous lives. Sometimes, I believe that they are of purely symbolic significance to the psyche in question and I think it is important to avoid jumping to conclusions and making judgments. We are dealing with an extremely sensitive and potentially dangerous area here and I think one has to approach it with an open mind and much humility."

[3]Having a very prominent Pluto in close aspect to Moon and Venus helps me.

[4]I was once giving a horoscope interpretation to two young women, both of whom had been related by marriage in a past life in ancient Antioch. They had been country girls who married two brothers and came to live in the family home. There were no dramatic events, just ordinary struggles adjusting to in-laws, husbands, children, and the various political and military disturbances that ruffled the life of the city. After I finished they asked with disappointment, "Is that *all* we did?"

[5]This has been a source of mucn soul-searching for me. I have known too many people to whom self-deception was second nature. I have had the best clairvoyant I know verify the accuracy of my impressions. She

gave me reassurance, but even so I am very cautious and rely primarily on my astrological knowledge.

[6]The Sign on the cusp of the 12th House is said to designate the Sign ruling the country or area of the person's last significant life. Aries (the Sign on this lady's 12th) is supposed to be the ruling Sign of Japan; see Manly P. Hall, *Astrological Keywords* (Totowa, N.J.: Littlefield, Adams & Co., 1975).

SUGGESTED READING

Basic Astrology Textbooks

Bills, Rex E. *The Rulership Book*. Richmond: Macoy Publishing and Masonic Supply Co., 1976.

Carter, C. E. O. *The Principles Of Astrology*. Wheaton: Theosophical House, 1972.

————. *The Astrological Aspects*. Romford, Essex, England: L. N. Fowler and Co., 1977.

Hall, Manly P. *Astrological Keywords*. Totowa, N.J.: Littlefield, Adams and Co., 1975.

Jones, Marc Edmund. *How To Live With The Stars*. Wheaton: Theosophical Publishing House, 1978.

Rudhyar, Dane. *The Practice Of Astrology*. Baltimore: Penguin Books, 1968.

Tyl, Noel. *The Principles And Practice Of Astrology*, 12 Vols. St. Paul: Llewellyn Publications, 1975.

Astrological Interpretation

Arroyo, Stephen. *Astrology, Karma And Transformation: The Inner Dimensions Of The Birthchart*. Vancouver, Washington: CRCS Publications, 1978.

————. *Astrology, Psychology And The Four Elements*. Vancouver, Washington: CRCS Publications, 1975.

Bacher, Elman. *Studies In Astrology*, 9 Vols. Oceanside, CA: Rosicrucian Fellowship, 1973.

Bailey, Alice A. *Esoteric Astrology*. N.Y.: Lucis Publishing Co., 1976.

Cunningham, Donna. *An Astrological Guide To Self-Awareness*. Vancouver, Washington: CRCS Publications, 1978.

Grebner, Bernice Prill. *Lunar Nodes*. Tempe, AZ: American Federation of Astrologers, 1976.

Greene, Liz. *Saturn: A New Look At An Old Devil*. N.Y.: Samuel Weiser, 1977.

Hickey, Isobel. *Astrology: A Cosmic Science*. Bridgeport, Conn: Altieri Press, 1970

Jones, Marc Edmund. *A Guide To Horoscope Interpretation.* Wheaton: Theosophical Publishing House, 1974.

Merriman, Raymond. *Journey Of The Soul Through The Horoscope.* Rochester, MI: Seek-It Publishing, 1978.

Karma, Reincarnation And Related Subjects

Bailey, Alice A. *Glamour: A World Problem.* N.Y.: Lucis Publishing Co., 1967.

Besant, Annie, and Leadbeater, C. W. *Man: Whence, How And Whither.* Wheaton: Theosophical Publishing House, 1947.

Blair, Lawrence. *Rhythms Of Vision.* N.Y.: Schocken Books, 1976.

Blavatsky, H. P. *The Secret Doctrine,* 6 Vols. Adyar, India: Theosophical Publishing House, 1971.

————. *An Abridgement Of The Secret Doctrine.* Edited by Elizabeth Preston and Christmas Humphreys. Wheaton: Theosophical Publishing House, 1968.

————. *The Voice Of The Silence.* Wheaton: Theosophical Publishing House, 1973.

Campbell, Joseph. *The Mythic Image.* Princeton: Princeton University Press, 1964.

Challoner, H. K. *The Wheel Of Rebirth.* Wheaton: Theosophical Publishing House, 1976.

Collins, Mabel. *Light On The Path.* Wheaton: Theosophical Publishing House, 1974.

Guirdham, Arthur. *The Cathars And Reincarnation.* Wheaton: Theosophical Publishing House, 1978.

Hanson, Virginia, ed. *Karma.* Wheaton: Theosophical Publishing House, 1975.

Isherwood, C. *Ramakrishna And His Disciples.* N.Y.: Simon and Schuster, 1965.

Krishnamurti, J. *At The Feet Of The Master.* Wheaton: Theosophical Publishing House, 1974.

Leadbeater, C. W. *The Masters And The Path.* Adyar, India: Theosophical Publishing House, 1975.

————. *The Inner Life.* Wheaton: Theosophical Publishing House, 1978.

————. *The Soul's Growth Through Reincarnation.* Adyar, India: Theosophical Publishing House, 1975.

Neumann, Erich. *The Great Mother: An Analysis Of The Ar-*